Clara Schumann:
A Dedicated Spirit

Clara Schumann:
A Dedicated Spirit

A Study of her Life and Work

BY

JOAN CHISSELL

'. . . I made no vows, but vows
Were then made for me; bond unknown to me
Was given, that I should be, else sinning greatly,
A dedicated Spirit.'
WORDSWORTH, *The Prelude*

A CRESCENDO BOOK
Taplinger Publishing Company
New York

First published in the United States in 1983 by
TAPLINGER PUBLISHING CO., INC.
New York, New York

Library of Congress Catalog Card Number: 83-50182
ISBN 0-8008-1624-2

To JAMIE and GERALD

Contents

Illustrations

8   Clara Schumann in London, 1888

In the Text

Acknowledgements

For access to Clara's programmes, as also to manuscripts, photographs, and relics of all kinds, I am deeply indebted to Dr Martin Schoppe and Dr Gerd Nauhaus, Directors of the Robert-Schumann-Haus in Zwickau: their kindness and help, both professional and personal, knew no bounds on both my visits to East Germany. Since it is not the easiest of journeys to make, I would also like to thank Dr Nauhaus for so generously finding time to answer the many questions I asked by post. Other friends to whom I owe gratitude for information and encouragement include Robert Layton, who kindly allowed me to listen to BBC tapes of recorded talks by several of Clara's pupils, also John Lade, John Warrack, Hans-Gerhard Kelber, Thomas Hemsley, Murray Perahia and the late Sir Clifford Curzon. Thanks no less warm are due to Mrs Anthea Gordon who conjured a type-script from my illegible hand-writing, and to my publishers for their infinite patience.

My major acknowledgement is nevertheless to Clara herself. She was an indefatigable writer of diaries and letters, and it was to these (predominantly as prepared for publication by Berthold Litzmann in his unrivalled, extensive biography, *Clara Schumann*, and his *Letters of Clara Schumann and Brahms*) that I turned first so as to allow her whenever possible to speak for herself at moments of strongest feeling. I also drew heavily on the letters of Robert Schumann, Brahms and Joachim, the three great influences in her life after her rift with her father, Friedrich Wieck, from whose own vastly entertaining résumé of his teaching method, *Clavier und Gesang*, I would have liked to quote very much more had space permitted. Of Memoirs consulted, inevitably those of Clara's youngest daughter, Eugenie Schumann, head the list. But my declaration of sources would not be complete without mention of the many illuminating passing impressions of Clara to be found in writings of contemporaries, including Edward Speyer, Ethel Smyth, Elisabet and Heinrich Herzogenberg, James Sterndale Bennett, Felix Moscheles, Amy Fay, Florence May, Liza Lehmann and last and certainly not least, Adelina de Lara.

JOAN CHISSELL
London, New Year's Day, 1983

Introduction

Clara Schumann, née Wieck, was a grateful daughter, a devoted wife, a caring mother, a loyal friend. She was also a conscientious composer, teacher and editor. But first and foremost she was a concert pianist. Music-making was the great motivating force of her life, a mission from which any deviation, whatever the counter claims of a warm and vulnerable human heart, was a betrayal. Nothing less than such a belief could have carried her through travels so arduous, and personal tribulation at times so bitter. It was as if she had experienced a Wordsworthian moment of truth: 'I made no vows, but vows were then made for me; bond unknown to me was given, that I should be, else sinning greatly, a dedicated spirit'.

Twelve hundred and ninety-nine programmes, extending from her début in Leipzig at the age of nine to her last public performance in Frankfurt at seventy-one, have been numbered and preserved in the Robert-Schumann-Haus at Zwickau. Their first disclosure is that the full-length solo recital as we know it today was for her the exception rather than the rule. Very many of her appearances, other than when playing concertos with orchestra, were in shared concerts, at which she would sometimes alternate solo groups with those of her collaborators, but often play with (or for) them as well as contributing solos. Hence the far larger number of chamber works in her repertory than might be found in that of a similarly renowned solo pianist nowadays. The Müller brothers (of Brunswick's well-known Müller Quartet) before her marriage, the Leipzig violinist, Ferdinand David, during the early 1840's, the Schubert brothers after her move to Dresden, and most notable of all, Joseph Joachim, with whom she appeared regularly throughout the last forty years of her life, stand out from a long list of instrumental colleagues (not forgetting the cellist, Piatti, and his friends in England) as do Pauline Viardot, Jenny Lind, Schröder-Devrient, Julius Stockhausen and Amalie Joachim (together with gifted younger artists like George Henschel, Antonia Kufferath and Liza Lehmann) from the singers with whom she was happy to share a platform – and to accompany in Schumann's songs. As for the pianists who partnered her in four-handed keyboard works, their names are legion: Pixis, Moscheles, Mendelssohn, Henselt, Liszt, Brahms, the teen-age Anton Rubinstein, her half-sister, Marie Wieck,

Otto Goldschmidt, Theodor Kirchner, Ferdinand Hiller, Ernst Rudorff, her pupil, Natalia Janotha, Arabella Goddard – and even Pauline Viardot – are among those most likely to have found a place in her own book of memories.

With regard to her chosen composers, nothing is more remarkable than the gulf separating programmes of her earlier youth from those of her maturity. She was born into an age when, as Schumann put it, 'at the piano nothing was heard but Herz and Hünten'. As an astute businessman, Clara's father, Friedrich Wieck, knew very well that only virtuosity, and the confections composed for self-display by every platform celebrity of the day, lured the public-at-large; in consequence until she was sixteen her platform repertory was predominantly comprised of Herz, Hünten, Hummel, Field, Kalkbrenner, Czerny, Pixis and Moscheles, together with a few show-pieces of her own. But enrolment in the mid-1830's as an honorary member of Schumann's fictitious Davidsbund opened her eyes to the brave new world for which his recently founded magazine, the *Neue Zeitschrift für Musik*, was fighting. Mendelssohn's arrival in Leipzig in 1835 was a further catalyst. In her later teens she was already exploring a very different kind of music in private – and risking some of it in public too. By the time her name had changed to Clara Schumann she was fully prepared to renounce all youthful dross to play her own part in the magazine's avowed aims of awakening interest in the forgotten past and of 'hastening the dawn of a new poetic age'.

Since of the younger romantics no-one's cause lay closer to her heart than Schumann's, it was ironical that it proved one of her hardest to win. Because it hurt her when he was not understood, at public concerts before her marriage she in fact only very occasionally played miniatures such as the Toccata, the first Novellette, and one or two numbers from the Paganini Studies, the *Études symphoniques* and the *Fantasiestücke*, Op.12 (there was also one performance of the Sonata No.1 in F sharp minor in Berlin). The rest of the great keyboard riches of his first composing decade she preferred to share only with sympathetic personal friends. The immediate popularity of the Piano Quintet and Variations for two pianos in the early 1840's helped to turn the tide: by the time of Schumann's breakdown her concert repertory included all his chamber works with piano as well as the Piano Concerto and its two single-movement companions for piano and orchestra. But it was not until after his death that she made her first major bid for the solo piano music at large, even then deeming it necessary to proceed cautiously with the larger suite-like works. Moscheles's son, Felix, recalls how at a party he once tried to outwit her reluctance to go to the piano by confessing his love for *Carnaval*'s concluding March and proposing just a page or two of that. 'Page or two' she indignantly exclaimed, 'Wenn man den Carnaval spielt,

spielt man ihn ganz'. Yet on the concert platform it was her regular custom to omit "Eusebius', 'Florestan', 'Coquette', 'Réplique' and 'Estrella', just as fearing public *ennui* she preferred to play only a selection from the eight pieces of *Kreisleriana* (never including No. 3), and usually only ten or so from the eighteen of the *Davidsbundlertänze*. From the Sonata No. 3 in F minor she seems only to have detached the variation movement (on her own theme), and not often. Its companions in G minor and F sharp minor (on the latter's return to her repertory in later years) gave her no qualms, nor did such works as the *Études symphoniques*, a particular favourite, the C major *Phantasie*, added in 1866 and never long put aside for the next twenty-one years, and a host of immediately endearing miniatures. But the song-cycles, like the longer piano suites, again found her wary. When at last essaying the *Dichterliebe* and *Liederkreis* (Eichendorff) cycles complete with Stockhausen in the early 1860's, having previously just kept to miscellaneous favourites, she liked to insert a group of piano solos midway through – often dips into *Kreisleriana*, but sometimes into Bach, Handel and even Kirchner. Still more strange is it that though in Vienna in 1866 and Rostock in 1867 she performed *Frauenliebe und-Leben* complete with two lesser singers, when she returned to this cycle a few years later with Amalie Joachim she usually omitted the last three songs, in the process presumably depriving audiences of the exquisite keyboard postlude.

With her two other youthful romantic heroes, Chopin and Mendelssohn, the way was easier. Surprisingly, she appears never to have publicly performed such masterpieces as Chopin's B flat minor or B minor sonatas, or his fourth *Ballade* in F minor, or the *Fantasia*, Op. 49, in the same key. But having introduced his *La ci darem* Variations to Germany when only twelve, she quickly followed it up with the G minor Piano Trio, the Fantasia on Polish Airs for piano and orchestra and the E minor Piano Concerto (not always played complete), all in her repertory by 1834, as well as miniatures of all kinds just as soon as they emerged in print. Of the bigger solo pieces, the B flat minor Scherzo, the A flat Polonaise and the Barcarolle became special favourites. Towards the end of her career she also returned to the F minor Piano Concerto, after a considerable period of neglect, as if to make amends in several exceptional performances for having omitted the first movement when first playing the work in Leipzig in 1841.

As for Mendelssohn, after the exhilaration of performing his B minor *Capriccio brillant* under his own baton in 1835, when just sixteen, and joining him in his four-handed A major *Allegro brillant* in 1841, she turned to his G minor Piano Concerto in 1842, playing it more often than its successor in D minor, taken up in 1856. By that time her repertory included his two Piano Trios and two Sonatas for cello and piano as well as many solo pieces (his Piano Sonatas, like Chopin's, she ignored on the platform), with groups of *Lieder ohne Worte* turning up time and time again in response to popular demand. She also played the *Variations sérieuses* often enough to suggest that its noteswere engraved on her heart.

Though for several years her programmes regularly included three or four highly popular operatic Fantasias by Thalberg, Henselt (whose early Variations, Concert Studies and Piano Concerto she also ardently pioneered) and Liszt (initially represented by his transcriptions of Schubert songs), her interest in their bravura challenge quickly waned after her marriage. Even Liszt's maturer keyboard music, composed after his withdrawal from the concert platform, she deemed unworthy of serious attention. As she approached middle age it was Brahms alone on the contemporary front, apart from a few minor friends like Kirchner, Rudorff, Hiller, Bennett, Scholz and her half-brother, Bargiel, for whom she was prepared to break lances. Sadly, several of Brahms's works she would most dearly have loved to champion came too late for her tiring, increasingly pain-wracked wrists and arms. The D minor Concerto proved enough of a strain eventually to have to be abandoned altogether, similarly the Handel Variations. Though learnt with an eye on the platform, the Paganini Variations in their turn seem never to have been publicly performed by her. As for the B flat Concerto of 1881, at sixty-two she knew better than to attempt it at all. But it was she who first introduced movements from his Piano Sonatas to the general public, also Hungarian Dances, Waltzes, Ballades and less physically demanding Variations. It was she who immediately seized on every chamber work involving the piano, from the Quartets and Quintet of the earlier 1860's right through to the Trios and Violin Sonatas of her last platform decade. And it was she who even after retirement from the public platform still initiated many a personal friend into the intimate confidences of the Intermezzi and their companion pieces written as Brahms's own farewell to the piano.

The past, whose treasures Schumann himself was so anxious to restore to honour, could for Clara be said to have begun in the 1680's. Scarlatti, represented by miscellaneous sonatas, she played much more often than Handel, remembered only through his seventh harpsichord Suite or, like Rameau, an occasional dance excerpt; none entered her repertory until after her husband's death. But Bach lay close to her heart from as early as 1835, when having started to explore the '48' (and already slipped a C sharp major Fugue into a Halle recital that July) she joined Mendelssohn and Rakemann in November in the D minor Concerto for three pianos. In early days of widowhood she went on to the C major Concerto for two pianos as well as the E major and A major Sonatas for violin and piano while also enlarging her solo repertory with her own transcriptions of organ Preludes and Fugues, the Chromatic Fantasy and Fugue, and somewhat later, the Italian Concerto, the G major Partita and groups of dances from various English Suites.

As for the mid-and-later eighteenth century, though Haydn's G major Sonata for violin and piano and 'Hungarian' Trio in G were great favourites in recitals with Joachim, she never essayed his solo piano sonatas in public – nor those of Mozart. But starting with the G minor Piano Quartet in 1842, Mozart was constantly saluted, whether through four-handed keyboard works (notably the D major Sonata for two pianos, K.448), or the half dozen or so Sonatas for violin and piano played with Joachim, or most notably, his Concertos in D minor, K.466, and C minor, K.491, added to her repertory in 1857 and 1861 respectively.

Weber she preferred to remember through his *Conzertstück* for piano and orchestra, first performed by her in 1842, rather than the piano sonatas, from which she only occasionally detached this or that Scherzo or Rondo. Schubert's sonatas in their turn had to wait until 1866 before she felt the public was ready for them, first the last in B flat (Op.posth), followed in the next few years by those in A minor (Op.42) and G major (Op.78) as well as the 'Arpeggione'. But she had long played his two piano trios, while numbers from the *Moments musicaux*, the *Impromptus* and the *Ländler* increasingly occupied the place in her affections once held by Liszt's transcriptions of his songs.

The great cornerstone of her classical repertory was nevertheless always Beethoven, starting with a Leipzig performance of the *Fantasy for Piano, Chorus and Orchestra* as early as December, 1833, when she was just fourteen. His piano sonatas she approached through the 'Appassionata' (though not risking it complete until 1837), following it with others of the middle period – the 'Waldstein', the 'Moonlight', the 'Tempest', the 'Pastoral', 'Les Adieux' and the E flat sonata, Op.27, No.1 (also its early predecessor in the same key) – which together with the 'Eroica' Variations and the 32 Variations in C minor, she could never play too often. Of the third period works, the A major Sonata, Op.101, proved an even more enduring favourite. The 'Hammerklavier', on the other hand, had only a few performances by her after the first in 1855, while the E major Sonata, Op.109, though learnt in 1857, she preferred not to play in public until she was over fifty. The A flat Sonata, Op.110 (though also learnt in 1857) and the C minor Sonata, Op.111, seem never to have been publicly heard from her at all. Nor were Beethoven's first two piano concertos. She even waited until 1868 before taking up the third Concerto in C minor. But the 'Emperor' and the fourth Concerto in G, introduced in 1844 and 1846 respectively, contributed almost as much to her life's happiness as her husband's constantly played A minor work. The chamber music was no less a source of stimulation and joy. Of the piano trios, the 'Archduke', the 'Geister' and the C minor, Op.1, No.3, were in her repertory before her marriage; others, along with the second, third and fifth Sonatas for cello and piano, soon followed. But it was the Sonatas for violin and piano that she came to know and love most of all, with the 'Kreutzer' (its first movement first played by her as early as 1835) and the G major Sonata, Op.96, heading favourites also including the earlier G major and C minor Sonatas – and of course the 'Spring'. Her performances of these works with Joachim were among the crowning achievements of her career.

ONE

Her Father's Daughter: 1819–27

'I was born at Leipzig, September 13th 1819, in the house called *Hohe Lilie* in the *Neumarkt*, (to which my parents had moved at Easter, 1818) and received the name of Clara Josephine. My godparents were a notary named Streubel, a friend of my father; Madame Reichel, a friend of my mother; and Frau Cantorin Tromlitz of Plauen, the mother of my mother, Marianne Tromlitz. My father kept a musical lending library and carried on a small business in pianofortes. Since both he and my mother were much occupied in teaching, and besides this my mother practised from one to two hours a day, I was chiefly left to the care of the maid, Johanna Strobel. She was not very fluent of speech, and it may well have been owing to this that I did not begin to pronounce even single words until I was between four and five years old, and up to that time understood as little as I spoke. But I had always been accustomed to hear a great deal of piano playing and my ear became more sensitive to musical sounds than to those of speech. I soon learned to walk, and in my third and fourth years could go out with my parents and cover miles of road.'

Throughout her long, active life, Clara rarely for long neglected the habit of diary keeping instilled in her from earliest childhood by her father, Friedrich Wieck. But in that first entry, as in accounts of her development for several years to follow, the words came from Wieck himself, even then sufficiently confident of his prowess as a teacher to take it for granted that every detail in the story of his first surviving daughter (an elder girl, Adelheid, died in infancy) would one day be of interest to the world. Already he could point to his young wife and pupil, Marianne, daughter of the Cantor at Plauen and grand-daughter of the eminent flautist and flute composer, Johann Georg Tromlitz: his systematic tuition had not only ripened her sufficiently to appear at the Leipzig Gewandhaus Subscription Concerts as soprano soloist in Mozart's *Requiem* and other works in 1817, the year after their marriage, but also to play piano concertos by Ries, Dussek and Field on this same eminent platform in 1821, 1822 and 1823.

Music had always been the strongest motivating force in Wieck's own life, so much so that when he left the Gymnasium at Torgau in 1803, an otherwise favourable report carried the reproof 'he has devoted too much time to music'. But his training was haphazard in the extreme, with everything entirely dependent on his own initiative and effort. His father, a small tradesman with five sons in the Saxon town of Pretzsch, had fallen on hard enough times not even to be able to pay school fees. Funds raised by local well-wishers only covered Friedrich's tuition and the cost of a bed in Torgau. For food he was dependent on the basic bread and butter his mother sent over by the local carter, on the occasional bowl of soup offered by his landlord, and best of all, on a once-weekly invitation from a lawyer ('this cheered me, weakly and sensitive as I was, and the good food which I enjoyed – generally roast mutton with beans or peas – revived and strengthened me during the best part of a summer') until eventually becoming eligible for the free dinners available to the Gymnasium's poorer pupils. The few groschen he earned by helping a child of one of the townsfolk to learn to read were not enough to pay for regular music lessons. But he managed to acquire an old table keyboard, and after winning the sympathy of the local organist and the town musician with his keenness, both of whom gave him a few hours of their time whenever they could, he had the great good fortune to come to the notice of the Oberförster Herr von Loewen, who let him attend the lessons arranged for his wife and children from the eminent, albeit by this time semi-paralysed pianist, Johann Peter Milchmayer. Out of kindness of heart, Milchmayer even gave Wieck some private tuition too.

Wieck's own maternal grandfather was a Lutheran pastor, so when a place was offered him at the University of Wittenberg as a student of theology, he suppressed musical promptings and took it. After three years' subsidized studies he preached his first sermon at St. Sophia's Church in Dresden. It was also his last. For sternly refusing to compromise with his conscience on realizing the ministry was not his true vocation, he at once left it to take a job as a private tutor. Entrusted with a certain young Emil von Metzradt, his sense of mission as a pedagogue grew sufficiently strong for some projected 'weekly notes' on his pupil, designed for his titled employer, to overflow into an earnest essay on the physical, intellectual and moral training of the young. After due insistence on the importance of fresh air and physical exercise, and of stimulating the child's enjoyment in work rather than just drilling him, his final message nevertheless remained that of the erstwhile theologian: 'Make it your central aim to train the child to become a good man, for this is the highest goal of humanity'.

At one of the two households where he worked, Wieck had the luck to find the pianist Adolf Bargiel employed as music tutor, and again turned this relationship to good personal advantage. Even so, nine years in the wilderness was enough. After a leisurely visit to Leipzig for treatment of an infection threatening his eyes, the lure of that city's musical riches could no longer be resisted. Seeking out his old university friend, Streubel, already well on his way up the ladder, he soon elicited some valuable introductions, not least to the critic, Johann Friedrich Rochlitz, who in his turn opened doors enabling Wieck to acquire a few pupils, and more ambitiously, in 1815, to dedicate a set of Eight Songs, numbered as his Op.8, to Weber – with a request for candid criticism. (While praising their 'deep feeling' and search for 'beauty and novelty', Weber also had some severe strictures to make about careless word-setting, unvocal melody, and harmony sometimes as incorrect as modulations were extravagant). A loan from Streubel also enabled Wieck to acquire that musical lending library and the piano hire business to which the first entry in Clara's diary refers, so that by May, 1816, not yet quite 31, he had settled into the first home of his own with his nineteen-year-old bride, Marianne.

'At Easter 1821', so Clara's diary continues, 'my parents moved to a house in the Salzgässchen, and it was here that I was fated to lose my mother. She left my father on May 12, 1824, and went to Plauen to arrange for a legal separation.' Still only twenty-seven, and by now not only the mother of Clara but also of Alwin (born 1821), Gustav (born 1823) and Viktor (born 1824), Marianne Wieck had in fact wearied of her husband's domineering albeit often caustically humorous mind; as her own person-ality ripened, so the relentless daily round he imposed increasingly irked her own independent spirit. She was permitted to keep her daughter only for that first summer at her parents' home in Plauen. On September 17, 1824, when just five, Clara was formally restored to the custody of Wieck. Short visits were allowed when, after Marianne's remarriage to Wieck's fellow tutor, Adolf Bargiel, in 1825, the two lived for a year in Leipzig. But on their removal to Berlin, Clara was again bereft of a mother. Wieck himself was to wait another four years before finding a new wife to care for his children – and give him more.

Dreams of creating a *Wunderkind* of his own had always been uppermost in Wieck's mind, and immediately Clara returned to him the lessons began. Though at five she could already play a few exercises 'without moving the hand' besides effortlessly picking out little dance-tunes by ear, difficulties of communication because of her retarded speech soon led him to experiment with a system of class tuition devised and widely disseminated in Europe by Johann Bernhard Logier (1777–1846), a German pianist and pedagogue of French descent who had chosen Dublin as his home. To their considerable financial gain Logier and his disciples instructed the young in groups, claiming that it gave them confidence to play their scales, exercises and early pieces together. At demonstration classes, beginners would often supply the tune while those a little more experienced supported them with chords or arpeggios, astounding musically naïve parents with the fullness of the resulting sound. For Clara the venture was a success in the rather different way Wieck no doubt always hoped for: she quickly found her tongue as a result of his decision to teach her not alone, but until Easter, 1825, in the company of two carefully selected young friends. For a while Wieck also tried out Logier's controversial 'chiroplast', an apparatus attached to the keyboard into which the hand was placed to assist wrist and fingers find the alleged right position. Celebrities like Clementi, described by Mozart as a 'mere mechanicus', the cleanly classical J. B. Cramer, and Kalkbrenner, whose playing was once hailed as being 'as polished as a billiard-ball', were among those who publicly testified to its virtues, though Kalkbrenner, so influential in Paris as a teacher, in time came to recognize its limitations. In Wieck's case, curiosity soon turned to active mistrust, just as had happened when a special board of professors set up under the aegis of London's Philharmonic Society investigated Logier's method in England as early as 1817. Wieck quickly realized that just resting the hand on a table or chair and gently moving the fingers up and down was a much more natural preparation for his own basic ideal, the production of beautiful tone, cultivated through 'quiet movement of the fingers and a correct position of the hand, without an uneasy jerking of the arm'. Even at this stage he always encouraged Clara to sing, believing that nothing better fostered true keyboard cantabile than the singing voice. So strong was his conviction that piano and singing 'should explain and supplement each other' that when he eventually published a general résumé of his approach to music teaching in 1853, he called the book *Clavier und Gesang*, and included several chapters on voice production pure and simple.

If making the piano sing was the first lesson Wieck taught, general musicianship, in other words an awareness of the mysterious natural laws determining the sequence of musical sounds, was the second. The intricacies of written notation he felt could wait. As he subsequently explained: 'With my own daughters I did not teach the treble notes till the end of the first year's instruction, the bass notes several months later'. It was the ear that he alerted first, through the recognition of variations of high and low pitch and contrasts of major and minor tonality, as well as the throb of the beat in all varieties of rhythm, duple and triple, fast and slow. Soon the basic cadences and little exercises of his own had to be memorized by ear and reproduced in all keys. When notes were eventually learnt, sight-reading without looking at the hands, so that the eye and mind could always be a bar or two ahead of the fingers, became an obligatory daily adventure.

Technical training was not long delayed, for too many people, in his opinion, shirked it until too late, when the muscles of the hands were already formed. He insisted on scales, though only for a quarter of an hour per day, and at first only with separate hands so that no unevennesses in the one should be covered by the other; he also advocated playing them with every variation of touch and gradation of dynamics to help the thumb pass under smoothly and strengthen weak fingers. He had great belief in studies for specific hurdles like thirds, trills, stretches and development of the fourth and fifth fingers – provided they were not undertaken just for their own sake but always in the context of a specific problem encountered in whatever composition was then being studied. He had strong views on the use and abuse of loud and soft pedals. Reliance on the soft pedal for finer gradations of *piano* was as much an admission of inadequate control of touch, in his opinion, as resort to the right pedal for an illusion of volume, though at the same time he thought Hummel went too far in hardly ever using the latter, sacrificing many fine effects possible on the instruments of Stein, Brodmann and Conrad Graff.

Always he encouraged his pupils to conquer one particular piece and play it daily for weeks on end so that 'by its perfect mastery they may gain a fearless confidence . . . they must regard that piece as a companion, friend and support'. Czerny's *Toccata*, Op.92, was one of his favourite recommendations for more advanced students. He was also tireless in developing a critical awareness of the quality of the instrument itself on which practising had to be done, or performance given, with special reference to pitch and tuning as well as action. Last but not least, he never let the young forget that technique was only the means to an end, making his point in a little jingle of his own: 'The artist's first rule is that skill is a tool; But your art's put to shame if skill is the aim'. His belief that even the simplest exercise could be made both musically expressive and tonally beautiful is clear from the detailed phrase markings and dynamic nuances in the collection of his own exercises assembled, edited and printed by his daughter, Marie, in 1884.

Never had any of his pupils thrived on it all more than Clara. As she approached seven, her stretch was already wide enough for her to manage octaves in both hands. Thanks to her father's gifted pupil from Chemnitz, Emilie Reichold, she was also a competent duet player, and having taken the bass part in a performance of Haslinger's little Concerto for four hands with quartet accompaniment, at once began to study her first orchestral concerto, Hummel's in G major, Op.73. As the diary proudly recalls: 'In 1827 my perception of music began to develop more and more quickly, and I could distinguish the keys with fair certainty simply by ear, nor was I unacquainted with the first elements of theory. I could quickly find the sub-dominant and dominant chords in every key, and could modulate at will or at command (as the chords led me) from major and minor keys through the diminished seventh, by using the leading note of the dominant. My playing also improved, my attack was good, firm and sure, and my fingers strengthened so rapidly that I could now play difficult pieces for two hours on end with fair persistency, and my father often praised my aptitude for natural and good execution, which I always liked'. Occasionally there were passing clouds, as when a short time afterwards she confessed: 'My father specially blames me now for a certain jealousy of disposition – love of pleasure – childish sensitiveness – and a curious inclination never to enjoy the present time or present possessions. This last troubled my father the most, because it made me appear seldom contented, since a perpetual "but" or "if" got in the way'. In the main, however, it was progress without tears. For just as with his first charge, Emil, so with his own daughter, Wieck always insisted on plenty of time spent out of doors ('active exercise, in all weather, makes strong, enduring piano fingers, while subsisting on indoor air results in sickly, nervous, feeble, overstrained playing. Strong healthy fingers are necessary for our present style piano playing, which requires such extraordinary execution, and for our heavy instruments'), and never demanded more than two or three hours' practice. Even schooling, which Clara began at six, was restricted to minimal requirements so as not to overburden her or destroy the 'joyousness of youth'.

So it was a natural enough child who wrote her very first letter in her own hand to her mother the day after her eighth birthday, still elated with the memory of playing her first concerto five days earlier at an orchestral rehearsal before a small, invited audience:

Dear Mother,
   You have as yet read nothing from me, but now I can write a little I will send you a little letter, which will please you. I had presents on my eighth birthday from dear Bertha and from my dear Father, from dear Father I got a beautiful dress, and from Bertha I had an ash-cake [*Aschkuchen*] and a plum-cake and a lovely knitting bag. And I played Mozart's E flat concerto which you used to play, with an orchestral accompaniment, and Herr Matthäi, Lange, Belke and a lot of others played with me. It went very well and I never stuck at all, only my cadenza would not go easily where I had to play a chromatic scale three times. I was not a bit frightened, but the clapping troubled me. Emilie Reichold and M. Kupfer played too. The day before my birthday I went to Malger with father. Please give my love to Grandmamma, and my brothers send their love to you. Now you will write to me, won't you?
   Your obedient daughter, Clara Wieck, Leipzig, September 14, 1827.

Dear Mother, I will come to see you soon and then I will play a great many pieces for four hands with you. And I have sung and played through ever so many operas already, such as *Oberon, Die Schweizer-familie, Der Schlosser, Die Zauberflöte*, which I have seen in the theatre too. My dear father has ordered me a beautiful piano from Herr Stein in Vienna, because I have been industrious and can play and sing at the same time all Spohr's songs and the concerto went without a mistake. Good-bye. C.

TWO

On the Leipzig Platform 1827–30

As sturdy tradesfolk, not artistically dependent on the munificence of a prince, the citizens of Leipzig were justly proud of their Gewandhaus Orchestra from which Clara's accompanists at that concerto rehearsal had mostly been drawn. Originating in a modest concert-giving society called *Das grosse Konzert*, the orchestra had begun to acquire an identity of its own when Johann Adam Hiller was appointed director in 1763, after the interruption of the Seven Years War, the more so when the old Gewandhaus ('cloth-house') building was purchased in 1781, giving the orchestra a distinctive name as well as a permanent home. Its present director was Christian August Pohlenz (described by Wagner as belonging 'to the type of fat and pleasant musical-directors . . . a great favourite with the Leipzig public') who with Heinrich August Matthäi as Koncertmeister was responsible for an annual series of twenty-four subscription concerts as well as many 'extras' called for by individual artists or charitable occasions. With Haydn, Mozart and Beethoven long accorded a place of honour, its reputation for enlightened programme-building drew a large number of eminent visiting soloists to the city, not least pianists. By this time Wieck had delegated his lending library to the care of a manager, so as to be able to give all his energies, apart from teaching, to his piano warehouse, to which every artist applied when wanting a concert instrument. Not only was his name becoming increasingly familiar amongst the leading performers of the day but also all the pre-eminent piano manufacturers. While he himself appreciated the richer potential of the so-called Clementi school, deriving from the deeper action of the English firm of Broadwood, Clara, already fastidiously aware of differences of touch and compass, was still much happier with the lighter Viennese instruments favoured by the virtuoso camp, particularly those of Andreas Stein, whose firm's earlier developments had proved such a stimulus to Mozart. So a cordial relationship grew up between Wieck and Stein, prompting an uncommonly personal letter from Wieck, almost forty-three, in the course of July, 1828: 'Dear Friend, I was married on July 3 to my dear Clementine Fechner, and we went to Dresden the next day – yesterday we returned, and today I write to beg you for your congratulations on the sudden event. I had been considering the matter for three years and had been wholly unable to make a choice. My children, my house, and I myself will now, if I mistake not, be splendidly cared for'.

He was not mistaken. Clementine, still only 23, was not a musician. But like Wieck's own mother, she was a daughter of the church, in this instance a pastor of enlightened views. One of her brothers was an artist, the other a still more esteemed professor of philosophy. Clara and her two younger brothers, Alwin and Gustav, were at the wedding (the baby Viktor, entrusted to Marianne, had died that same year), after which Clara, almost nine, went off with her father and stepmother on their honeymoon, still child enough to confide to her diary 'I was amazed at Dresden and also at the beautiful country around; but I liked even better to be in the Simons' garden with little Ida and Thekla, and the lamb, or under the cherry and gooseberry and currant trees. I enjoyed myself thoroughly until the 15th, when we left'. During Leipzig's Easter festivities that year she had found equal pleasure, away from music, in 'the wax-works, the elk, Weisse the juggler from Paris, the horse-breakers, and the Panorama of Gibraltar'.

Her performing experience throughout 1828 was mostly gained at musical evenings in their own home, such as one in February when she played Schubert's four Polonaises for piano duet with her father, or in the houses of music-loving friends, notably Dr Ernst August Carus, recently moved from a Colditz practice to the Chair of Medicine at Leipzig University, where on March 31 she took part in a trio by Hummel and, as she put it in the diary, 'made fewer mistakes than the gentlemen who accompanied me'. But in Dresden Wieck allowed her to perform at the Institute for the Blind, and back in Leipzig he saw no harm in allowing her to appear at the Gewandhaus, not as a Wunderkind making her official début, but in just one supporting item in the course of a concert given by a certain Caroline Perthaler ('Pianoforte-Spielerin aus Grätz in Steyermark') – and even then only as primo in a duet by Kalkbrenner with the up-and-coming Emilie Reichold, with whom she so often made music at home, using a six octave Stein piano with two pedals for different levels of soft tone as well as a third sustaining pedal. The date was October 20, 1828, and it was an evening Clara never forgot. Eagerly awaiting the arrival of the splendid Gewandhaus glass coach in which artists were traditionally transported to the hall, she was dismayed, when summoned by the maid, to find a rather ordinary conveyance awaiting her with several young girls already aboard, and still more upset when it set off in the wrong direction, stopping on the way to collect yet others in party dress. Eventually she plucked up courage to ask when they would return to the Gewandhaus, only to discover that they were en route for a country ball at Eutritzsch, and that she had been picked up in mistake for the porter's daughter, also a Clara. Though soon overtaken and rescued by the rightful coach, she arrived at the Gewandhaus in tears. But Wieck, contriving to greet her with a bag of sugar plums, allegedly saved the day by commenting 'I quite forgot to tell you, Clärchen, that people are always taken to the wrong house the first time they play in public'.

In her own diary Clara recorded 'It went very well and I did not play any wrong notes but got much applause'. The critic of the *Allgemeine Musikalische Zeitung*, in what was her first press notice of importance, appeared just as content: 'It was with particular pleasure that we listened to the performance of the very talented nine-year-old Clara Wieck, with whom was associated Demoiselle Emilie Reichold, in Kalkbrenner's Variations for four hands on a march from *Moses*. Under the guidance of her distinguished father, who is especially distinguished by his knowledge of the art of piano playing and the enthusiasm with which he devotes himself to its furtherance, her future may be anticipated with the highest hopes'.

If Clara herself thought the occasion had earned her a little relaxation, the tenacious Wieck did not. Only nine days later the diary records 'My father, who had long hoped in vain for a change of disposition on my part, noticed again today that I am still lazy, careless, disorderly, obstinate and disobedient, and that I play as badly as I study. I played Hünten's new Variations, Op.26, to him so badly, without even repeating the first part of the variation, that he tore up the copy before my eyes, and from today onwards he will not give me another hour, and I am to play nothing but scales, Cramer's Etudes Book I, and Czerny's trilling exercises'. But the penance was short-lived. Before long she was even tackling one or two separate movements from works by Mozart and Beethoven as well as stocking up her repertoire with the show pieces by Ries, Hummel, Moscheles, Field and Herz, besides Hünten and Kalkbrenner, that her astute father knew only too well were what the general public would want to hear.

1829 brought an exciting new catalyst into her life. In February of that year, the legendary forty-seven-year-old Paganini, on his first north-German tour, stopped a short time in Leipzig on his way to Berlin. Thwarted in attempts to arrange a last minute 'extra' concert at the Gewandhaus, Wieck followed him to Berlin, where, totally bowled over by what he heard, he would not rest until four concert dates had been secured for Leipzig that autumn. On the morning of October 4, Wieck reintroduced himself to the great man at his Leipzig hotel, taking along Clara too, who was at once invited to play, albeit 'on a wretched old piano with black keys which had been left behind by a student. I played my Polonaise in E flat, which he liked very much, and he told my father that I had a vocation for art, because I had feeling. He at once gave us permission to attend all his rehearsals – which we did'. On these occasions Paganini was uncommonly gallant to Clara. He introduced her to celebrities, and allowed her to present others to him just like a grown-up colleague, while at two of the four concerts he offered her a special seat of honour on the platform. Meanwhile Wieck had surreptitiously replaced the inferior piano at the hotel with an excellent new one from his warehouse, gaining him a second invitation to take Clara along to play – on this occasion predominantly with himself in duets, including some Variations on themes from Paganini's concertos by Wieck's Dresden friend, Krägen (Court pianist to the King of Saxony). Praise was now tempered with the advice not to play 'too restlessly and with too much movement of the body'. Her happiness was complete when on the day of departure Paganini inscribed her autograph album with an extract from one of his Scherzos and a harmonization of the chromatic scale in contrary motion together with the words 'al merito singulare di Madamigella Clara Wieck'.

For Clara, just ten, the experience was a milestone. Life from now on was to bring her into continuous contact with renowned artists, intellectuals and aristocrats, all of whom, as a little friend of Paganini, she could approach with a new confidence, as if suddenly aware of her own potential. On a return visit to Dresden at Easter, 1830, when invited by a certain Count Kospoth to play duets with his wife, an amateur pianist of some repute, she replied, 'I will come, but are you sure your wife can play?', continuing, after an answer in the affirmative, 'Indeed? Then take me to her, I should like to make her acquaintance'. Throughout the month's stay her reception was sufficiently warm in aristocratic circles, not least at the two court soirées given by Princess Louise, to cause Wieck some private worries. As he wrote to his absent wife: 'I am afraid lest the admiration and notice should have a bad influence on Clara. If I see any harm, I shall leave at once so that she may return to her middle-class surroundings, for I am too proud of her simplicity to exchange it for any honour in the world. People find her very lovable. She is still the same simple, natural child, but she often shows deep understanding and rich imagination. She is unruly, but noble and sensible. When playing she is incredibly self-possessed, and the larger the company the better she plays'. That her own powers of self-criticism were also developing was proved when after receiving great applause for a laboured performance of some virtuoso variations on a hard, unyielding piano, she stood up gravely and told the audience she had not played well – and then burst into tears. Wieck, pressed on all sides to publish his method, soon conquered his own qualms. 'It is impossible to describe the sensation your two monkeys from the Leipzig menagerie are making here', he wrote in a later letter to Clementine. 'No one would believe that Clara could also compose, and all present went into raptures when she extemporised on a given theme (from *La Muette de Portici*)'.

With this new acknowledgement of improvisational ability (consider-

ably developed by Czerny's 'Guide to the Art of Improvisation') on top of
Paganini's encouraging words about the E flat Polonaise, one of Wieck's
first moves on returning to Leipzig was to put Clara's creative activities
under specialist supervision. He had always valued general musicianship
more than mere prestidigitation, and had tried to help Clara with her
harmony and counterpoint. But recognizing his own limitations in this
sphere, he now turned to the fifty-years-old Christian Theodor Weinlig,
an erstwhile pupil of Martini in Bologna, who since 1823 had occupied the
same position of Cantor at St Thomas's Church once held by Bach. It was
a wise choice, as no less a person than Richard Wagner also discovered
when going to Weinlig in his late teens during the winter of 1831–2.
Though initially irked by endless exercises in four-part harmony, Wagner
quickly came to recognize Weinlig's uncanny skill as a teacher of counterpoint and form, and never ceased to thank him for the new clarity and
fluency in his own musical reasoning that resulted from their six months
together. Clara, too, acquired the same sterling grounding, writing
chorales and miniature fugues galore for Weinlig while continuing, like all
the grown-up virtuosi of the day, to produce pieces for herself to play,
including sets of variations on a Tyrolese theme and an original theme
(now lost). When three more Polonaises in C, D and C major followed
her first in E flat, Wieck even persuaded the firm of Hofmeister to publish
the four as her collective Op.1, a venture quickly condemned as premature
by the pungent Berlin critic, Rellstab (to whom she had been introduced
by Paganini) in a review in the Berlin *Iris*. In simple ternary form, they
rarely extend in harmonic or melodic invention beyond the pretty drawing-room platitudes of the day – as a child she had played many such
pieces by Spohr and Field. But they are neatly shaped and attractively
pianistic, with the central trio of each, always in a different key, marked by
a delicate charm in contrast to the robuster main section. The *espressivo* G
minor trio of No. 3 in D is the most winning: even Chopin at the same age
could have been proud of it.

By the autumn of 1830 Wieck decided the moment was ripe for her
official Gewandhaus début: November 8 was the selected day. In the customary manner of the time she emerged not just as a pianist but composer
too. The programme included her Variations on an original theme, also
one of her very first songs (in all probability 'Der Traum', to words of
Tiedge, specifically mentioned by name in several subsequent programmes), sung by the same Henriette Grabau who took part in Caroline
Perthaler's concert two years before. She also joined her father in a curio
of his own composition, a Romanze for piano and physharmonica,[1] the
latter a tiny, three-octave embrionic harmonium invented by Anton

---

[1] Wieck's instrument is still preserved in the Schumann-Haus at Zwickau.

Montag, den 8. November 1830,

wird

CLARA WIECK

eine

musikalische Akademie

mit

Unterstützung des hiesigen Concert-Orchesters

im

SAALE DES GEWANDHAUSES

zu geben die Ehre haben.

Erste Abtheilung.

1) OUVERTURE aus Fra Diavolo, von Auber (neu).
2) VARIATIONEN über „An Alexis send' ich dich" von Lindpaintner, gesungen von Dem. Henriette Grabau.
3) RONDO BRILLANT für Pianoforte mit Orchester, O. 101 von Kalkbrenner (neu), gespielt von Clara.
4) LIED mit Pianoforte-Begleitung, componirt von Clara, gesungen von Dem. Henr. Grabau.
5) VARIATIONS BRILLANTES für Pianoforte solo, O. 23 von H. Herz, gespielt von Clara.

Zweite Abtheilung.

6) QUATUOR CONCERTANT für 4 Pianoforte mit Orchester, über mehrere beliebte Melodien, von Carl Czerny, O. 230, gespielt von Herrn Musikdirector Dorn, Herrn Knorr, Herrn Wendler und Clara (neu).
7) ROMANZE für die Physharmonica mit Pianoforte.
8) ARIA aus Donna del Lago mit Orchester, gesungen von Herrn Hammermeister.
9) VARIATIONEN über ein Originalthema für Pianoforte solo, componirt und gespielt von Clara.

Einlasskarten zu 16 Gr. sind bei Friedrich Hofmeister, im Leihinstitut für Musik (Bülows Haus in der Reichsstrasse No. 579, 2 Treppen hoch) und an der Casse zu bekommen.

Einlass halb 6 Uhr. Anfang halb 7 Uhr.

Häckel in Vienna in 1818 (the left of its two pedals acting as bellows and the right as an immediate silencer) often used by Wieck in his lessons for accompanying pupils in concertos – as also by Clara in early days for practising improvisation.[1] For the rest she played Kalkbrenner's *Rondo Brillant*, Op.101, for piano and orchestra, Herz's *Variations Brillantes*, Op.23, and Czerny's Quartet Concertante, Op.230, for four pianos and orchestra (with Heinrich Dorn, the youthful music director of the Leipzig Opera, as one of her colleagues) 'with a finished execution and the brilliant virtuosity of the day that ensured the approbation of the audience' as the *Allgemeine Musikalische Zeitung* subsequently wrote. In her diary, Clara had only one reservation to make: 'I played to the satisfaction of my father and of the public. My bows were not very successful, except for the first; they were too quick'. That her father had already alerted her to the financial aspects of her career is revealed in the added comment that out of the concert's thirty thalers profit, 'I gave my father 20 thalers for his trouble and I am sorry that he will not take more, but from now on I shall frequently treat my family at the *Kuchengarten*'.

[1] In subsequent concerts she frequently followed the Romanze with a solo improvisation on it.

Out into the World 1830–32

1830 brought two newcomers into Clara's family circle, the immediate favourite a baby half-brother, Clementine's first-born, christened Klemens. And after some deliberation, in the autumn Wieck accepted a young man of twenty, by the name of Robert Schumann, as a resident piano pupil in their house at Grimmaische Gasse No. 36. They had first met in 1828, when in deference to pressures from his merchant guardian and his mother, Schumann had agreed to adopt the safe profession of law rather than following the musical and literary inclinations of his own heart so encouraged by his bookseller-cum-publisher father in Zwickau until the latter's untimely death in 1826. Enrolment at the University compelled him to visit Leipzig during the first week of March, 1828. Though intending to leave again as soon as possible in view of his brother Julius' impending wedding, he could well have been cajoled into staying over the weekend to attend the party on March 31 at which Clara took part in a Hummel trio,[1] for the Carus family were old friends of Schumann's too. He had already written some songs for Agnes, Dr Carus's attractive young singer wife, who affectionately nicknamed him Fridolin (after Schiller's guileless young page). But even if not at this party, his meeting with Wieck was certainly not long in coming. After a characteristically impulsive holiday trip with a new-found Heidelberg law-student friend, Gilbert Rosen, during which they were received in Bayreuth by the widow of their mutual literary idol, Jean Paul, and in Munich by the already renowned thirty-one-year-old Heine, Schumann was back in Leipzig in legal harness by mid-May.

In one of those mercurial mood-changes over which he had no control, almost immediately his youthful confidence and high spirits dissolved into despair as he realized the full extent of his boredom with 'chilly jurisprudence', also his lack of sympathy for his fellow students with their fencing clubs and their wild and hazy notions about nationalism. Amidst the noise and bustle of a big city he was bitterly homesick for Zwickau and the solace of its so much more attractively hilly surrounding countryside. His only comfort was music, to be found with friends like Ernst and Agnes Carus, and through them, Wieck. 'I am very often with Wieck who teaches me the

---

[1] See p. 80.

piano', so he informed his mother in August, 1828, 'and there I get the chance every day of making the acquaintance of the most excellent musicians in Leipzig. I often play duets with Mlle Reichold, who is quite the best pianist, and am going to perform a four-hand concerto with her at one of the grand concerts next winter'. Though a casual hint to his family that he would like to buy a splendid Stein piano for 400 thalers met with no response, not even from a mother who loved spoiling her youngest son, he managed to hire a good instrument for a ducat a month, and spent far more time in his uncommonly comfortable student lodgings than in the lecture room, either practising alone, or else playing chamber music with two or three keen amateurs encountered among fellow students. Schubert's piano trios were top favourites: when Schubert died that November a friend heard Schumann sobbing all night. He also began to compose again with even more zest than in boyhood, starting a Piano Quartet in C minor besides completing a set of Schubert-inspired Polonaises for piano duet, and several songs which he sent for criticism to Gottlob Wiedebein, Music Director at Brunswick and himself the composer of a then much-praised album of Lieder. 'Your songs have many, sometimes very many shortcomings' Wiedebein replied, 'but I should call them sins not so much of the spirit as of nature and youth, and these are excusable and pardonable where poetic feeling and genuine spirit shines through. And it is precisely that which has pleased me so much'.

Alarmed at this increasing preoccupation with music, Schumann's mother raised few objections when he himself proposed leaving Leipzig in May, 1829, to join his friend, Rosen, for a few terms at the University of Heidelberg, where he claimed there were better professors of law. She humoured him still more by allowing him an extravagant summer holiday exploring Switzerland and Italy, requested under pretext of improving his languages. So happily reunited with Rosen and keenly aware of Heidelberg's own natural beauty, he went through most of that winter on the crest of a wave, throwing himself into its social life – the balls and sleigh-parties, the eating and drinking, the love-making and music-making – with a zest quickly winning him the title of the 'Heidelberg favourite' even if at the same time alarming his family with his personal indulgences (such as new clothes and having his portrait painted) and constant requests for money, albeit always couched with irresistible charm and humour. He was of course fully aware of the town's inferiority as a musical centre in comparison with Leipzig. But this was offset by secret satisfaction in the knowledge that nobody in Heidelberg could play the piano as well as he, his greatest triumph coming in a concert with the Grand Duchess of Baden in the audience at which he performed Moscheles's Alexander Variations so brilliantly that there was 'absolutely no end to the "bravos" and "encores".'

For a while, he even managed to summon up a little interest in the lectures of Mittermayer and Thibaut, especially the latter, an eminent authority on Roman Law and the Pandects. 'Good heavens! What a difference there is between the Leipzig professor, who stood at his desk and rattled off his paragraphs without any sort of eloquence or inspiration, and this man Thibaut, who although about twice as old as the other, is overflowing with life and spirits, and can hardly find words or time to express his feelings', so he wrote home. A keen amateur musician, Thibaut was almost as renowned in artistic as in legal circles on account of his book, *On Purity in Musical Art*, and the weekly choir practices he organized and directed in his own house to champion Handel and still earlier neglected composers. At first Schumann thought his tastes too exclusively antiquarian. Later, the bond between them strengthened. And when the moment came for Schumann to return to Leipzig University, where as a Saxon citizen he was compelled to take his degree in Saxon law, it was Thibaut who at last made it clear to him that any further attempt to adapt himself to a way of life for which he had neither interest nor talent was futile. Rising at 5.30 a.m. on the morning of July 30, 1830, Schumann accordingly took up pen to write the most important letter of his life.

> Heidelberg
> 30th July 1830, 5 a.m.
>
> Good morning, Mamma!
> How shall I describe my bliss at this moment? The spirit lamp is hissing under the coffee pot, the sky is indescribably clear and rosy, and the keen spirit of the morning fills me with its presence. Besides, your letter lies before me and reveals a perfect treasury of good feeling, common sense and virtue. . . .

The blandishments completed, he at once came to the point. Claiming that his life had been a twenty years' struggle between poetry and prose, otherwise music and law, he continued:

> At Leipzig I did not trouble my head about my career, but went dreaming and dawdling on and never did any real good. Here I have worked harder, but both there and here have been getting more and more attached to art. Now I am standing at the crossroads and am scared at the question which way to choose. My genius points towards art, which is, I am inclined to think, the right path. But the fact is – now, do not be angry at what I am going to say, for I will but gently whisper it – it always seems to me as if you were putting obstacles in my way. You had very good reasons for doing so, and I understood them all perfectly, and we both agreed on calling art an 'uncertain future and a doubtful way of earning one's bread'. There certainly can be no greater misery than to look forward to a hopeless, shallow, miserable existence which one has prepared for oneself. But neither is it easy to enter upon a career diametrically

opposed to one's whole education, and to do it requires patience, confidence and quick decision. I am still at the height of youth and imagination, with plenty of capabilities for cultivating and ennobling art, and have come to the conclusion that with patience and perseverance, and a good master, I should in six years be as good as any pianist, for pianoforte playing is mere mechanism and execution. Occasionally I have much imagination and possibly some creative power. . . . Now comes the question: 'To be, or not to be,' for you can only do *one* thing well in this life, and I am always saying to myself: 'Make up your mind to do one thing thoroughly well, and with patience and perseverance you are bound to accomplish something.' . . .

If I stick to law I must undoubtedly stay here another winter to hear Thibaut lecture on the Pandects, as every law student is bound to do. If I am to go in for music, I must leave this at once and go to Leipzig, where Wieck, whom I could thoroughly trust, and who can tell me what I am worth, would then carry on my education. Afterwards I ought to go to Vienna for a year, and if possible study under Moscheles. Now I have a favour to ask you, my dear mother, which I hope you will grant me. *Write yourself to Wieck and ask him point blank what he thinks of me and my career. . . . If you like you can enclose this letter to Wieck. In any case the question must be decided before Michaelmas*, and then I shall pursue my object in life, whatever it may be, with fresh vigour and without tears . . .

Goodbye, dear mother, and do not fret. In this case heaven will help us only if we help ourselves.

Ever your most loving son,
Robert Schumann.

Disturbed and perplexed, the more so since her three elder sons eyed the whole proposal with such displeasure, Frau Schumann at once approached Wieck, ending her letter with the plea:

All rests on your decision – *the peace of a* LOVING MOTHER, THE WHOLE HAPPINESS FOR LIFE of a young and inexperienced man, who lives but in a higher sphere and will have nothing to do with practical life. I know that you love music. Do not let your feelings plead for Robert, but consider his years, his fortune, his powers and his future. I beg, I conjure you, as a husband, a father and a friend of my son, act like an upright man and tell me your opinion frankly – what he has to fear or to hope.

Already Wieck had sized up Schumann well enough to foresee problems. But it was a challenge he could not resist:

Leipzig,
August 1830.

Honoured Madam,

I hasten to answer your esteemed favour of the 7th inst. without further assuring you in advance of my warmest sympathy. . . . My suggestion would be that in the first place (for many and far-reaching reasons of which I hope to persuade your son) he should leave Heidelberg – the hotbed of his imagination – and should return to our cold, flat Leipzig.

At present I merely say that I pledge myself to turn your son Robert, by means of his talent and imagination, within three years into one of the greatest pianists now living. He shall play with more warmth and genius than Moscheles and on a grander scale than Hummel. The proof of this I offer you in my eleven-year-old daughter, whom I am now beginning to present to the world. . . .

1. Robert very mistakenly thinks 'that the whole of piano playing consists in pure technique'; what a one-sided conception! I almost infer from this, either that he has never heard a pianist of genius at Heidelberg or else that he himself has advanced no farther in playing. When he left Leipzig he knew better what belongs to a good pianist, and my eleven-year-old Clara will show him something different. But it is true that for Robert the greatest difficulty lies in the quiet, cold, well-considered, restrained conquest of technique, as the foundation of piano playing. I confess frankly that when – in the lessons which I gave him – I succeeded, after hard struggles and great contradictoriness on his part, after unheard-of pranks played by his unbridled fancy upon two creatures of pure reason like ourselves, in convincing him of the importance of a pure, exact, smooth, clear, well-marked and elegant touch, very often my advice bore little fruit for the next lesson, and I had to begin again, with my usual affection for him, to expound the old theme, to show him once more the distinctive qualities of the music which he had studied with me, and earnestly to insist on my doctrines (remember that I cared only for Robert and for the highest in art). And then he would excuse himself for the next week or fortnight or even longer, he could not come for this or that reason, and the excuses lasted – with a few exceptions – until he went to a town and to surroundings which in truth are not designed to restrain his unbridled fancy or quiet his unsettled ideas. Has our dear Robert changed – become more thoughtful, firmer, stronger, and may I say calmer and more manly? This does not appear from his letters.

2. I will not undertake Robert (that is if he means to live wholly for art in the future) unless for a year he has an hour with me almost every day.

Why? For once I ask you to have unquestioning confidence in me. But how can I do this now that I have a business at Dresden as well, and at Christmas am going to found a similar one in Berlin, Vienna and probably also in Paris? What will Robert's so-called Imagination-Man say to it if the lessons (lessons in touch, with an unemotional theme) have to be stolen from me and he is left to himself for from three to six weeks, to go on in the right direction? Honoured lady, neither of us can tell that; Robert himself knows best; he alone can say if he really has any determination.

3. Without committing myself further at present, I declare that the piano virtuoso (if he does not happen to be the most famous composer whose name has been honoured for years) can earn his living only if he gives lessons – but then, very easily and well. Good, intelligent teachers who have received an all-round education are wanted everywhere, and it is known that people pay 2–4 thaler an hour in Paris, Vienna, St Petersburg, Berlin, etc.; and 6–8 thaler

in London. I am educating my daughter to be a teacher first of all, though – child as she is – she is already far superior to all other women pianists in the world, for she can improvise freely – yet I do not allow this to mislead me in any way. Robert would be able to live very comfortably in such places, as a piano teacher, since he has a small income of his own. . . .

But I wish to know if Robert will decide at once to give lessons here, since teaching needs years of training? Robert surely remembers what I demand from a good piano teacher? That is one question which I cannot answer; nor can I say whether Robert also himself can answer it.

4. Can Robert determine to study dry, cold theory, and all that belongs to it, with Weinlig for two years? With instruction in the piano I always combine lessons in the practical study of simple chords by means of which I impart a beautiful and correct touch, etc. etc. – in a word, everything that is not and never will be found in any piano school.

Has Robert condescended to learn even this small amount of theory, although in any case my lessons are sufficiently interesting? I must say, No. Will Robert now decide like my Clara to give some hours every day to writing exercises in three- and four-part composition? It is work which almost wholly silences the imagination – at least such a one as our Robert enjoys. . . .

Most honoured friend, do not be anxious – compulsion is of little use in such matters: we must do our part as parents; God does the rest. If Robert has the courage and the strength to clear away my doubts when he is with me – and they might practically be removed in six months (so that in the contrary case everything would still not be lost) – then let him go in peace and give him your blessing. In the meantime you will be awaiting his answer to these few lines, the writer of which respectfully signs himself

Your most devoted servant,
Fr. Wieck.

Thus it was that when Clara's Polonaises, Op.1, appeared in print, one copy was specially reserved for 'Herr Schumann, who has lived with us since Michaelmas, and studies music'.

*

After a warmly received return visit to Dresden over Christmas and the New Year, Clara spent most of the first nine months of 1831 at home, working hard at her harmony, counterpoint and instrumentation (she even took some violin lessons to help her scoring) as well as widening her repertoire for the projected autumn tour. Having a good-looking, exuberantly imaginative young musician in the house with whom to share her discoveries and achievements was a great new spur, though as Wieck had anticipated, in matters of theoretical discipline Schumann was anything but a good influence, refusing even to consider any kind of systematic course with Weinlig when there were winged creators like Schubert and Jean Paul Richter from whom he felt he could learn so much more.

Already by the end of May Schumann's diary had noted Clara's 'enormous passion', followed a few weeks later by a still more revealing observation: 'What a creature Clara is! She certainly talked more cleverly than any of us . . . whims and fancies, laughter and tears, death and life, mostly in sharp contrasts, change in this girl with the speed of lightning.' He himself was unconsciously opening up new realms of experience for her. Never previously encouraged by her father to read, she now became aware of a world of Greek and Latin classics that held Schumann in thrall no less than romantics like Byron and E. T. A. Hoffmann as well as his one and only Jean Paul – and a host of younger poets too. By midsummer she was undoubtedly let into the secret of the musical novel, *Die Wunderkinder*, he had begun to plan in his diary, in which she and her father, Paganini, Hummel and various others were to appear under fanciful pseudonyms. She had already discovered that his own creative urges found just as ready an outlet in words as in music: his bedtime stories were always one of the most eagerly awaited treats of the day – for her young brothers, Alwin, Gustav and Klemens no less than herself. 'During your absence I have been in Arabia collecting fairy-tales for your benefit', he wrote when she eventually left on her first major tour outside her native Saxony, 'six new stories of men and their doubles, a hundred and one charades, eight amusing riddles, and then some awfully fine brigand stories, and the tale of the white spirit. Oh! how it makes my flesh creep!' Sometimes he would dress up and dim the lights to make his tales the more scarifying, as he was to recall several years later in a poem written for her in Vienna, its first lines:

> 'At night when you were very small
> I oft came dressed as a spectre tall
> And rattled at your door –
> You bade me begone, as you shrieked, afraid'.

Wieck himself, often reproached for not allowing Clara enough childish relaxation, for the most part looked on benevolently. Nevertheless as a hard-headed, self-made man, compelled to struggle for every penny, he sometimes suspected a strain of the dilettante in his pupil, besides wincing at his frequent extravagances, notably as regards clothes, cigars, champagne and travel – and the consequent continuous appeals for money to his fond family. Their worst clash was nevertheless when Schumann, impatient as ever for results and aware that Wieck's imminent tour with Clara would keep him away for a long time, innocently proposed a course of piano lessons with Hummel, second to none in acclaim as a teacher. 'He took it ill', so Schumann wrote to his mother in December, 1830, 'and asked me whether I mistrusted him, or what; and whether, as a matter of fact, he was not quite the best master? He saw that I was startled by such unnecessary anger, but we are now quite friendly again, and he treats me most affectionately, like his own child. You can hardly have a notion of his fire, his judgement, his view of art, and yet, when he speaks of his own or Clara's interests, he is as rude as a bear'. As the moment of departure with Clara drew nearer, Wieck and Schumann in fact came closer than ever before, despite temperamental differences, enough so for Schumann to beg his mother to write and thank Wieck for all his kind interest and help. Their discovery of Chopin's *Là ci darem* Variations, Op.2, at this time also drew all three of them into a kind of conspiratorial bond in their determination to champion a composer so able to infuse the popular virtuoso-variation style of the day with a new poetic magic all his own. Schumann's fanciful article of praise for this work, dating from September 1831, eventually appeared (albeit cut) in the *Allgemeine Musikalische Zeitung* on December 7, 1831, marking his début as a critic. Wieck followed it up with one of his own, published early in 1832 in the Hamburg *Cecilia*. As for Clara, her diary records that the work, learnt in eight days, 'is the most difficult piece of music which I have ever seen or played. This original, inspired composition is still so little known that it has been considered incomprehensible and unplayable by nearly all pianists and teachers. At the next concert that I give, here or in Berlin, or anywhere else, I shall play it in public for the first time'.

Clara's imminent attack of measles, together with an outbreak of cholera in Berlin, caused last minute changes of plan. But ten days after her twelfth birthday, with Paris still the ultimate goal, she set out with her father on a journey destined to keep them away from home for just over seven months. And it was in the Town Hall at Weimar, their first stop, that on October 7, 1831, Clara realized her ambition of introducing Chopin's Op.2 to Germany. For the first few days their welcome in this city was decidedly chilly. But as soon as Clara had played to the perceptive Geheimrat Schmidt, one by one doors began to open – even that of the eighty-two-year-old Goethe, who a decade earlier had shown similar interest in another little Wunderkind of twelve called Felix Mendelssohn. 'He received us very kindly', so the diary records after their first visit on October 1, 1831, at noon. 'Clara had to sit by him on the sofa. Soon afterwards his daughter-in-law came in with her two very clever-looking children of ten and twelve. Clara was now asked to play and as the piano stool was too low Goethe himself fetched a cushion from the ante-room and arranged it for her. She played Herz's *La Violetta*. While she was playing more visitors arrived and she then played Herz's Bravura Variations, Op.20. Goethe estimated these compositions and Clara's playing very justly, spoke of the pieces as bright, French and piquant, and admired Clara's intelligent rendering'. When invited to play to him a second time,

nine days later, she included one of her own sets of variations, in sum
pleasing him enough to win her a farewell present in the shape of a
medallion of himself with a note inscribed on its box in his own hand: 'To
the artistically highly gifted Clara Wieck. In kindly remembrance of
October 9, 1831. Weimar. J. W. Goethe'. The sincerity of his interest was
reaffirmed in a letter to his friend, Zelter, mentor of the young Mendelssohn: 'Yesterday a remarkable phenomenon appeared before me: a father
brought his daughter (a pianist) to see me. She was on her way to Paris and
played some recent Parisian compositions; the style was new to me, it
demands great ease in execution, but at the same time is always light; one
listens readily, and enjoys it. As you are certain to understand the sort of
thing, please explain it to me'.

Erfurt, Gotha, Arnstadt, Cassel, Frankfurt-on-Main and Darmstadt,
their next ports of call, brought mingled success and frustration, including
an unexpected warning in Frankfurt that unless Clara played more
Mozart and Beethoven and fewer virtuoso variations, she could never
hope to conquer that particular city. Her biggest encouragement, other
than Weimar, came in Cassel, where as well as melting the Elector's heart,
she also made a considerable impression on the critic and theorist, Moritz
Hauptmann (Wieck briefly considered sending her back to Hauptmann
after the tour for composition lessons), and still more on the composer,
Spohr, whose songs she had sung since the age of eight, and who now gave
her some useful advice about extending and strengthening the endings of
one or two of her compositions as well as a generous letter of introduction.
'Such is her skill', he wrote, 'that she plays the most difficult works that
have been written for the instrument with a combination of certainty and
skill which is to be seen only in the greatest living artists. Her playing is
further distinguished from that of the ordinary prodigy in that it is not only
the result of vigorous classical training, but also springs from her own
heart, as is testified by her compositions, which belong, as does the young
artist herself, among the remarkable phenomena of art'.

Paris was at last reached on February 15, 1832. 'Great God! What a
journey! What hardships during those four nights on the way to Paris! And
now we are much hampered by our inability to speak French', so Wieck
wearily complained in his diary, even though rooms had been booked for
them, and a warm hand of welcome extended, by Clementine Wieck's
artist brother, Eduard Fechner, who had made Paris his home. Their
mood was predominantly one of bewilderment at the sheer size of the
place, and the overwhelming number of musicians, writers and painters
lured there by its current reputation as Europe's artistic centre. Pianists,
especially of the virtuoso-composer school, were the most prolific of all,
including the highly influential, fashionable Kalkbrenner, and the scarcely less notorious Herz and Pixis (both major favourites in her repertory at

this time, the latter increasingly so after his concert in Leipzig on October 8, 1833, when she joined him in his *Grosses Duet* for two pianos) as well as the young Liszt and Chopin, already recognized by connoisseurs as in a place apart. Soon after his own arrival in the city, only five months earlier, Chopin had caustically written: 'I really don't know whether any place contains more pianists than Paris, or whether you can find more asses and virtuosos anywhere'.

Dashed in his secret hope that Clara might nevertheless still set the city talking if able to appear as supporting artist in a concert with Paganini, Wieck reconciled himself to an introductory round of late night receptions at which Clara just took her turn with whoever else this or that society hostess could procure, frequently struggling with heavier, stiffer pianos than she had ever encountered before. He himself wrote ironically to his wife of his own preparation for these ordeals: 'You should see me at the soirées (most pedantically attired by Fechner beforehand) with yellow gloves and a white stock, my hat always in my hand, careering about from 10 at night to 2 in the morning, half French, half German, and half despairing, perpetually straining my ears in order not to miss anything. Child, you would not recognize your Friedrich, for you never saw a more interesting-looking lackey. Just so well do my sturdy boots and shoes (they are made something after the fashion of the ferry-boats in which one used to cross the Mulde near Wurzen) fit with my blue frock-coat with the velvet collar and little brass buttons, and black trousers. In this get up I look something like a young oak in the Rosenthal'. One specific soirée on March 2 at Princess Vandamore's drew still livelier comment: 'What a place for it! There was an audience chamber decorated with heavy, old-fashioned tapestries, which with its adjacent rooms was a veritable emporium of porcelain, huge old vases, cups, figures, stuffed birds etc. etc. Here we found nothing but princes, ambassadors, and ministers as audience. Clara made a beginning upon an old, English ramshackle piano whose every note jerked and quivered. . . .' On this occasion Clara's co-artists included a handsome, ladykiller-type Spanish guitarist in national costume, an Italian soubrette soprano ('her method was that of the latest, frivolous, coquettish school, with all its merits and defects, its eternal ritardandos and cadenzas'), and the great Kalkbrenner himself, who despite teasingly condemning the German keyboard style and teaching methods in conversation with Wieck, was nevertheless politely approving of his daughter. Once or twice they were at parties when Chopin played his own compositions, including the *Là ci darem* Variations, which they found 'hardly recognisable on the rough and stubborn piano of Kalkbrenner's', as Wieck put it in the diary, commenting elsewhere that 'Chopin is a handsome fellow, but Paris has made him slovenly and careless in himself and in his art'. There is no record of any personal exchanges between them at this time. Possibly Chopin even tried to avoid him. He is known to have intensely disliked Wieck's well-intentioned but over-picturesque review of the *Là ci darem* Variations, even managing to get it suppressed when with Fechner's help, Wieck submitted it to the editor of Paris's *Revue Musicale*.

Two official appearances were eventually arranged for Clara on March 19 and April 9, both at Stöpel's Music School (with a congenial piano kindly lent her by the manufacturer, Erard) though only alongside others in programmes reflecting the superficial tastes of the time. For the second, Wieck had initially booked the bigger Hôtel de Ville. But when an outbreak of cholera half emptied the city, he quickly resolved on compromise – and more important still, to pack their bags the moment the concert was over. Clara impressed her small audience by including an extemporization, and by playing all else in the programme from memory. But no important doors were opened, and there was little financial gain. They left on April 13, and after delays occasioned by obligatory quarantine as well as a few days' illness of another kind for Clara herself en route, they were back in their own home by 11.30 a.m. on May 1, 1832. A quarter of an hour later, so the diary records, 'Clara was cleaning knives in the kitchen'.

FOUR

First Pangs 1832–35

During Wieck's absence Schumann had moved into lodgings of his own, but young Gustav and Alwin immediately rushed round to tell him the travellers had returned. In the constant meetings of the next few weeks Schumann's impression of Clara was that she had 'grown prettier and taller, stronger and more self-possessed, and speaks German with a French accent which Leipzig will soon drive out of her'. It was springtime, so there was one happy excursion to the zoo besides several evening reunions with relations and friends at Leipzig restaurants like the Brand and Wasserschenke. At close quarters with a panther she was 'foolish and frightened', though soon afterwards Schumann found her adorably childish in not knowing the difference between a duck and a goose. This incident remained in his mind with sufficient fragrance for him to recall it in one of those verselets he was later to send her from Vienna:

> 'You saw a duck and thought it a goose,
> Certainly things play fast and loose'.

Now in her thirteenth year, Clara was in fact at a difficult stage of adolescence, often 'charming and lively', but sometimes recalcitrant and tearful. 'She is being very self-willed just now towards her stepmother, who is certainly the worthiest of women', so Schumann wrote on June 1, 1832. 'The old boy scolded Clara. All the same he will soon be under Clara's thumb; already she gives orders like a Leonore – though at the same time she knows how to beg and coax like a child.'

But once the initial excitements of home-coming were over – and they included welcoming a baby stepsister, Marie, born on January 17 of that year – order was gradually restored. One of Clara's first responsibilities was to give piano lessons to Alwin, now eleven. Wieck also deemed the moment right for her to leave Weinlig and start a new course in harmony, counterpoint and composition with Heinrich Dorn (one of her partners in her Gewandhaus concert on November 8, 1830) with whom Schumann himself had consented to study during Wieck's absence. Dorn in fact soon terminated those lessons, recognizing that though Schumann genuinely respected him and even, in principle, the value of contrapuntal discipline too, he was far too elated in the knowledge that his fanciful *Papillons*, Op.2, were soon to appear in print, in succession to his equally freely conceived *Abegg Variations*, Op.1, of the previous year, to consent to don any kind of academic straight-jacket. For Clara there were no such problems. From her father she had learnt to accept the rigours of her calling with a professionalism far in advance of her years, and in all matters of instruction did exactly what she was told. A manuscript copy of a little folk-like song, composed for and affectionately inscribed to her teacher, survives as proof of her happy relationship with Dorn.

Nevertheless it was towards the unfettered, imaginative world of Schumann's *Papillons*, with which he had been so preoccupied in their house before the tour, that she looked in her own Op.2, a set of *Caprices en forme de Valse* recently published in Paris. Though naïve, her pieces have the same Schubert-inspired waltz-lilt of his, deriving unity from an uprising scale motif (with an accented passing note on the first beat of the second bar) that stems direct from the leading theme of his first number (subsequently quoted in *Carnaval*). The *ritard e morendo* ending of her No.2, its melody expiring on an unresolved leading note, is also pure Schumann. Still more interesting, in view of its symbolic importance in the future for them both, is the falling five-note motif, marked *doloroso*, introduced in F minor in the course of her No.7. Significantly, another variant of this same motto, again in F minor and marked *doloroso*, made its way into the *Valse Romantique* published by Hofmeister in Leipzig as her Op.4. This piece, too, is strongly influenced by *Papillons*, though one of its episodes makes a passing nod at Chopin, whose early mazurkas and waltzes she could well have heard from his own hands in Paris.

Ex. 1

A

Caprice en forme de Valse

doloroso

B

Valse Romantique

doloroso

When first hearing her play again, after her battles with French pianos which even in Kalkbrenner's house she had found tough and stubborn, Schumann ungallantly observed that she sounded 'like a hussar'. But by the end of May he was already praising her mercurial lightness and grace in his *Papillons*. And Gewandhaus audiences were no less appreciative of the imaginative charm behind technical ease when she returned as soloist with the orchestra in two virtuoso-type programmes in July, 1832, the second including the first movement of Field's second Concerto, and still more when on September 30, just thirteen, she appeared at the first of the official autumn subscription series (all her previous concerts had been 'extras') in the G minor Piano Concerto of Moscheles.[1] That she played everything from memory, then a far from common feat, made everyone marvel the more.

After the exhaustion of their previous winter's adventures, Wieck decided to restrict travelling to a short November tour first to Altenburg, and then to Zwickau, where Schumann's mother still lived, and Schneeberg, where her other sons carried on the family publishing trade. The concert in Zwickau's Gewandhaus on November 18 not only at last allowed Frau Schumann to hear the Wunderkind of whom Robert had recently remarked 'we are like brother and sister', but also the first movement of a Symphony in G minor which he had recently completed, as proof of his industry as a student. Clara herself was represented as composer by a Scherzo for orchestra, now lost, probably written as an exercise during her lessons in composition and instrumentation the previous year (its most likely first performance was at her concert in Altenburg on May 18, 1831). From Wieck there was another duet for piano and physharmonica to play with his daughter, this time a Notturno in B flat displaying how prettily the physharmonica[2] can sing over a gently rippling piano accompaniment as well as bringing reminders of links with the organ loft (in passages of quasi-improvisational chordal modulation) within the work's imposing piano introduction and benign coda. Besides this and a duet for violin and piano by Herz and Beriot (undertaken with the leader) Clara also played three formidable bravura works with the orchestra by Pixis, Herz and Moscheles (the Grande Polonaise from his E flat concerto). It was soon after this concert that standing at a window with Clara as Robert walked by and smiled up at them Frau Schumann was allegedly moved to exclaim: 'Some day you must marry my son'.

Schumann himself decided to remain with his family over the winter – and not only because he wished to try and revise and complete the symphony, also various other keyboard projects, in peace. Either because of using a mechanical finger-strengthener (then much in vogue) or merely because of over-practice in an attempt to catch up on his late start as a

[1] At a chamber concert only the month before she had taken part in his *Der Abschied des Troubadours* for voice, guitar, violin and piano, written in collaboration with Giulini and Mayseder.

[2] A manuscript sketch of this work is preserved in the archives of the Schumann-Haus at Zwickau.

Sonntag, den 18. November 1832.

GROSSES CONCERT
im Saale des Gewandhauses.

ERSTER THEIL.

1) Ouverture aus „der Felsenmühle" von Reissiger.
2) Recitativ und Chor aus „der Schöpfung."
3) Grosses Concert von Pixis, für Pianoforte mit Orchestre, vorgetragen von Clara Wieck.
4) Duett und Chor aus „der bezauberten Rose" von Wolfram.
5) Grosse Polonaise, aus dem Esdur-Concert von Moscheles, für Pianoforte mit Orchestre, vorgetragen von Clara Wieck.

ZWEITER THEIL.

6) Erster Satz der ersten Symphonie, componirt von Robert Schumann.
7) Chor aus „der bezauberten Rose" von Wolfram.
8) Duo für Pianoforte und Violine von Herz und Bériot, vorgetragen von Clara Wieck und Herrn Musikdirector Meyer.
9) Scherzo für Orchestre, componirt von Clara Wieck.
10) Notturno für Pianoforte und Physharmonica, vorgetragen von Herrn Wieck.
11) Bravour-Variationen von Herz für Pianoforte mit Orchestre, vorgetragen von Clara Wieck.

Billets à 6 Gr. sind bis Sonnabend Abend zu haben in der Richter'schen Buchhandlung.
Der Eintrittspreis an der Kasse ist 8 Gr.

Anfang halb 7 Uhr. Ende um 9 Uhr.

Zwickau.   **DER SINGVEREIN.**

serious piano student, he had recently lamed the weaker fingers of his right hand. After several months of treatment ranging from brandy-and-water bathing, herb poultices and *Tierbäder* (immersing the affected part in the blood of a freshly killed ox) to the electrical and homoeopathic, he now realized that all further thoughts of a pianist's career were out of the question. And though reconciled to the disaster by this time, and even in a way glad to know that his true future lay in composition, the experience had been traumatic enough to make a few quiet months with his family, away from the pressures of Leipzig musical life, almost essential.

As for Clara, she went down with scarlet fever the moment she returned, profitably spending her convalescence in learning to sew. But a long letter from Leipzig to Zwickau on December 17, 1832, reveals where her thoughts always lay:

My dear Herr Schumann,

. . . On the very day – a few days after our return – when I was to have played at Molique's concert, I got scarlet fever, and until a few days ago I had to stay in that wearisome bed. But it was only a slight attack and already I can be up for several hours every day, and have played the piano again. But I was not able to play at the Gewandhaus. I played to Hermstedt and Molique; since then they have not appeared again, for fear of infection. But you, dear Herr Schumann, must not let yourself be prevented from coming here, for everything will be over by the New Year. I am playing in the Gewandhaus on January 8, and immediately after that I am playing Hummel's septet, for which everything is prepared already. I wager that the time would not have seemed long to you here, as it probably does in Zwickau, ... Ah, what a lot of news I had to tell you. But I will not do it, or else you will stick at Zwickau; I know you. I will just make you curious, so that you shall long for Leipzig. But out of pity I will tell you one thing, since the time must hang so on your hands.

On Saturday my Father was at the Euterpe. Listen: Herr Wagner has got ahead of you; a symphony of his was performed, which is said to be as like as two peas to Beethoven's symphony in A major. Father said that F. Schneider's symphony, which was given in the Gewandhaus, was like the freight-waggon which takes two days to get to Wurzen always keeping to the same track, and a stupid old waggoner with a great peaked cap keeps on growling to the horses: 'Ho, ho, ho, hotte, hotte'. But Wagner drives in a gig over stock and stone and every minute falls into a ditch by the road, but in spite of this gets to Wurzen in a day, though he looks black and blue. . . . Father helped me with this part of my letter. . . . I am looking forward to Christmas very much, and the piece of cake that I am going to save for you is already waiting for you, so that it may be eaten by you, although it is not baked yet. Give my love to everybody, and write me an answer soon, only write nice and clearly. Hoping to see you soon, I end my letter and remain your friend, Clara Wieck.

A Gewandhaus subscription concert on January 10, 1833, with Herz's

Variations on a theme of Rossini and Hummel's Septet in the programme marked Clara's return to health, followed only a few days later by an invitation recital at the Wiecks' home, now Reichstrasse 579, courageously including Chopin's very recently published Mazurkas, Op.6 and Op.7 and his E flat Nocturne, Op.9, No.2, together with two of Schumann's *Paganini Caprices* and her own *Caprices en forme de Valse*, Op.2, alongside trivialities by Pixis (his third and fourth trios), Moscheles, Reissiger and her father's Romanze for physharmonica and piano.

Illness then struck a more dastardly blow at the Wieck family when Klemens, Clementine's three-year-old son, adored by them all, died within a few hours of first symptoms on February 5. But after a brief recuperative visit to Dresden, where Alwin and Gustav were entered at the Freemasons' School, life resumed its strict course, with instruction for Clara in French and English as well as a daily singing lesson from her father on top of her work for Dorn. It was at this time that she also first began to contemplate a piano concerto. Apart from the fact that all itinerant virtuosos of the day wrote their own to play at their concerts, there was the still stronger stimulus of wanting to share the orchestral adventures on which her absent Herr Schumann had recently embarked, especially when he encouraged her, in a letter to Wieck of January 10, 1833, by suggesting that the concerto's key should be C major or A minor.

*

Schumann himself returned in March. Though his Symphony was still incomplete, its revised first movement had been played again at Schneeberg in January, and on April 29 he managed to squeeze it into a programme at the Gewandhaus where it was somewhat eclipsed by Mendelssohn's *Midsummer Night's Dream* Overture as well as a *Concertsatz* by Kalkbrenner and Pixis's *Concert-Rondo, mit orchestra und 3 obligaten Glockschen*,[1] both brand new, with Clara as the soloist. Nevertheless the experience boosted his morale, as did reunion with many old friends. His happiness was further enhanced by finding delightful new lodgings on the city's rural fringe. As he put it in a note to Clara on May 23: 'Good morning! In your prosaic town you can have no idea of what a morning is like in Riedel's Garden, when everything, from the birds to myself, is singing, humming and rejoicing.' As for Clara's delight in his return, a letter from Schumann to his mother soon after his twenty-third birthday tells it all:

'Clara is as fond of me as ever, and is just as she used to be of old, wild and enthusiastic, skipping and running about like a child, and saying the most intensely thoughtful things. It is a pleasure to see how her gifts of

---

[1] Much in demand from her in the next few years.

mind and heart keep developing faster and faster, and, as it were, leaf for
leaf. The other day, as we were walking back from Connewitz (we go for a
two or three hours' tramp almost every day), I heard her saying to herself:
"Oh, how happy I am! How happy!" Who would not love to hear that? On
that same road there are a great many useless stones, lying about in the
middle of the footpath. Now, when I am talking, I often look more up than
down, so she always walks behind me, and gently pulls my coat at every
stone to prevent my falling; meantime she stumbles over them herself!'

When confined to his rooms with a severe fever, he wrote a letter to
Clara on July 13, 1833, outlining what he called 'a plan of sympathy – this!
tomorrow on the stroke of 11 I shall play the adagio from Chopin's
variations and at the same time I shall think of you very hard, exclusively of
you. Now the request is that you should do the same, so that we may see
each other and meet in spirit. The place will probably be over the little
Thomaspförtchen, where our doubles will meet'. Her reply, at once fond
and teasing, was despatched by return:

Dear Herr Schumann,
   With great difficulty I have at last, with my mother's help, made out your
letter, and at once sit down to answer you. I am very sorry that you have been so
shaken by the fever, and all the more since I have learned that you are not
allowed to drink any Bavarian beer, a prohibition which you must find it very
hard to obey. You want to know if I am alive? Well you may tell that by the
number of compliments I have sent you already – to be sure I do not know if
they have been delivered, but I hope so. How I live, you can easily think for
yourself. How can I live happily when you no longer come to see us! As to your
request I will grant it, and shall find myself at 11 o'clock tomorrow over the little
Thomaspförtchen. I have finished my *"Doppelgänger"* chorus, and have added a
third part to it. To my great sorrow I cannot write you a longer letter, as I have
so much to do. Please write to me again. From her heart there wishes you a
quick recovery,
                                      Clara Wieck.

When I got your letter I thought, now you too shall write really badly for once,
and I have done so, as you may see.

In her next letter of August 1 she was able to enclose her newest
published composition, the *Romance Variée*, Op.3, proudly dedicated to
him. As she knew he was also currently working on a set of Impromptus on
her own theme, she added: 'Your able re-casting of this little musical
thought will make good my mistakes, and so I beg for this – I can hardly
wait to make its acquaintance'. There was a cryptic remark in his fanciful
letter of thanks to set her thinking: '. . . To you I have nothing but a
heartfelt "thankyou" to give, and if you were here (even without your

father's permission) a hand-clasp; and then I would say something of the hope that the union of our names on the title-page may be a union of our views and ideas at a later day. I am too poor to offer more'. By August 18 his own *Impromptus* arrived, rushed into print in time for the forty-eighth birthday of her father, the dedicatee, while he was escorting Clara on a brief tour of Chemnitz, Schneeberg and Carlsbad. Like Beethoven's 'Prometheus' Variations, Op.35, Schumann's Op.5 *Impromptus* are strengthened by a strong bass motif (the notes C F G C) as important to the argument as the theme itself, not least in the fugal finale. But though Clara's variations are more simply argued, more naïvely pianistic, with several little decorative flourishes and cadenzas in the virtuoso style of the day, they affirm the orderly elegance of her thinking and contain one or two charming streaks of fancy. Whether by accident or design, there is even a recall of that five-note falling motif, to become so important to them both, as a means of modulating from C to A flat for the penultimate variation.

Schumann's dedication to Wieck was in fact a gesture of reconciliation. Shortly beforehand, he had not concealed his bitterness when in response to a request for help in founding a new music journal, Wieck had replied: 'If you take up the matter energetically I promise you my help, but if you get lukewarm . . .'. Always a realist, Wieck knew his old pupil's impulsive enthusiasms, and feared this might prove just another passing whim. But this time he was wrong. Schumann and a group of progressive young friends had genuinely tired of the superficialities passing for art in the musical world around them, equally the impotence of current criticism in the press. Meeting night after night, often at Leipzig's *Kaffeebaum* restaurant, they thrashed out a policy designed to revive interest in the great classical past, not forgetting recent heroes like Schubert and Beethoven, as well as to hasten the dawn of a new poetic age. Publishing problems, together with Schumann's nervous breakdown in the autumn after the successive deaths of his much loved sister-in-law, Rosalie, and his brother, Julius, caused serious delay. But the first number of the *Neue Zeitschrift für Musik*, as they elected to call it, eventually emerged in April, 1834, with Julius Knorr as editor (a post very soon taken over by Schumann himself) and with the initially sceptical Wieck himself on the board of directors. Nothing quite like it had ever previously appeared in print. For resurrecting the fantasy of the *Harmonische Verein* projected by Weber a quarter of a century before, Schumann enlisted all his contributors, always concealed by pseudonyms, into the Davidsbund, an imaginary society pledged to wage war on music's Philistines in every possible way. Still obsessed by the *Doppelgänger* world of Jean Paul and Hoffmann, he himself most liked to write under the twin names of Eusebius and Florestan representing him as dreamer and man of action respectively, a division of his own personality first adopted in his unrealized novel. On the rare occasions when their views concurred, he would sign himself Master Raro – a pseudonym which at other times hid the practical, down-to-earth opinion of Wieck himself.

There was some initial conflict for Wieck on realizing that one of the paper's main targets of abuse was just that kind of empty virtuoso music in which Clara had scored most of her early successes, with Herz and Hünten highest on Schumann's list of 'dross'. But while a wily enough business man to give the public what they wanted rather than face the financial loss of empty seats, he had always managed to silence his critics – and his conscience – with the irrefutable rejoinder that such music lay more within the mental grasp of a child than mature Bach, Haydn, Mozart or Beethoven (on whom he had once been privileged to pay a call in Vienna). He also had the comfort of knowing that he encouraged Clara to explore the classics in private, whether in their own home, or with friends who were connoisseurs. At this moment she was in fact already studying such works as Beethoven's C minor (Op.1) and 'Archduke' Trios also his Choral Fantasy – soon to be followed by the 'Appassionata' – as well as Preludes and Fugues by Bach. On the contemporary front, every available new work by Chopin was immediately learnt,[1] besides any from Schumann. As a proud, honorary member of the Davidsbund, in which she was known as Chiara, or Zilia, she herself was now increasingly aware of where musical goodness and truth really lay. That Wieck himself recognized signs of a growing maturity and self-determination in every aspect of her character is abundantly clear from the letter he wrote soon after her confirmation on January 10, 1834.

My daughter,
You must be independent now; that is most important. I have dedicated nearly 10 years of my life to you and your education; it is for you now to think of your duties. Fix your mind then, on noble and unselfish deeds, on doing good, on a true humanity which shall grow more and more at every opportunity, and consider the practice of virtue to be true religion. When you are bitterly misunderstood, calumniated, envied, do not let this lead you astray in your principles. Ah! this is a hard struggle and yet in this consists true virtue. I remain your helpful adviser and friend, Friedrich Wieck.

*

Up till this time Clara's closest girl friend had been Emilie List, daughter of the American Consul in Leipzig, who was confirmed at the same time.

---

[1] By this time she was playing Chopin's E minor Concerto, Op.11, his Fantasia on Polish Airs for piano and orchestra, Op.13, and his G minor Trio, Op.8, as well as solos.

But when playing at Plauen early in 1834, Clara was introduced to a girl of seventeen and a half called Ernestine, whose ostensible guardian (in reality her natural father), Baron von Fricken, was a keen enough amateur flautist and music-lover to propose sending her to Leipzig to study piano with Wieck as a resident pupil as from April 21. No one was more excited about the new lodger than Clara, even though three years younger than Ernestine, and it was not long before she was confessing 'Ah, when only you get to know Schumann! I like him best of all our acquaintances'. At first Ernestine was indifferent. But as Clara subsequently confessed to Schumann: 'I had not long to wait before she became more and more fond of you, and soon it got to a pitch that I had always to call her when you came. I was glad enough to do so then, for I was only too pleased that she liked you. I wanted her to, and I was satisfied. You always talked to her alone when she came, and you only talked nonsense to me. I was not a little hurt by this, but I comforted myself with the thought that it was only due to the fact that you always had me, and also that Ernestine was more grown up than I was'.

Though a new-found pianist friend, Ludwig Schunke, with whom he now shared lodgings, and the start of a lovely warm spring were gradually helping Schumann to overcome recent heartbreak and worries about his right hand, he still could not forget a remark made during his breakdown by his doctor: 'Medicine is no good here. You need a wife'. In the circumstances, Ernestine's sudden arrival seemed so providential that it was not long before he was whispering to his mother that she was 'just such a one as I might wish to have for a wife'. Wieck at once took stock of the situation, writing to reassure the Baron that though there was a 'strong feeling' between Schumann and Ernestine, their meetings were always adequately chaperoned (little did he know what in fact went on behind his back with the discreet help of friends). More important, as soon as it could be arranged, he sent the now patently unsettled Clara to Dresden, ostensibly for further composition studies under Karl Reissiger, Weber's successor at the Dresden Opera, also a course of singing lessons under Miksch, chorus master at the opera house, who had studied with Caselli, a pupil of Bernacchi, and in Wieck's opinion knew more about voice production than anyone living.

Distressed as she was, Clara maintained a brave face, admonishing her old friend, on his birthday, with a smile:

Dear Herr Schumann,
    Today, Sunday the 8th of June, on the day when the good God let fall so bright a musical spark from heaven, and you were born, I sit here and write to you, although I have had two invitations for this afternoon.
    The first thing I have to write is that I send you my good wishes, that you may

not always be contrary, may drink less Bavarian beer, may not stay behind when others go, may not turn day into night and *vice versa*, may show your friends what you think of them, may compose industriously, may write more for the newspaper because the readers wish it, and firmly resolve to come to Dresden etc. etc.

But is it permitted Herr Schumann, to take so little notice of a friend that you do not even write to her? Every time the post arrived I hoped to get a letter from a certain Herr Enthusiast, but ah! I was disappointed. I comforted myself with the thought that at least you were coming here, but my father has just written to me to say that you are not coming with him as Knorr is ill. Emilie too is not coming with him as she is going to a watering place – that is misfortune upon misfortune. Well, one must take things as they come! I am much looking forward to your new rondo, it will give me something to work at. Here in Dresden everybody, and Sophie Kaskel (a pretty girl) in particular, is quite in love with your Impromptus and practises them industriously. She – and Becker and Krägen – are quite unhappy that you are not coming here, and it is really quite unpardonable of you.

There is a notice fixed to my door: "Clarus Wieck, officially appointed contributor to the latest musical paper". Before long you shall have 6 pages from me, and then you will have to pay me a lot.

I hear that Gustav has written to you – Fine stuff I expect! And you really mean to answer him? In that case I too may expect an original letter – the handwriting need not be original (i.e. illegible) – may I not, Herr Schumann? This ingenious, original and witty epistle commends to you with due deliberation (you do not like haste) your friend

Clara Wieck

Clara Wieck

Double.

A brief return to Leipzig for the christening of another baby step-sister, Caecilie, for whom Ernestine and Schumann stood as godparents, brought home the reality of the situation rather more acutely for Clara, nor was her pain much eased on learning soon after that the Baron had removed Ernestine from Leipzig so that she should not be compromised before the engagement was officially announced – in secret he was also legitimizing her birth for that moment. Wieck's next step was to plan a new concert tour for the whole of the winter of 1834–5, with Magdeburg, Schönebeck, Halberstadt, Brunswick, Hanover, Bremen and Hamburg as the principal ports of call. In a further attempt to divert Clara he invited Carl Banck, a young song composer who also contributed occasionally to the *Neue Zeitschrift*, to join them on the first part of the tour. But it was not till reaching Brunswick, where she played a lot of chamber music with the four brothers, Karl, Theodor, August and Franz Müller, of the eminent Müller String Quartet, that Clara found any real solace. In a letter to her stepmother, she even pretended to have fallen in love with Karl.

Professionally, the tour brought the usual mixture of successes and harassments. Interviewers either intimating that he was a slave-driver, or questioning his choice of repertoire, proved the main source of Wieck's irritation, while Clara's big cross, as ever, was indifferent or impossible pianos. By April 4, 1835, Wieck's diary records 'Clara plays with reluctance and does not want to do any more'. By now he, too, was weary enough to cancel plans for a Berlin concert, and by the middle of the month the travellers were back in Leipzig.

Schumann called the first afternoon after their return. As Clara later put it: 'How well I remember how you came into the room and hardly gave me even a passing greeting, and how I went in tears to Augusta, who was with us, and said: "Oh! I love no one as I love him, and he did not even look at me!"' Nor was it any consolation to find him writing variations on a theme by Baron von Fricken, subsequently to emerge as the *Etudes symphoniques*, or to discover that he had just finished another set of variations on the letters of Ernestine's birthplace, Asch, translated into musical notation – even if this particular work, entitled *Carnaval*, did in fact include her own musical portrait under the pseudonym of 'Chiarina', alongside Ernestine's 'Estrella'. But Ernestine was no longer in the house. And as the days passed, Clara slowly began to perceive that something in Schumann's attitude had changed. At the time it was of course impossible for him even to try to explain to her his inner conflict on discovering the true facts of Ernestine's birth and meagre financial expectations, and still more, his sudden awareness that Clara herself was no longer a child with whom he could just 'laugh and play'. All that he reserved for a long letter much later. Music, for the moment, was the cloak under which deeper feelings were hidden, drawing them into the same almost daily contact as of old. And by the end of the summer she was the proud possessor of a Sonata in F sharp minor significantly inscribed 'To Clara, from Florestan and Eusebius', its first movement based on the same two motifs (originating in a sketched fandango that Schumann for a while lost) on which she had written a piano piece entitled 'Le Ballet des Revenants' (subsequently published as No.4 of her *Quatre Pièces caractéristiques*, Op.5).

There was a brief separation when Clara left to play in Halle, and Schumann to visit his mother in Zwickau. But with Mendelssohn's arrival in Leipzig as conductor of the Gewandhaus Orchestra, and the attendant stream of distinguished musical visitors to the town, most of whom made a call at the Wieck household, the new autumn season threw Clara and Schumann into still closer social contact. Mendelssohn was guest of honour at her sixteenth birthday party on September 13, 1835, amusing them all by imitating Chopin and Liszt at the piano as well as playing Bach and works of his own both alone and with Clara, who in her turn, at his special request, performed the Scherzo from Schumann's new Sonata

which she had introduced to him complete a few days before. Significantly, Mendelssohn refused to listen to anything in her repertory by
Herz. Champagne flowed freely, and the evening was yet more heart-
stirring for Clara when she was presented with a new Capriccio by
Mendelssohn as well as a birthday ode and a gold watch from 'the
Davidsbund'. Not long afterwards there was another red-letter day when
Chopin called. Now twenty-five, he was on his way back to Paris after a
reunion with his parents in Carlsbad, and Schumann was of course
summoned to meet him too. Clara herself admired his beautiful French
manners as much as his very delicate *pianissimo*, but found his rubato too
capricious for her own taste. He in his turn was lavish in praise of her
playing of his own music, and gave her one of his newest pieces.
Moscheles's visit was another landmark for them both. Schumann had
never forgotten hearing one of his recitals way back in 1819 (he had even
kept the programme) and at this moment hoped to secure him as London
correspondent of the *Neue Zeitschrift*. Clara of course played him Schumann's Sonata, which he at first found 'laboured, difficult and somewhat
intricate', and its composer 'a retiring but interesting young man'. For
Clara's own playing, not least in Beethoven's 'Archduke' and one of
Schubert's piano trios, his praise was unbounded, particularly for its total
lack of affectation. Of his own G minor Concerto he wrote to his wife: 'No
better interpretation or execution of the work is possible. I myself could
not give it more effect. She plays it just as though it were her own
composition'. Moscheles also enormously enjoyed joining Clara and
Mendelssohn in a private performance at Wieck's house of Bach's then
unpublished and practically unknown D minor Concerto for three pianos,
which he at once decided to have copied for London.

The musical climax of these increasingly happy autumn days came on
November 9, when with Mendelssohn as conductor (and he was making
history at the Gewandhaus as the first to stand in front of the orchestra and
beat time with a baton) Clara was soloist in a programme which included
not only his own recent (1832) B minor Capriccio (playing it 'like a little
demon and I liked it very much', as he wrote to his sister) and Bach's D
minor Concerto for three pianos with Mendelssohn and the young
Bremen pianist, Louis Rakemann, as her partners, but also a Piano
Concerto in A minor of her own, dedicated to her old friend and admirer,
Spohr. First projected in the winter of 1832/3, this Concerto had reached
an advanced enough stage by October 22, 1833, for Clara to describe it (in
her own handwriting) in her diary as finished, though a reference (in
Wieck's handwriting) exactly four months later to the completion of its
finale suggests that this movement was either a later addition or else had
been substantially revised. The diary also reveals that Schumann himself,
much involved at the time with problems of instrumentation in his own G

minor Symphony, orchestrated it for her.[1] (She was business-woman
enough to record that the copying of instrumental parts cost her precisely
4 Thaler 12 Silbergroschen). Both at Leipzig's Hotel Pologne on May 5,
1834, and in Plauen four months later Clara's programmes had included
a *Concertsatz* by herself. But the performance of the work in its entirety
at the Gewandhaus under Mendelssohn in November, 1835, was the
official christening.

In a crop of mixed reviews the most favourable came from the critic of
the *Komet*, who assessed the Concerto as 'written throughout in a grand
style' and admired its 'interchange of the softest and most tuneful
melodies with the fieriest and most fantastic passages', also 'the poetic
unity which governed the whole'. In view of the largely monothematic
piano concerto in the same key Schumann himself was eventually to write,
nothing in Clara's work is in fact more interesting than its attempted unity:
the uprising A minor motif heard from the orchestra at the outset
influences the opening of the central *Andante non troppo, con grazia*, also
the rondo theme of the closing movement. In a personal letter to Clara
three years later, Schumann himself confessed doubts about the first
movement: admitting that some of its ideas were gems, it still left him with
an impression of incompleteness. In form, this opening movement (or
section) is in fact no more than a quasi-improvisational exposition and
development, without a recapitulation. An enharmonic modulation then
carries the music into A flat major (rather more cunningly than the swerve
into that key in the course of the first movement) for the central *Andante*,
an idyllic song-without-words. Mainly for solo piano, this music is very
close in spirit to the Aria in Schumann's F sharp minor Piano Sonata
(which he developed from his youthful song-setting of Kerner's poem,
'An Anna'), with its main motif inverted in A major in a brief central
section before the arrival of a solo cello to transform the recapitulation
into a love-duet. The lively final movement is an extended sonata-
rondo, with well-sustained development of its first and second subjects in
lieu of the easier expedient of a new central episode. Some charming
exchanges between piano and orchestra near the end do credit to the
youthful Schumann's ear for instrumental colour. But except for a few
salubrious introductory or linking tuttis, the orchestra plays only a very
subservient, supporting role: the Concerto is primarily a soloist's show-
piece, and as such shows Clara's ability to soften note-spinning with a
feminine charm of her own.

Schumann's young English friend, Sterndale Bennett, aptly summed it
up in his diary as a work that needed 'weeding', adding, however, that
Clara was a very clever girl, and that he wished all girls were like her. She

---

[1] Part of the manuscript survives in the Staatsbibliothek, Berlin.

herself, while aware of its weaknesses, was still sufficiently proud of her achievement to play it quite often on her tours in the next few years – performances which brought her censure from Schumann, increasingly opposed to any echoes of the virtuoso-composer school. But at the first performance he concealed all secret reservations in flowers. 'What we first heard took flight before our eyes like a young phoenix soaring up from its own ashes' was how he began his anonymous article in the *Neue Zeitschrift* (included in his 'Letters of an Enthusiast' series about daily events in Leipzig). 'Here white yearning roses and pearly lily calyxes inclined their heads; there orange blossoms and myrtle nodded, while alders and weeping willows spread out their shadows. In the midst of it all a maiden's radiant countenance gently moved, seeking flowers for a garland. I often spied little boats, hovering daringly over the water. There lacked only a master's hand at the helm, a smartly spread sail, to send them cutting swiftly, triumphantly and surely through the waves'. As the article continued, so the metaphors became increasingly mixed. For Schumann's head was by now completely ruled by his heart. Shortly before Clara left with her father towards the end of November for another brief tour including Zwickau, Plauen, Glachau and Chemnitz, he called to say goodbye, and kissed her as, light in hand, she saw him out down the stairs. He followed her to Zwickau, where they kissed again – a kiss passionate enough for him to recall it even three years later when writing to her from Vienna. With that kiss, both knew that a new chapter in their lives had begun.

FIVE

Professional Triumphs, Personal Vacillations
1835–38

Throughout the second half of 1835 Wieck was sufficiently relieved at finding Clara restored to something like her old equanimity to accept Schumann's frequent presence in their house without protest. He knew no one spurred her to greater effort: even while completing her concerto she was at work on new solo pieces eventually published as her Opp. 5, 6 and 8. In any case, Wieck still considered him emotionally bound to the absent Ernestine. He had no knowledge of that Zwickau kiss, or, at first, of its consequences. So that back in Leipzig, where Clara was soloist in Beethoven's Choral Fantasy under Mendelssohn at the Gewandhaus on December 15, Schumann could confide to his diary 'happy hours pass in her arms at Wieck's house in the evenings'. At Christmas he even gave her pearls. But as Frau Wieck observed at the time, 'pearls mean tears'. And when Wieck himself suddenly realized the way the wind had turned, his reaction was as drastic as when he saw his daughter upset by Schumann's attentions to Ernestine eighteen months earlier. On January 14, 1836, she was again sent off to Dresden, where he knew she had friends and interests enough to console her while preparing for two concerts in late January and early February – at the first of which Wieck's diary records that she showed signs of nervousness and even shed some tears.

Her spirits rose on receiving Schumann's latest *Paganini Etudes* as 'token of his regard', but infinitely more when on February 7, he suddenly arrived in person on learning that Wieck had been called away for a few days. Sympathetic friends contrived that they could meet alone, and in a great uprush of love intensified by the long-delayed, official termination of his engagement to Ernestine, and the still more recent death of his mother, Schumann laid bare his heart to her as never before when eventually forced to tear himself away to attend to family affairs:

'From the Coach-Office at Zwickau. Past 10 at night. February 13, 1836.

How close you seem to me, my darling, darling Clara, so close that I feel as if I could hold you. . . . Today has brought me many different emotions – a letter of instructions from my mother; the story of her death. But your radiant image shines through the darkness and helps me to bear everything better. At Leipzig my first care shall be to put my worldly affairs in order. I am quite clear about my heart. Perhaps your father will not refuse if I ask him for his blessing. Of course there is much to be thought of and arranged. But I put great trust in our guardian angel. Fate always intended us for one another. I have known that for a long time, but my hopes were never strong enough to tell you and get your answer before. . . . The room is getting dark. Passengers near me are going to sleep. It is sleeting and snowing outside. But I will squeeze myself right into a corner, bury my face in the cushions and think only of you. Your Robert.'

Schumann subsequently admitted that despite their temperamental differences and passing tiffs, he had always secretly assumed Wieck's continued interest and kindness to him to mean only one thing – that he had been accepted as Clara's future husband. Young as she was, Clara felt the same. So her father's wrath on discovering what had happened in his absence was the most traumatic experience of her life. Never had she heard any family friend so mercilessly vilified. All further contact with Schumann, whether personal or by letter, was totally forbidden. In his rage Wieck even threatened to shoot Schumann if he ever tried to approach Clara again.

Self-interest of course played its part, for Wieck was a self-made man. Clara's career was his biggest potential source of income as well as self-advertisement, gaining him entrée into the most distinguished musical society throughout Europe. But at this moment he was concerned for Clara too. She was only sixteen, and on the threshold of fame. To throw away such gifts and opportunities for impecunious domesticity seemed nothing less than sacrilege. Moreover in eight years Wieck had discovered Schumann's irresponsibility over money, his acute susceptibility to the fair sex, his frequent weakness of will, his over-addiction to drink, and last but not least his indifferent health – all pardonable enough in a personable young pupil and friend but not in a prospective son-in-law. Even Schumann's potential as a musician seemed negligible in comparison with that of his own daughter.

Distressed and wounded as she was, Clara had no alternative but to obey. She recognized her total dependence on her father in every practical detail of daily life, and sensed the devotion underlying everything he had done for her. Despite his railing she could neither stop needing nor loving him. But on her return to Leipzig, after a short visit to Breslau, her conflict was at times unendurable, not least one evening at the Wasserschenke restaurant when, as she subsequently confessed, 'you passed by our table. Ah! Robert – then I could have wished I were in my grave, I became quite ill, and trembled violently, and this lasted the whole evening, and that night in bed I should have liked to weep, but I could not, only I prayed to God I know not what'.

Schumann's confidence was at first not too seriously shaken, even if news of her had to be wormed out of friends, even passing acquaintances, such as Dr Kahlert of Breslau, to whom he wrote on March 1, 1836:

'Clara Wieck loves, and is loved in return. You will soon find that out from her gentle, almost supernatural, ways and doings. . . . The happy ones acted, met, talked and exchanged their vows without the father's knowledge. He has found them out, wants to take violent measures, and forbids any sort of intercourse on pain of death. Wieck is sure to call upon you at once, and will invite you to come and hear Clara play. Now, this is my ardent request, that you should let me know all about Clara as quickly as possible – I mean as to her state of mind, the life she leads, in fact any news you can obtain, either directly or indirectly. Please consider all that I have told you as a sacred trust, and don't mention this letter either to the old man or to anybody else. If Wieck speaks of me, it will probably not be in very flattering terms. Don't let that put you out. You will learn to know him. He is a man of honour, but has got a screw loose'.

But as the spring and summer wore on, Clara's subservience to her father increasingly baffled Schumann. She made no acknowledgement when he sent her his newly printed F sharp minor Sonata at the end of May, and when soon afterwards she returned a packet of his letters to her, accompanied only by a curt request for hers to him, his hope began to fade. There was a worse blow when his erstwhile friend and colleague, Carl Banck, now Clara's singing teacher and a regular and to all intents warmly welcomed visitor to the Wiecks' home, informed him how quickly she was reconciling herself to changed circumstances and new faces. Giving way to total despair and dissipation, not merely heavy drinking but also a return to a girl called Christel, often in his bed back in 1831 when Wieck and Clara left for a long winter tour, he was soon begging money from his brothers, Karl and Eduard, while his rowdiness even brought a threat of eviction from his landlady, Frau Devrient – though as a motherly widow, formerly of Zwickau, she soon relented when he told her the whole sorry tale.

A musical phoenix soon rose from his shattered dreams. It was in June, 1836, that he sketched his three movement *Phantasie* in C, of which on its completion two years later he wrote to Clara: 'the first movement is the most passionate thing I have ever composed – a deep lament for you'. Nothing from his pen ever surpassed this profound love-poem, which besides weaving Clara's falling five-note motto into both first and last movements, also in the first surreptitiously quotes the sixth of Beethoven's *An die ferne Geliebte* songs ('Take them, then, these songs I sang thee, songs of passion, songs of pain. Let them like an echo tender all our love call back again') – a quotation the more pointed since he originally intended to donate proceeds from sales of this work to Liszt's fund for a Beethoven monument in Bonn. Though less distinguished in material as well as less perfectly designed, a new F minor Sonata, Op.14 (originally a

five-movement work called *Concert sans orchestre*) also reflects his turbulent emotion throughout the whole of that winter and spring, with the
five-note Clara motto the main seminal force of the whole work as well as
being openly acknowledged for the first time in the slow movement,
'Variations on an Andantino of Clara Wieck'.

Personal frustrations apart, there was no more stimulating place for
either Schumann or Clara to be at this time than Leipzig, with Gewandhaus concerts under Mendelssohn's direction reaching unprecedented
standards when he appointed his brilliant young friend, Ferdinand David,
as leader of the orchestra after Matthäi's death towards the end of 1835.
Before Mendelssohn's marriage Schumann dined with him most days at
the Hôtel de Bavière, lost in admiration of his effortless perfectionism in
every branch of music-making. As he put it to his family: 'I look up to him
as to a high mountain. He is a real God'. The bright hope of English
music, the twenty-year-old Sterndale Bennett, and the maturer Polish
violinist, Karl Lipinski, so devoted to Bach and Beethoven, were two
others newly arrived in Leipzig whose friendship brought Schumann
particular relief, indeed joy – as he acknowledged by dedicating his *Etudes
symphoniques* to the one and *Carnaval* to the other.

Since Wieck already had ambitious travels planned for early 1837,
during the autumn of 1836 he restricted Clara's concerts to Naumburg,
where she was knocked down and badly bruised on the way to the hall, yet
still managed to play and sing two songs as well, and later, Freiberg. She,
too, found plenty to stimulate her musically in Leipzig, not least when her
old champion, Spohr, revisited the city, and still more, her idolized
Chopin, now frail enough in health to cause her real concern. After long
hours of his own with Chopin on that same visit, Schumann wrote to
Dorn: 'He played me [besides the G minor Ballade] a lot of new studies,
nocturnes, mazurkas; it was all simply incomparable. It is touching to see
the way he sits at the piano. You would like him immensely; but Clara is a
greater *player*, and invests his compositions with an almost deeper
meaning than he does himself'. Chopin subsequently declared that Clara
was the only female pianist in Germany who knew how to play his music.
Clara herself was particularly elated that both Chopin and Spohr were so
enthusiastic about her newest compositions, the *Quatre Pièces caractéristiques*, Op.5, the six *Soirées Musicales*, Op.6, and the *Variations de Concert sur
la Cavatine du 'Pirate' de Bellini*, Op.8, all of which she was now practising
hard for her approaching New Year tour. The Op.5 pieces were dedicated
to her pianist friend, Sophie Kaskel (the 'Sara' of the Davidsbund) who
had recently introduced the Bavarian pianist-composer, Henselt (he had
relations in Dresden) to their circle. And it was to Henselt, five years her
senior, that Clara dedicated her Op.8 Variations.

Though still adhering to the old virtuoso tradition, these Variations reveal her total assurance in that moribund sphere. The arresting introductory recitative, artfully growing from the first three notes of Bellini's tune, is followed by a brief poetic fantasy on snippets from the theme before its unadulterated presentation (albeit with cunning touches of canonic imitation in under parts) as Bellini's 'Tu vedrai la sventurata'. An eloquent little ritornello used as a recurrent link relieves the ensuing pyrotechnics, not least when expanded into a harp-like *quasi fantasia a capriccio* before the final burst of brilliance, where exhilaration is underlined by instructions like *brillante e passionato, sempre forte e fuocoso, strepitoso, stringendo, spiritoso, pomposo* and *trionfonte*.

The Variations are nevertheless outclassed by the two more or less contemporaneous Suites of Op.5 and Op.6. With Schumann and Chopin as her models, she totally eschewed all empty note-spinning to write ten genuine 'character' pieces, which as a subsequent (1837) *Neue Zeitschrift* review by Florestan and Eusebius put it, 'belong to those who can delight in music without the piano, whose hearts swell to bursting point at the sound of intimate yearning and inner song'. The gem of each set is its slow movement, with the 'Notturno' (No.2) from Op.6 telling the most personal tale. In simple ternary form with a lilting siciliano-type middle section, it opens with a yearning melody (lavishly embellished on its returns) directly growing from the five falling notes of her motto. Schumann subsequently quoted the opening of this piece, albeit in a different key, as a 'Stimme aus der Ferne' in the last of his own *Novelletten* of 1838. (See Ex.2, A and B.) The penultimate of the *Quatre Pièces caractéristiques*, Op.5, a 'Romance' in B major, is no less remarkable for a teenager – daring in chromatic harmonisation of the opening section (which incidentally is winsomely recapitulated in B minor), and with a central episode in D major as ardent as any song by Schumann (adorned by some of his characteristic gruppettos too). Schumann's influence is again very strong in the central section of Op.5, No.2, entitled 'Caprice à la Bolero', incorporating a melody in broken chordal accompaniment with passing alternations of triple and duple rhythm within its three-four time signature. Though less effective as a concert piece than the crunchingly accented 'Impromptu: Le Sabat' (No.1), the concluding 'Scène fantastique: Le Ballet des Revenants' (No.4) has the special interest of growing from the same two motifs found in the first movement of Schumann's F sharp minor Sonata, in its turn derived from an early projected Fandango of which a sheet was for a while lost – hence perhaps Clara's title. As for her Op.6, Schumann's influence can again be discerned in the lyrical flow of the middle section of the Toccatina (No.1). But in the Ballade (No.4), the Polonaise (No.6) and most of all the well contrasted Mazurkas in G minor (No.3) and G major (No.5), her guiding star was Chopin. Schumann showed his affection for the G major Mazurka by using its opening

Ex. 2

A CLARA

Andante con moto

B ROBERT

Stimme aus der Ferne

motif to launch his own *Davidsbündlertänze*, embodying all the ups and downs of their love the following year.

*

On February 7, 1837, Wieck and his daughter set out for the Prussian capital, Berlin. It was the city which had nurtured Mendelssohn. Clara herself was now seventeen and a half. So weighing up all factors Wieck decided to put aside childish things and for the first time to present her as a fully-fledged artist in programmes emphasizing musicianship more than virtuosity. Admittedly she introduced herself at the Opera House on February 16 in nothing more substantial than her own Concerto and Herz's *Variations brillantes*, Op.76. But her appearance on this occasion was no more than a curtain-raiser before a pantomimic ballet in three acts entitled *Robinson* (in early years she quite often played virtuoso items before, after, or during the intervals of various theatrical entertainments, such as at Carlsbad in August, 1833, Breslau in March, 1836, and Prague in November, 1837). Her first full-length recital at the Hôtel de Russie on February 25 (incorporating vocal solos from two male singers) was a very different story. The Andante and Finale of Beethoven's 'Appassionata' (she had previously only risked its Finale in cities of lesser importance) stood as the centrepiece of the first half, with Bach's C sharp minor Fugue from the '48' (in her repertory since 1835) and recent pieces by Mendelssohn (the A minor Capriccio, Op.33, No.1) and Chopin (the F sharp major Nocturne and 'black key' study) as its companions. A set of Variations by Herz was her only concession to box-office after the interval. For the rest she played her own Bolero and Mazurka, and an almost as recent Andante and Allegro, also a concert study 'Wenn ich ein Vöglein war', by her newly discovered young friend, Henselt. Her subsequent five programmes included the 'Appassionata' complete as well as Beethoven's 'Kreutzer' sonata (with Hubert Ries), a variety of other works by Bach, Mendelssohn and Chopin, and her own Bellini Variations.

Critical response was mostly favourable, not least in the *Preussische Staatzeitung* where her playing was compared with that of Mendelssohn ('only the latter controls his performances to greater repose; his rival allows herself to be more carried away by her enthusiasm, without, however, exceeding the limits of feminine grace') and also Czerny's Austrian-born pupil, Theodore Döhler (like Henselt just five years Clara's senior) who in this paper's eyes offered 'graceful facility and soft elasticity' as against Clara's 'powerful impulse and passionate expression'. A year or two before, Schumann had arrived at a similar estimate of Clara's personal style when comparing her with the eleven-years-older Anna Belleville, from France, also a pupil of Czerny: 'Belleville's playing is technically the finer of the two; Clara's is the more impassioned. . . .

Anna is a poetess; Clara is poetry herself'. All Berlin was amazed at her boldness in playing everything from memory, though to some this feat savoured of ostentation. As the poetess Bettina von Arnim put it 'How pretentiously she seats herself at the piano, and without notes too! How modest is Döhler on the other hand, who has the music in front of him!' Clara herself was content enough in the city where her mother lived, where she could fit in some counterpoint lessons from the distinguished pedagogue, Siegfried Dehn, and where she found a true friend in the composer, Spontini, then in charge of the Opera House. But Wieck himself had hoped for more. Upset by certain critics who found his carefully chosen programmes 'monotonous', by less than sold-out halls, and by the sheer exhaustion of organizing concerts amidst so much red tape, he railed at the city in his diary, and could scarcely wait to remove Clara to Hamburg, where she played her own Concerto at a Philharmonic concert on April 1 and gave recitals on April 8 and 12. By May 3 they were back in Leipzig after brief stops at Bremen, Hanover and Brunswick.

Clara was neither surprised nor displeased to find Carl Banck at Clementine Wieck's side to greet them. Letters had passed between them during the tour, and it was in fact to Banck that Clara had poured out her indignation over the review of her piano concerto in the *Neue Zeitschrift* after its publication by Hofmeister early in 1837. Schumann had sent the score to his colleague, C. F. Becker, organist of St Nicholas Church in Leipzig, explaining 'I dare say you know my relations with the old man are such as to prevent my writing anything about the concerto myself, and I don't think it would be in good taste. Perhaps you will consider this all the more reason for granting my request. Half a page would be enough, but I should like to have your signature, C.F.B. The criticism might be joined to that of Herz's concerto, and the series closed with a few words about Bennett's concertos. Perhaps this will give you an idea'. In the event Becker failed him by writing only a few evasive words to the effect that there could be no question of real criticism 'since we have to do with the work of a lady'. And when Schumann himself stepped in with an ecstatic review of the latest concerto by Sterndale Bennett, a composer very much more admired by him than by either of the Wiecks, Clara[1] took the whole thing as a personal affront. Insult was added to injury in her eyes when soon after her return another article appeared entitled 'The Editor's Ball'. Though in essence a review of an assortment of recently published dance-music by Chopin, Liszt and lesser luminaries, Schumann fancifully wove his critical comment into an account of an imaginary ball attended by an assortment of characters including an upstart Flemish bassoonist called de Knapp (a thinly disguised caricature of Carl Banck)

---

[1] At this time Clara was very reluctant to learn any of his works.

and two sisters, of whom the elder, perspiring Ambrosia, because a pianist attended by de Knapp, Clara took to represent herself. Despite early initiation into Schumann's world of 'doubles', she failed to appreciate that even if Ambrosia was the Clara who was breaking his heart, the exquisite younger Beda (who in the article had secretly painted Chopin's portrait) was the Clara he still worshipped, and once again she turned to Banck for sympathy. Sensing a new danger, Wieck at once asked Banck to go, meanwhile resorting to the old expedient of despatching Clara to Dresden, this time under the protective eye of himself and Clementine for a fortnight before she joined the music-loving family of Major Serre and his wife (a household which Schumann, after his own first visit a year later, described as 'all mirth and money') at their elegant, spacious home overlooking rolling fields, woods and hillocks in the pretty nearby village of Maxen.

The consequences of this long, happy summer holiday were far from what Wieck intended. For among the Serres' guests was a certain Ernst Adolf Becker, a magistrate of mature years from Freiberg, whose admiration for Schumann's music was rivalled only by that for Clara's playing. Recognizing a true friend, Clara told him the whole, bitter story – to receive assurances from him almost at once of Schumann's unfaltering love that sent her back to Leipzig with new courage. At her morning recital in the Börsenhalle on August 13 she played not only Chopin and Henselt as well as her own Bellini Variations, but also three numbers from Schumann's recently published *Etudes symphoniques*. Becker himself took Schumann along to hear them, and it was to Becker that Clara at last entrusted a personal plea that Schumann should give her back all his love-letters to her which, in obedience to her father, she had been compelled to return. Through Becker, Schumann replied no, but that she could have new ones. And the day after the recital, accompanied by flowers, the first arrived: 'Are you still faithful and true? Firmly as I believe in you, yet the stoutest heart may become confused when nothing is heard of the being whom one loves best in the world. And you are that to me. A thousand times I have thought it all over, and everything tells me: it must be, if we will, and act. Write me the simple word "Yes" if you will yourself give your father a letter from me on your birthday. Just now he is well disposed towards me, and will not reject me if you beg for me. I write this on Aurora's Day. Would that nothing but a dawn parted us [in the Saxon calendar August 12, 13 and 14 are the days of Clara, Aurora and Eusebius respectively]. I mean all this as it stands, with my whole soul, and sign it with my name'. Clara's reply was immediate: 'So one little "yes" is all you want? What an important little word it is! Surely a heart as full of inexpressible love as mine can utter it freely. I can indeed say it. My inmost soul whispers it unceasingly' she wrote on the day of Eusebius. Deeming discretion the better part of valour, they resisted all temptation to meet until four days before Clara's birthday, when on the way home from the Lists with her maid Nanny, always 'faithful and silent', a brief reunion was contrived – understandably, after eighteen long months' separation, with some embarrassment. 'You were so stiff, so cold', Clara wrote afterwards, 'I, too, should have been glad to be warmer, but I was too much excited. I could hardly control myself. . . . The moon shone so beautifully upon your face when you took off your hat and passed your hand over your forehead. I had the most delightful feeling that I ever had, I had found again what I loved best'. And on September 13, although warned by Becker that it was all too soon, Schumann once again opened his heart in a letter to Wieck (with separate enclosures for Frau Wieck and Clara), pleading his own growing awareness of his creative potential, his unwavering constancy during long months of enforced separation and his willingness to undergo any further tests of devotion Wieck might wish to impose. 'If you find that I have been proved to be true and manly', he wrote, 'bless this union of souls, for nothing but a parent's sanction is wanting to our highest happiness. It is no momentary excitement, no passion, nothing external, which binds me to Clara by every fibre of my being, it is the deepest conviction that a union can seldom have come into existence under such a favourable concurrence of circumstances'.

But as Clara subsequently wrote: 'This was the unhappiest of all my birthdays. It was not only that my Father did not even show me your letter, but neither did he give me the one which you had enclosed for me. . . . I cried the whole day long. . . . A few days later I was still unable to calm myself, tears stood always in my eyes, till at last Father began to feel a little pity, and asked me what was the matter; whereupon I told him the truth. Thereupon he took your letters out of his secretaire and placed them before me saying: "I did not mean to let you have them, but since I see how unreasonable you are, read them". I was too proud, and would not read them. The wound which I had received could not be healed in this way'.

Schumann's subsequent interview with Wieck was no less painful. 'My conversation with your father was terrible', he wrote to Clara on September 18. 'Coldness, his ill-will, his confusion, his contradictoriness – he has a new method of destruction, he drives blade and haft into one's heart. . . . Today I am so dead, so *degraded*, that I can hardly conceive a beautiful thought, even your image has fled from me, so that I can hardly picture your eyes. Faint-hearted enough to give you up I am not; but embittered, wounded in my most sacred feelings. He treats me like the dirt beneath his feet. . . . If only I had a word from you. You must tell me what I am to do. Otherwise I shall abandon myself to scorn and mockery, and let fate carry me where it will. Not even to be allowed to see you! He said that we might meet on neutral ground, before everybody, a spectacle to all the world. All this is so chilling, it rankles so! And we may write when you are away! That was all he would consent to . . .'.

As for Wieck himself, his only real concern at this moment was preparing Clara for Vienna, that legendary musical Mecca on which he had set the highest hopes of her whole career. To keep her calm he knew he had to make a few small concessions, such as granting an open exchange of correspondence with Schumann after their departure. With Nanny's help, the two lovers also secretly managed to exchange rings. But by the end of the month it was clear that in his fight for time Wieck had won yet another round. Even on the afternoon of her tearful birthday he had inveigled her into composing variations for a two-piano 'Duo on a theme from Maskenball'[1] in collaboration with the twenty-five-year-old visiting Russian pianist, Anton Gerke, which they in fact played together at his own Leipzig concert just three days later. And it was from a chastened daughter, her sights for the present far removed from the domestic hearth, that Schumann received his goodbye letter: 'Till now I have been continuously unhappy, but write me a word of reassurance after this letter and I shall go out into the world without a care. I have promised Father to be cheerful and to live for some years more for art and the world. You will hear so many things of me, many a doubt will arise in your mind when you learn of this or that, but then think to yourself – She does all that for me: Could you ever waver? Well – then you would have broken a heart that loves but once. Clara.'

*

Clara's official farewell to Leipzig was at the Gewandhaus on October 8, in a programme conducted by Mendelssohn that included her own Concerto. A week later, with her father and Nanny, she set out for Dresden (where she introduced Schumann's newly published *Carnaval* to friends at a private party) en route for Prague and Vienna. Bitter-sweet as recent events had proved, experience had matured her. She knew, irrefutably, that she was loved, and that knowledge strengthened and enriched every note she played. After her first concert at the Prague Conservatoire on November 12, with a *Rhapsodie* by Thomaschek in deference to Bohemia, alongside pieces by Henselt, Chopin and herself, she was recalled thirteen times. 'Again and again I had to come out of my hiding-place, and then there were all the curtsies which you know I make so abominably! The thought of you inspired me so while I was playing that the whole audience became inspired too. I have already had letters and visits of congratulation today – the people have run mad' she wrote to

[1] Now lost, the Duo was summed up by Wieck as 'one eighth Czerny, one eighth Kalkbrenner, one eighth Herz, one eighth nothing at all, one eighth Gerke and one eighth Clara' (the arithmetical error is his own).

Schumann immediately after the concert, in one of the many secret letters, as opposed to the formal ones vetted by Wieck, they managed to exchange in ensuing months with the help of Nanny and certain friends in Leipzig willing to address Schumann's envelopes in an unfamiliar hand. Two more appearances, one in Prague's larger Konvikt Hall, the other with orchestra in the theatre, brought still more enthusiastic acclaim – besides two languishing personal admirers, one who spoilt a whole evening set aside for a letter to Schumann, the other who 'threatens to devour me with every glance, and if I sit down to the piano all is over, I make up my mind to an embrace every time; luckily, as you know of old, a stool always stands by my side, over which he falls first'. By November 24, the eve of departure, success as both artist and woman had even proved heady enough to prompt a few observations painful for the Leipzig-bound Robert to read, even though he sensed that Wieck was behind her pen: 'I have been thinking a great deal about my circumstances during these days, and I must call your attention to something. You rely on the ring! Good heavens! that is but an external bond. Had not Ernestine too a ring from you, and what is of more importance, your promise? And yet you have torn that bond asunder. . . . One thing I must say to you; I cannot be yours until circumstances have entirely altered. I do not want horses or diamonds, I am happy in possessing you, but I wish to lead a life free from care, and I see that I shall be unhappy if I cannot always work at my art, and that I cannot do if we have to worry about our daily bread. I require much, and I realize that much is needed for a comfortable life. Therefore Robert, ask yourself if you are in a condition to offer me a life free from care. Remember that simply as I have been brought up, I have yet never had a care, and am I to bury my art now?'

First impressions of Vienna were mixed. While immediately recognizing the genuine enthusiasm and good taste of the city's many amateur music-lovers, such as Baroness Pereira at whose house Clara successfully broke the ice on December 3, Wieck found the professionals – and even their welcoming friend, Josef Fischhof, a professor at the Conservatoire – somewhat limited and complacent. 'Mendelssohn ought to come here – Good God! how a really good musician is wanted here – there is such beautiful material', so he confided to his diary. For Clara there was nevertheless one colossus against whose every scale, arpeggio, trill and tonal gradation she knew her own would be mercilessly weighed and measured. As the influential critic, Bäuerle, put it: 'Vienna is to decide whether this modest young artist, who in Germany ranks beside Liszt and Chopin, can be mentioned in the same breath as Thalberg'. The handsome, illegitimate son of two Swiss aristocrats, and a pupil of both Hummel and Moscheles, Thalberg, only seven years Clara's senior, had been the idol of Vienna ever since his début there in 1829. Famed in his own operatic fantasias and other virtuoso pieces for a special effect whereby the melody was played by both thumbs in the middle of the keyboard between wide-ranging arpeggio swirls to its extremities (in such a way as to suggest three hands at work) he was usually considered Liszt's one and only serious rival in supernatural brilliance – even though his style was quite different. 'Like Liszt he could play the apparently impossible, but unlike Liszt he never indulged in any affectation or extravagance of manner in achieving his mechanical triumphs' so one admiring critic wrote. 'His strength and flexibility of wrist and finger were amazing, but he always tempered his strength with delicacy. His loudest fortissimos were never noisy'. Already Clara's repertory included several of his compositions, which even the astute critic, Hanslick, was misled into rating as high as Liszt's in transcending virtuoso superficialities of the day.

Sensing the easy-going temper of the Viennese public at large, Wieck proceeded much more warily in programme-building than in Berlin. At her first concert in the Musikvereinsaal on December 14 her bid was largely made in show pieces by Pixis, Henselt and herself (the Bellini Variations), with only Chopin to represent the new poetic age. An enthusiastic reception emboldened her to risk Bach instead of Pixis in the second concert on December 21, also her own Concerto instead of her Variations, while at the third on January 7 she at last dared to include the 'Appassionata' complete. Though her fourth concert on February 4 went exclusively to Thalberg and Liszt, just to show that she could do the impossible too, at her fifth on February 11 she made a point of including Mendelssohn, and would have risked a selection from Schumann's *Etudes symphoniques* at the sixth on February 18, despite Vienna's total ignorance of him, but for the fact that all her other solos happened to be in minor keys. The last three programmes also included piano trios by Schubert and Beethoven, as well as Beethoven's 'Kreutzer' sonata.

For both father and daughter, these six concerts, together with two further appearances at the Kärthnerthor Court Theatre and, of course, many private soirées, were the realization of a lifetime's hopes and dreams. Never had either experienced a satisfaction as great as knowing that they had this legendary city of music at their feet – formidable box-office profits elated Wieck still more. Even as early as December 22 his joy overflowed in a letter to Clementine: 'Dear Wife, Clara is the theme of all Vienna. She has won all hearts even at court. The papers no longer write notices; they have become enthusiastic and emotional and weave laurel wreaths. It is touching and costs me many a tear, I can tell you'. Searching for an explanation for such a victory over Thalberg and others, the *Allgemeine Musikalische Zeitung*, in a retrospective review of her concerts on March 7, 1838, came to much the same conclusion as Wieck himself, that she played with greater feeling: 'Her performances created a sensation on each occasion only to be compared with the enthusiasm roused by a Paganini, a Lipinski; and which was excited, not only by her technical bravura, but, in an incomparably greater degree, by her invariably individual, sympathetic conception and interpretation of the music she played. An original feature in her programmes, the inclusion of several short pieces played in succession, sufficiently shows the standpoint from which she must be judged, her aim to present clearly the individuality of each master, to reproduce his inmost being with understanding, feeling and enthusiasm. The instrument itself becomes, under such treatment, the means to an end, deriving a warmly pulsating life from the intellectual conception breathed into it. The interest of a public which is accustomed as a rule to mere firework effects – rondos, fantasias, caprices and the like – was secured even for a work of Bach, and desire was expressed for a second hearing, not only of some bagatelles by Chopin and Henselt, but also of the difficult fugue movement.'

A more detailed appraisal of her accomplishment appeared in the *Neue Zeitschrift für Musik* on April 27, 1838. Rating her, though still only eighteen, in the same class as Thalberg, Liszt and Henselt, the anonymous writer (subsequently identified as the Viennese musician, Josef Fischhof) devised a list of criteria by which the four could be judged and compared:

Purity of style: Thalberg, Clara, Henselt, Liszt
Improvisation: Liszt, Clara
Warmth of feeling: Liszt, Henselt, Clara, Thalberg
Depth of innate musicianship: Liszt, Clara
High-soaring spirit: Liszt
Sophisticated ease: Thalberg
Affectation in presentation: Henselt(?)
Wholly self-determined originality: Liszt
Total absorption: Clara
Ability to sight-read: Liszt, Thalberg, Clara
Versatility: Clara, Liszt, Thalberg, Henselt
Musical scholarship: Thalberg, Henselt, Clara, Liszt
Musical judgement: Liszt, Thalberg
Beauty of touch: Thalberg, Henselt, Clara, Liszt
Audacity: Liszt, Clara
Egoism: Liszt, Henselt
Recognition of others' merits: Thalberg, Clara
Objectivity in performance: None
Adherence to metronome: None
As an example to future artists in accuracy, proper preparation and avoidance of platform grimaces: (In these separate contexts only Clara and Thalberg came through all unscathed).

The final verdict was that while the refined, sensuously bewitching Thalberg could be hailed as the outstanding representative of the Italian school, and the demonic Liszt of the French romantic, Clara and Henselt stood for all that was best in the German field of lyrical sentiment, he earning the epithet 'exciting', and she 'ennobling'.

Still more gratifying to Clara, personally, were the private tributes. As she wrote to Schumann on Christmas Eve, 1838: 'You may already have heard of one delicate attention towards me. Schubert left behind, among other things, a Duo for four hands [Op.140] which has just been printed by Diabelli and dedicated to me. This has affected me very much, I can hardly say why, myself. It is extraordinary how easily I am upset now, sometimes I think I am quite sentimental'. She was equally touched when on January 9, 1838, the *Wiener Zeitschrift* published a poem by Grillparzer inspired by her performance of the 'Appassionata'.

Clara Wieck and Beethoven

A great magician, tired of world and life,
Locked his murmuring genii
In a casket, diamond-hard, secure from all,
Then casting key into the sea, he died.
A horde of little men strove hard
In vain! No lever loos'd the rigid bolt
Its magic, like the master, slept.
A shepherd child in play upon the shore
Watching the hasty, uncommanded search
Thoughtful yet unthinking as girls are
Sinks her white fingers in the flood
And seizes, raises, holds: she has the key!
She hastens with a quickened, beating heart
The casket gleams, all-seeing, as she comes.
The key takes hold. The lid flies back. The spirits
Rise, and bow submissive heads
Before this gracious, guileless mistress
Who leads them with white fingers as she plays.

Her greatest personal honours were nevertheless in being made an honorary member of Vienna's illustrious Gesellschaft der Musikfreunde, and equally, in view of the fact that she was a foreigner and a protestant as well as so young, when the Emperor and Empress, to whom she had often talked as well as played at court, nominated her a 'Kammervirtuosin' of the Imperial household.[1] 'She is a great virtuoso; I have never heard such

---

[1]　She was sufficiently proud of this title to print it in her programmes for years to come.

playing, but I am still more pleased with her personality' was the Empress's comment. On receiving the letters patent on March 15, Wieck himself confided to his diary: 'I never paid 4 florins – which the stamp cost – and a new Austrian ducat with such pleasure'. She herself subsequently commemorated her visit in a *Souvenir de Vienne* published by Diabelli in that city as her Op.9. Cast as a set of virtuoso variations on the Austrian National Anthem, the work opens with the same kind of introduction stealthily hinting at the tune and ends with the same excitedly grandiose kind of coda found in her earlier Bellini Variations.

Whatever her own mood, Robert was never long forgotten. 'I have just come from the Empress, I am eating a plate of soup, and will finish my letter. Although the Emperor, the Empress, and the rest have been talking to me, do you not think I would rather talk to you?' she wrote late one night, in the same letter confessing that only the day before her father had again told Nanny 'If Clara marries Schumann, I would say upon my death-bed that she is not worthy to be my daughter'. Realizing the extent to which he was basking in her triumphs, sometimes she begged Schumann for more understanding of Wieck's pride in and ambition for her. Sometimes there were even veiled hints that Robert himself did not quite appreciate the full extent of her platform potential, or the gruelling social strains imposed by such success. Occasionally she was woman enough to enlarge on more personal conquests: 'I shall arrange to go away from here soon, for these visits from all my adorers are more than I can bear', she wrote on March 8. 'I can understand that you love me, because I love you so much, but I do not know why these others love me. I am cold, not pretty (I know that) and as for art? that counts for nothing, for the greater number of my suitors know nothing about it'. Several times she even dropped cautionary remarks about his own musical activities, such as asking if he knew his instruments well enough to embark on some projected string quartets, or begging for greater lucidity at all times in whatever he wrote since 'it hurts me too much when people do not understand you'.

Yet always there was the assurance that her love could never change, as in a letter of April 3, 1838: 'In the carriage today we spoke of you, and I told him (father) again that he could say what he liked to me, I would never give you up, and I say to you again that my love knows no bounds, if you wanted my life today I would give it for you'. Her suggestion, prompted by her father, that they should leave Leipzig and eventually make their married home in Vienna, where she was more enthusiastically acclaimed and financially recompensed, and where he might possibly obtain a professorship at the Conservatoire, gave Schumann particular hope as a practical solution to their *impasse*. Whatever their content, her letters were his lifeline. As he wrote in mid-March: 'If only you knew how I value your opinions about everything, even those which do not directly concern art itself; how your letters refresh my spirit – so write to me of what goes on around you, of men, customs and cities. You have a good eye, and I so much enjoy following you and your thoughts. . . . In other respects my life has gone on so quietly for the last three months that it can only offer the most glaring contrast to yours, which would bewilder me if I were in your place. I am up early, generally before 6 o'clock; these are my most sacred hours. My room is my chapel, the piano my organ, and your picture, well, that is the altar piece'. Admitting, too, that nothing gave greater wings to his imagination than expectation and longing 'such as I have experienced during the last few days while I was waiting for your letter', he was also soon able to tell her of his new *Kinderscenen*, Op.15, following hard on the heels of the *Fantasiestücke*, Op.12, already sent to her in Vienna, of the eight *Novelletten*, Op.21 ('jests, Egmont stories, family scenes with fathers, a wedding') and last but not least, of *Kreisleriana*, Op.16, completed in a four-day flood of inspiration during April, 1838 ('a positively wild love is in some of the movements, and your life and mine, and the way you look').

Despite regrets that Clara only felt able to play his works at private gatherings, inwardly he knew where he stood, and had no fears. On April 13 he was particularly explicit: 'I am affected by everything that goes on in the world, and think it all over in my own way, politics, literature and people, and then I long to express my feelings and find an outlet for them in music. That is why my compositions are sometimes difficult to understand, because they are connected with distant interests; and sometimes striking, because everything extraordinary that happens impresses me, and impels me to express it in music. And that is why so few modern compositions satisfy me, because, apart from all their faults of construction, they deal in musical sentiment of the lowest order, and in commonplace lyrical effusions'. Moreover he was aware that there were connoisseurs who already understood – like Moscheles, for instance, who had recently privately commented 'the proper ground for finger gymnastics is to be found in Thalberg's latest compositions. For "mind" (*Geist*) give me Schumann. The romanticism in his works is a thing so completely new, his genius so great, that to weigh correctly the peculiar qualities and weaknesses of his new school I must go deeper and deeper on to the study of his works'.

Tired as she was, Clara had still to play twice at the theatre in Pressburg in fund-raising concerts for Budapest's flood victims, at the Imperial Castle in Vienna by the express wish of the Emperor, and finally in Graz. But before the return to Leipzig on May 13, via Dresden, Wieck contrived a fortnight's holiday in Vienna to coincide with the arrival of Liszt, already a legend in his twenty-seventh year. He presented his visiting card at once, and with a sight-reading ability as phenomenal as his virtuosity, immediately made Clara feel like a schoolgirl. Even awareness of his eccentricities could not damp both the Wiecks' enthusiasm, as a diary entry after his first concert on April 13 reveals: 'He cannot be compared to any other player – he stands alone. He arouses terror and amazement, and is a very attractive person. His appearance at the piano is indescribable – he is an original – he is absorbed by the piano. . . . His passion knows no bounds, not infrequently he jars on one's sense of beauty by tearing melodies to pieces, he uses the pedal too much, thus making his works incomprehensible if not to professionals at least to amateurs. He has a great intellect, one can say of him that "his art is his life".' Later, in a letter to Robert, she admitted 'When I heard Liszt for the first time in Vienna, I hardly knew how to bear it, I sobbed aloud (it was at Graff's), it overcame me so'. Meeting and hearing the urbane Thalberg shortly afterwards, though gratifying enough, was a routine event for her in comparison. Liszt in his turn was deeply impressed by what he subsequently described as Clara's 'mastery of technique, depth and sincerity of feeling, and thoroughly noble bearing', especially praising her performance of Beethoven's 'Appassionata'. At the time, however, it was Liszt's response to Schumann's music that thrilled her most. 'He rates your compositions extraordinarily highly, far above Henselt, above everything he has come across recently. I played your *Carnaval* to him, and he was delighted with it. "What a mind!" he said, "that is one of the greatest works I know". You can imagine my joy' she wrote to Robert from Graz on April 23, fully aware that she would soon be back in Leipzig where a new round of battle with her father would inevitably begin.

SIX

Love's Victory 1838–40

Whatever more personal issues played their part in Wieck's growing animosity (and recent researchers have suggested that he might already have attributed Schumann's bouts of ill-health, and even his lamed right hand, to syphilis), the main cause of his opposition to Clara's marriage at this moment lay in a new awareness of her professional potential. Vienna had opened his eyes as never before to the wealth as well as fame now within their grasp. To lose it all, just when the magic door had opened, was a negation of his whole life's work. 'Schumann can operatize, philosophize, be as enthusiastic, idealize, as much as he likes, it remains settled that Clara can never live in poverty and obscurity – but must have over 2000 thalers a year', he had written in his diary on March 3, 1838. To humour her he proffered some sort of airy consent to the union on those financial terms (together with an agreement that they should leave Leipzig so that their living standards would not be compared with those of the wealthy Mendelssohn and David) in the full belief that Schumann could never command that sum anywhere – even if he could bear to uproot himself from his increasingly warm and welcoming circle of Leipzig friends.

As for Schumann, he had always suspected there was a touch of the charlatan, 'modelling his mannerisms on Paganini', in Wieck, whose slightly Jewish facial features had not escaped his notice, and who in the secrecy of his diary he nicknamed Meister Allesgeld. And by now Clara's pleas for more understanding of her father's concern for her well-being had exhausted his patience. As he put it:

'Clara, there are the most important things to be discussed – for in truth, we are not advancing, and it appears that I shall never get a wife if it depends on her. Well then! that your father has begun to growl and grumble again has once more made me very angry with him. I begin to think he is a Philistine who is wholly encrusted by material thoughts and interests, who has become entirely devoid of feeling, who looks upon young love as a kind of childish disease, like measles, etc. which everyone must go through, even if he dies of it. Add to this arrogance, because you have received such great honours. . . . Hatred towards him often rises in me again, so deep a hatred that it does indeed look strange beside my love for his daughter. But if he has so many times taken back what he promised, he will do it again – in a word, I expect nothing from him, we must act for ourselves. Listen, therefore, my Clärchen – as soon as possible I will go to Vienna and I wait for your consent to this. . . . There is however one important question as to which you must set my mind at rest. Can you trust yourself, regardless of your father's consent, to give me an approximate date for our union? I think if we settle on Easter (two years from now) you will have fulfilled all the duties of a child and need not reproach yourself, even if you have to tear yourself away by force. . . . I have almost given up all hope of seeing you in the summer. I have had to put up with it for two whole years, so let it be the same for another two. What is it, when we have to steal a few minutes in deadly anxiety in order to get a couple of distracted words together? No, I want you altogether, for whole days, whole years, the whole of eternity. I am no longer a knight of the moonshine. If you very much want me, I will come, but otherwise let us leave it, it leads to nothing further. . . . I will have you for my wife, it is my sacred, earnest determination.'

With unfaltering love Clara at once gave her promise. Aware of physical stirrings that made it impossible to contemplate a life lived for the platform alone, the woman in her longed for his comforting arms, and always intuitively realized that it was for his creative genius that her lesser career as a performer would eventually have to be sacrificed, or at any rate curtailed. But she, like her father, had returned home flushed with success. Moreover she was still only eighteen. For her there was not the same urgency to rush into matrimony, a fact which Schumann, nearly a decade her senior, frequently failed to understand. Another visit to Dresden from July 2 to August 7 temporarily eased the tension, for though slightly embarrassed by the attentions of the Bremen pianist, Louis Rakemann (one of her Gewandhaus collaborators in November, 1835, with whom she had again played two piano works in Bremen in April, 1837), she had the compensating pleasure of a new girl friend of seventeen, the Spanish singer, Pauline Garcia, who with her mother and brother-in-law, the violinist Charles de Beriot, had introduced themselves to the Wiecks before leaving Leipzig in the course of a concert tour. 'She seems to be an exception to all other singers – she takes a vivid interest in music', so Clara's diary shrewdly observed. 'She sings very dramatically, always without notes, and accompanies herself without looking at the piano, and she can play anything by ear. They were the pleasantest artists who had visited us for a long time'.

Eventually summoned by her father to resume work, Clara returned to the Gewandhaus to play the first movement of Chopin's E minor Concerto on September 8, with three transcriptions of Schubert songs by her new-found friend, Liszt, 'Ave Maria', 'Lob der Tränen' and 'Erlkönig', the most recent additions to her repertoire, as solos. She was even forced to repeat 'Erlkönig' ('truly a great exertion') in response to overwhelming applause. Frequently reproached by Wieck for not often enough using the *Neue Zeitschrift* to further Clara's cause, this time Schumann hailed the recital as 'the finest and most fragrant flower of romance which has been offered us for a long time, and a demonstration of technique brought to faultless perfection'. He also published a poem, which though mysteriously signed 'A.L.', he subsequently admitted to writing himself:

Dream Picture on the evening of the 8th
To C.W.

An angel-child floats down from on high,
Sits at the keys, and the songs sweep by;
As her fingers wander over the notes,
In magic circles above her floats
 Ring upon ring
 Of figures wild;
 The old elf-king,
 And Mignon mild,
 A hot-mettled knight
 Arrayed for the fight.
 A nun on her knee
 In ecstasy.
And the people who heard it began to rejoice
As if they applauded an earthly voice.
But the angel-child shrank from the tumult, and flew
Back to her home in the heavens blue.

But a personal letter to Clara the day after the concert reveals that his priorities had not changed. 'Come and let me kiss you again and again for the way you played to me yesterday – you, my own Clara, with your beautiful soul and your wonderful talent! You played magnificently! People don't half deserve what you give them. As you sat there all alone, supreme in the mastery of your art, and people spoke of you as if it were all a matter of course, I thought how happy I was to call such a treasure my own, and also felt very strongly that I could dispense with the crowd who were there simply to say they had heard you. You are too dear, too noble, for the career which is to your father the aim, the crown of existence. Are these few hours worth so much expenditure of time and energy? Can you look forward to a continuation of this as your whole vocation? No; my Clara is to be a happy wife, a contented beloved wife! Indeed I reverence your art, and dare hardly think of all the happiness promised me in connection with it; but unless we are really in want, you shall not touch a note to please people for whom scales are too good – unless you wish it.'

 Schumann was in fact now deep in negotiations for transferring the *Neue Zeitschrift* to Vienna, where with the help of Clara's friends, Josef

Fischhof and Frau von Cibbini, lady-in-waiting to the Empress, he fully believed that after his arrival in early October he could secure a licence and find a publisher in time for the first number to appear on January 1, 1839. On learning that Wieck, in his consequent alarm, had rescinded all promises to Clara besides seeking the help (gallantly refused) of the jilted Ernestine, Schumann at once counselled Clara to leave home and stay either with the Serres at Maxen or else with Eduard and Therese, his brother and sister-in-law, drawing on the 1000 florins he had left for her, in the event of emergencies, in Leipzig. Once more filial love prevailed, this time exasperating Schumann enough to write 'I do not know what to say about your having once more come to an understanding with your father. You cry, he rages – and then it all goes back to what it was before and we never get any farther'. When, on realizing that Viennese negotiations were not going too smoothly for Schumann, Clara then proposed that they should postpone marriage for another six months after the suggested 1840 date, their good friend, Dr Reuter (who had helped so much in their clandestine correspondence) even stepped in, begging her to understand that her equivocation, though so well-intentioned, was driving Schumann to dangerous extremes of depression. Torn as it was, her tender young heart again found the right comforting words: 'My good dear Robert, love me still; for your sake I will give up that which I love next to you – my Father. I will follow you without his consent'. And after two highly successful Dresden concerts, harmony was sufficiently restored for her to write from Maxen: 'How beautiful the snow looked on the pine-twigs – oh! I thought so much of you! You asked me if I cared for the beauties of nature. I thank you for it, my love for you; since I have loved you, it is strange, I love nature too. Formerly my love was too childish, and besides my mind was not ripe to receive the beautiful, but now it is different.'

In Leipzig her happiest hours were at Sunday night music parties at the Mendelssohns', or Davids', or even her own home, when 'whatever anyone brings is played'. An F minor Trio by Robert's one-time greatly admired Prince Louis Ferdinand found special mention in her letters, still more a Quartet by the Dutch composer, Verhulst, one of the few young musicians congenial enough to her, and genuine enough in his own devoted admiration, to cause Schumann a few pangs of jealousy. But the pressing problem was her next tour – with Paris, where the Garcias were going, and possibly London, the cities on which sights had been set. Determined to teach her once and for all how much success depended on him, Wieck, under pretext of business, elected at the last minute to stay at home, refusing her even the comfort of Nanny (rightly suspected as an accomplice in romance) and engaging a totally strange French woman instead. It was a daunting prospect. But determinedly, she packed her bags, not forgetting a little piece called 'Wunsch' (eventually published as No.1 of *Bunte Blätter*, Op.99) sent her by Robert as a special Christmas Eve greeting from Vienna, also a set of beautifully inscribed verselets[1] in which only a few weeks before he had tried to enshrine their whole life together, past, present and future.

'Little Verses to Clara from R.S.
Vienna 1838'

*

'Do you not admire my courage in travelling alone with an entirely unknown person? Indeed I did tremble a little the first night that I slept with her', so Clara wrote from Nuremberg, their first stop, on January 11, 1839. For Robert the letter contained just two reassuring items – of a pleasant morning coffee encounter with Therese and Eduard Schumann en route, and much more important, the discovery that Ernestine had just married a certain Count Zedwitz. 'Now I am exculpated in everything and quite free and belong to no one but her whom I love above all. Only don't leave me. Stay true to me, otherwise I shall make a deep cut in my life and bring it to rest', was his eventual reply. For the rest the hazards of Clara's undertaking were all too apparent. Severe snow often compelled the coach to drive across fields and ditches ('how often did I pray to God that he would let us get happily through it all, just this once more') and even the Nuremberg concert had to be postponed a day because of severe flooding. 'The orchestra has refused to play and so I have rapidly to study Thalberg's *Caprice*, in which I am a little out of practice. I have to write every note to do with the concert myself, send round the tickets, see about tuners and men to carry the piano in addition. It is rather much; I do not know where to begin first, and then there are all the uninteresting visits'. Whether in public or at court, yet again at Ansbach, Stuttgart and Karlsruhe the warm response to her playing brought her some comfort. Yet without letters from her father or Robert (who had addressed everything to Paris) she felt bereft. In Stuttgart loneliness even drove her to make a confidant of a certain Dr Schilling, the local musical eminence, who went so far as to propose that Schumann should join him in some music magazine project of his own ('but if we come here, you must allow him to love me' she admitted to be among Dr Schilling's conditions) as well as persuading her to take a young girl, Henriette Reichmann, to Paris as her pupil. Schumann's boiling indignation, on realizing what the 'bungling Don Juan' was really after, only seemed to bring home her inexperience and insecurity to her the more.

Friends of her father's, including her uncle Eduard Fechner, in fact

---

[1] Reproduced in Appendix I.

wasted no time in trying to frighten her, after her arrival in Paris on February 6, about the dangers of life in a big city and the impossibility of going into society without some old lady to chaperone her. But taking rooms first in the Hôtel Michodière, where Pauline Garcia and her mother were staying, and then going to live with her old friend, Emilie List, whose parents were now officially domiciled in Paris, dispelled worries on this score – enough, even, for her to dismiss the French woman engaged by her father, whom she had found to be 'malicious and deceitful' as well as out all day. Henriette Reichmann, however, turned out to be pure gold, despite the man who had introduced her. That life had its carefree moments for all three young girls was very clear in a letter written to Robert in March: 'Emilie and Henriette . . . have commanded me to write and tell you that I can cook a really excellent breakfast, and am quite in my element! They are now enjoying it. . . . You must often be anxious lest I should not be able to cook. You can be at ease about it, I shall soon learn to (when once I am with you). Here Emilie puts in "You will only burn your piano-fingers". What rubbish the two girls chatter to me, about tea, coffee, and heaven knows what, with which I am told to amuse you, you poor fellow'.

Her descriptions of Parisian musical life, both to Robert and to her father (to whom she dutifully wrote once a fortnight), betoken a lively though far from uncritical interest in what came her way, from private parties ('unendurable . . . over 50 ladies sit around the piano in one tiny room and behave in the silliest fashion'), concerts ('wearisome because lasting from three to four hours'), the Opera (where she enjoyed Donizetti's *Lucia* but loathed *Les Huguenots* and strongly condemned their unstylish *Figaro*) to leading composers and instrumentalists including Meyerbeer, who was particularly nice to her, Berlioz ('quiet, has extraordinarily thick hair, and always looks on the ground'), who in his turn initially pleased her greatly by showing such an interest in Schumann's activities, and the self-satisfied Kalkbrenner. Chopin, to her sorrow, was at death's door in Marseilles, after his ill-starred Majorcan winter with George Sand, but she was much impressed by his cellist friend, Franchomme. Apart from musicians, she also dined with several ambassadors and one or two writers, including Heine ('he speaks bitterly of Germany'). But there was none of the glamour of her recent experiences in Vienna – the reason, as she knew only too well, being her uncertainty of how, when and where to launch herself in a city already overrun by pianists of every persuasion. Right from the start she had been worried about her actual instrument. 'I have an Erard in my room which is dreadfully stiff', so she wrote to Robert. 'I have lost all heart, but yesterday I played on a Pleyel and they are a little more manageable. I must study for another three weeks before I can play a note in public. I could have three grand pianos in my room already – everyone wants me to take his. If only I knew how to begin playing on a Pleyel without offending Erard, who has shown me every possible kindness.'

Her début was eventually made on March 21, not at the Conservatoire as she had hoped, but in Erard's hall, in a matinée series run by the publisher, Schlesinger. That same evening she played again at the house of Pierre Zimmermann, a piano professor at the Conservatoire, whose soirées had acquired a fashionable notoriety. Her first independently promoted concert, again at Erard's hall, followed on April 21, with Pauline Garcia's brother-in-law, Charles de Beriot, to help her.

In programme building she proceeded cautiously, with nothing more intellectually demanding than finger dazzlers by Henselt and Thalberg, Liszt's Schubert arrangements and some of her own Opp.5 and 6 for solos. Only at private gatherings of friends did she ever dare risk the music closest to her heart. But an admission to Robert that she had been playing his *Carnaval* at 2 a.m. at a certain Countess Perthuis's brought the usual intimation that it had not really been appreciated: 'Listen Robert! will you compose something brilliant, easy to be understood, something that has no directions written in it, but is a piece which hangs together as a whole, not too long and not too short? I should so much like to have something of yours to play at concerts, something suited to the general public. It is indeed humiliating for a genius, but policy sometimes demands it'.[1] As for her own reception, she could write after April 21, 'I created a genuine sensation, such as no artist has produced for many a day'. Yet though the hall was well filled, there was little profit margin in so expensive a city – nor did that or any other appearance open doors to the London concert platform, as she had dearly hoped. For by late February it was clear that all Schumann's prospects of transferring the *Neue Zeitschrift* to Vienna were being dashed to the ground: already his thoughts were turning to London and the possibility of a professorship at the Royal Academy of Music – with the help of his old friend, Sterndale Bennett.

By early April Schumann was in fact back in Leipzig, his return both hastened and darkened by the illness and death of Eduard, the eldest, staunchest and dearest of all his brothers. While glad enough to have explored Vienna, its beautiful surrounding countryside no less than its opera and ballet, and to have unearthed a pile of unknown Schubert manuscripts (including the 'great' C major Symphony, which he persuaded Breitkopf and Härtel to print) and to have found an old steel pen, which he kept as a kind of talisman, on Beethoven's grave, he was also desperately disturbed by the cabals and intrigues that had thwarted his

---

[1] At this moment she apparently forgot the existence of his Toccata, several times played by her soon after its publication in 1834.

own plans as well as disillusioned by superficiality of standards and taste. 'As for artists, I have sought them in vain', he wrote to his sister-in-law, Therese, 'I mean artists who not only play one or two instruments pretty well, but who are large-minded men who understand Shakespeare and Jean Paul'.

Aware, even before Schumann's return, that castles-in-the-air had tumbled, as also of Clara's professional uncertainties in Paris, Wieck decided that now was the moment to strike again – this time approaching Clara through Emilie List. With its threats of disinheritance and a lawsuit, his first letter achieved nothing. But his second, a direct appeal to the heart, reawakened all those old ties that had bound them for nearly two decades. In a sudden flood of compassion, coupled with the realization that she badly needed some more piano lessons, Clara wrote to propose that her father came to Paris at once to prepare her for another winter tour of Belgium, Holland, and ultimately, in the spring of 1840, England.

In her explanatory letter to Schumann, she asked only for a postponement of their marriage for six months or a year while he found ways of guaranteeing an annual income of 1000 thalers (her father had stipulated 2000). There was no question of any wavering in her love. An accompanying letter from Emilie, expressing concern at the extent to which conflict was playing havoc with Clara's health, was expressed with equal discretion – even its suggestion that Schumann could perhaps find security by taking over Eduard's bookshop. But both letters chanced to cross with a particularly optimistic statement of income from Robert, prepared with Dr Reuter, designed to prove that they were giving themselves a great deal of unnecessary anxiety, and that 'if you, you obstinate person, only liked, we could take each other tomorrow. . . . I am frightened at our wealth:

Your fortune	4000 thaler
My fortune	
1. In Government bonds	1000 ,,
2. In Karl's business	4000 ,,
3. In Eduard's business	3540 ,,
4. From what Eduard left	1500 ,,
	14,040 thaler
That gives an interest of	560 thaler
Other receipts yearly	
From Friese (*Neue Zeitschrift*)	624 ,,
Sale of music	100 ,,
Earned from compositions	100 ,,
Receipts during the year	1384 thaler '

This time Schumann's replies were bitter enough to cause him to destroy them in later years – as he also did a second letter from Clara that hurt him enough to confess, on May 18, 'that I was ready to put an end to myself with all possible speed a few days ago. . . . Everything seemed to fall on me at once. Your father has again been most insulting. . . . From my friends, from Therese, who was here just for a few days – from everybody without exception, I had to hear things that chafed my sense of honour unbearably. They all insisted that I had been abominably treated through-out, that you could not have any great love for me if you were content to let it go on'.

Such was the sting behind this last reproach that Clara knew she could never attempt appeasement again. Before Robert's birthday, for which she sent him her portrait and a cigar-case worked by herself, she had signed his appeal to the High Court for permission to marry without her father's consent. Insurrection in Paris (at first intriguing her enough to risk the street-firing in order to see what was happening) had meanwhile disrupted all musical and social life, and after moving out to Bougival on June 22 for the summer, she had little to do but give lessons to two boring English women and the ever sympathetic Henriette. When Robert requested that she should be back in Leipzig by mid-August, the Court having suggested one last attempt at reconciliation under the chair-manship of Pastor Fischer before proceeding to litigation, she said goodbye to France with few regrets.

From the viewpoint of composition, however, the Paris visit was not in vain. Though her first Scherzo in D minor, Op.10, because more showy, was the piece that went down best at soirées, it was into three miniatures eventually published by Mechetti in Paris in November, 1839, as *Trois Romances pour le piano, dédiées à Monsieur Robert Schumann par Clara Wieck*, Op.11, that she poured her heart. So strong was the conviction behind them that she flatly refused Schumann's suggested improvements for No.3, a Moderato in A flat, also his proposal that her original title, 'Idylle', should be changed to 'Notturno', or even 'Heimweh' or 'Mädchens Heimweh'. 'It is more of a valse than a nocturne' was her own emphatic comment, perhaps in recognition of Chopin's influence on its extended middle section. If No.1, a sighing Andante in E flat minor (in fact written last) is the most graciously pianistic in its restless semiquaver flow, No.2 in G minor, again marked Andante, is the most Schumannesque. 'I have heard anew that we must be man and wife. . . . Every thought of yours comes from my soul, just as I have to thank you for all my music' was his own immediate response, pointing out the extraordinary similarity of a phrase in its middle section to one that he had recently used in his *Humoreske*, as yet unknown to her.

Ex. 3

A CLARA

Allegro passionato

B ROBERT

Parts of this second Romance, especially the *Nach und nach schneller*
approach to the middle section, have an urgent speaking eloquence more
intimately personal than anything from her pen before. Significantly,
Schumann published it on its own in a supplement to the *Neue Zeitschrift*
in September of that year.

Ex. 4   Andante
Nach und nach schneller

Obtaining the support of Clara's mother, Schumann now regarded as an urgent necessity. Before meeting his fiancée at Altenburg, after nearly a year apart, and spending happy days with her visiting his relations at Schneeberg and Zwickau, he had been to Berlin on his own to introduce himself to the Bargiels. Immediately sympathetic, Marianne was only too willing to cooperate in the proposed family discussion in Leipzig, where on August 30, at the home of her married sister, she was reunited with Clara, who had arrived only the day before and for the first time ever not slept at her father's house. But all hopes of negotiation were dashed when Wieck failed to keep the appointment. Fearful of what might follow in Leipzig, Clara left at once with her mother for Berlin, leaden-hearted in awareness that a Court confrontation was now inevitable.

October 2 was the appointed day, and she duly returned. This time Wieck excused himself in writing – having already appealed to Clara to meet him in Dresden for private discussion, which her lawyer forbad, and then to accept a new set of conditions giving most of her concert-savings to her brothers while at the same time demanding two-thirds of Schumann's own capital as a marriage settlement together with the assurance that she was his sole legatee. Faced with refusal of this, he then proposed a three-month concert tour together for a guaranteed sum of 6000 thalers provided she delayed marriage until her coming-of-age. Her rejection of that, too, was more than his irascible temperament could take. When Clara was compelled to send her maid to his house to ask for Mlle Wieck's winter cloak, his alleged reply was 'Who is Mlle. Wieck? I know only two Fräulein Wiecks; they are my two little daughters here. I do not know any other'. Back in Berlin with her mother, Clara had not long to wait for further evidence that something inside him had now snapped.

Needing money to pay her way with the none too well-off Bargiels, she arranged one or two appearances in provincial centres, notably with her old friend, Karl Müller, in Stettin on November 7 and 8,[1] as well as concerts at Berlin's Opera House and Theatre Royal. Response to the last two, even from the King of Prussia himself, was warm enough to soften the blow of learning that her father had surreptitiously tried to prevent a

---

[1] In both programmes they included just the central variation movement from Beethoven's 'Kreutzer' Sonata.

kind friend from lending her the piano she wanted, also the King from giving her his support. But it was galling to be told that in Leipzig he was falling over backwards to champion the attractive young pianist, Camilla Pleyel, probably her own greatest female rival in musicianship, as opposed to mere prestidigitation, especially when friends described his ecstatic demeanour on the platform, when turning over pages for her, as 'as ridiculous in itself as it was wounding to the feelings of those who witnessed it'.

The climax came on December 18, 1839, when Wieck was ordered to appear in Court. 'I shall never forget it', Clara's diary sorrowfully records that night. 'I could not look at him without feeling the deepest compassion; all the pains he had taken, all his many sleepless nights, the explanation at which he had been working for months – all this is of no use to him. He was most passionate, so that the President of the Court had to call him to order, and each time it cut me to the heart – I could hardly bear that he should have to experience this humiliation. He looked at me with terrible anger, but he only once said anything against me. I would so gladly have once more entreated him, there before the court, but I was afraid that he might thrust me from him and I was nailed to my seat. This day has separated us for ever, or at least it has torn to pieces the tender bond between father and child – my heart too feels as if it were torn in pieces'.

The happiness of brief reunions with Robert, whether in Leipzig or Berlin, could not blind her to the growing effects of the struggle on her lover's none too hardy constitution. Snide remarks from Wieck like 'Where is his *Freischütz*, his *Don Giovanni*?' had begun to reach his ears. And though willing enough to admit to 'a certain amount of dissipation before I met Clara', Schumann was totally unprepared for the defamation of his personal character which, under the fictitious signature of Lehmann, Wieck circulated to all their associates immediately after the Court's eventual refutation, on January 4, 1840, of his every charge against Schumann except one – over addiction to drink. Never able to endure slings and arrows with half of Clara's fortitude (even though guilty of reproaching her of a hypochondriacal lack of confidence in her own talent) Schumann shrank into a shell of despair, avoiding society, composing only with the greatest effort. 'Set out on your journey soon' he counselled Clara, in one of his strangely erratic, irregular letters at this time. 'Change of air and fresh faces at least distract one's thoughts. If only I too had energy to wander out into the world! I do not want to see you until the final judgment has taken from me the disgrace which your father has brought upon me. . . . If only the strength to work would come back to me, how happy I should be. . . . I think, and think, and think, the whole day long – Ah! pray for me often'.

Strong in physique as Clara was (and in this respect Wieck's early

insistence on regular open-air exercise had paid dividends), worry now
took an increasing toll on her too. When a Berlin concert already delayed
by a hand pain eventually took place on January 19, 1840, she was on the
point of collapse. 'I could hardly fling myself into my concert clothes, I
could not stand, my limbs were so weak that I could not raise my hand' she
subsequently explained to Robert. 'The doctor was caught in the street at
half past five, but he could not do much for me, so I was packed into the
carriage and taken to the concert room. During the concert I strengthened
myself with champagne, but in spite of this several times while I was
playing everything went black before my eyes, and the whole evening I was
nearer to fainting than to any musical enthusiasm, and yet no one noticed
it and everything went splendidly' (the programme included Beethoven's
'Archduke' Trio as well as her own Bellini Variations). Several days of
severe face-ache followed ('As a rule I can conquer a good deal of pain,
but now I should often like to lay myself down and die') though a second
concert on February 1, at which she played Schumann's F sharp minor
Sonata for the first time in public, was another triumph of mind over
matter.

The very next day she left with her mother for concerts in Hamburg,
Bremen and Lübeck, and as Schumann had predicted, music and travel
began to work their customary therapeutic miracles. As always there were
passing embarrassments, such as finding the right piano, receiving
unwanted callers, discovering that the general public preferred the showy
Czech virtuoso, Dreyschock, to Thalberg, and that Hamburg's musical
city fathers, Cranz and Avé-Lallemant, were sufficiently intoxicated with
Camilla Pleyel only to find words to admire her own ear-rings, not her
playing, after her own first concert. She was still more upset, initially, to
discover that her erstwhile suitor, Rakemann, now her father's ally, had
circulated the slanderous Lehmann letter in Bremen – prompting Schumann to threaten to sue him. But as always, her dedicated musicianship
and simple sincerity of personality won all hearts – enough for her even to
enjoy life's ordinary pleasures as they came along, such as the discovery of
the freshest and most beautiful oysters before they boarded a boat to cross
the Elbe ('In my love-sick mind I determined to send you a small barrel,
and gave the commission to Cranz, who will send them off tomorrow, or
the day after, as soon as they come from the ship'), and still more
memorable, her very first sight of the sea – at Travemünde. 'We went out
to sea in a little boat with three sails till we could no longer see any shore,
and not one of us knew where we were . . . although I was rather nervous,
still I shouted for joy. The day was misty, but it looked all the prettier when
a faint sunbeam broke through the clouds and turned the waves to silver.
How many thousand times did I utter your name – oh! if only you could
have been with us.' Back in Berlin by March 11 her immediate thrill was a

performance of Goethe's *Faust*, evoking her meeting with the octogenarian author eight years earlier as vividly as had it been yesterday. She could also proudly report that having paid all travelling expenses and made certain obligatory purchases for her mother's family as well as herself, she still had 490 thalers left out of her takings of 970 thalers.

Even though now driven to plan a libel action against Wieck, Schumann, too, found that 1840 had its compensations. Good friends like Mendelssohn and David had pledged their support in any Court of Law. And by March, the University of Jena had awarded him an honorary doctorate of philosophy. Though indifferent to such titles himself he knew that Wieck would be impressed, and had accordingly explored every avenue open to him both at Leipzig University, through his sister-in-law, Therese, and at Jena through his friend, Keferstein – with the latter even volunteering to write a thesis on Shakespeare and music in the mistaken belief that the honour might come to him as a musical doctorate. His greatest joy was nevertheless in finding that musical ideas had started to flow again almost more spontaneously and pressingly than he could fasten them down – this time in the previously unexplored (except in adolescence) realm of romantic song. Last but not least there was the stimulating intoxication of meeting Liszt for the first time; after almost daily interchanges both confessed to a feeling of having known each other for twenty years. 'How extraordinary his playing is, so bold and daring, and then again so tender and delicate! I have never heard anything like it', so Schumann wrote, qualifying his enthusiasm, nevertheless, with the words: 'But his world is not mine, Clärchen. Art, as we know it – you when you play, I when I compose – has an intimate charm that is worth more to me than all Liszt's splendour and tinsel'. Away in Berlin, Clara began to feel as artistically deprived as she had done in December, when the 'Great' Schubert C major Symphony discovered by Schumann in Vienna had so thrilled everyone when first tried out at the Gewandhaus. So she jumped at an invitation from both Schumann and Liszt to return to Leipzig for the latter's charity concert on March 30, albeit expressing sadness that in loyalty to them Liszt had chosen to ignore her father. His playing this time she found a little more fallible than before, but his personality as enchanting as ever even if exhausting because so lacking in repose. Happy days followed for both Robert and herself when they returned to Berlin, not least in finding Mendelssohn on a visit to his native city, and being able to make music together. 'He is the pianist I love best of all' was Clara's admission in her diary. Schumann's pleasure overflowed in a letter to his friend, Dr Krüger: 'We passed a few hours at the piano which I shall never forget. I have lately written much for the voice. Well, he sang everything, accompanied by my betrothed (who plays *well*, as I dare say you know) so that I felt perfectly blissful'. Schumann's Eichendorff setting, 'Mond-nacht', embodying the German word for marriage, Ehe (translated into musical notation) in its bass, grew from this visit – and fittingly he sent it to Clara's mother for her birthday on May 15.

For Schumann's own birthday on June 8 Clara was back in Leipzig. Music-making together, and with friends including Lwoff, the composer of the Russian national anthem who was very anxious for Clara to tour his country, helped the time to pass agreeably enough, and there was a tremendous new fillip to Clara's own practising (she was at this time learning Chopin's F minor Concerto as well as more of Thalberg's operatic fantasias) when to her complete surprise she returned home on the evening of July 4 to find a splendid new Härtel grand piano awaiting her as a present from her beloved, with a little poem tucked inside the accompanying flowers. Three days later he was able to tell her the unexpectedly good tidings that Wieck, for lack of evidence, was unable to proceed with his charges. And on August 1 the Court at last gave its verdict: they were free to marry without parental consent. Realizing the game was up, Wieck lodged no appeal in the ten permitted days, so the first banns went out on August 16. 'I cannot grasp this happiness' so Clara's diary records (even though lamenting lack of money for a proper trousseau) as she and Robert started to look for a home, soon finding 'small but cosy' rooms in the house of Maurermeister Scheitel at No. 5, Inselstrasse.

But there was still work to be done. On August 8 she played at Jena, and three days later at the Grand Ducal Court in Weimar, where the Empress of Russia and a number of other foreign luminaries were among the guests, to her displeasure keeping up a lively conversation and even allowing their dogs to bark throughout most of her programme. A return visit the next evening, when the foreigners had left, was much more to her liking – especially as the Grand Duchess showed such interest in her forthcoming marriage. Moving on to Liebenstein to stay with her old friends, the Lists, she several times played to the Duke and Duchess of Meiningen at their nearby castle (with Emilie List to vary the programme with songs), finding herself touched to the point of tears by the motherly kindness of the Duchess. 'I shall never forget this woman with her tenderness and her angelic gentleness, and yet at the same time with her truly royal dignity'.

Other concerts followed in Gotha, Erfurt, and finally at the Town Hall in Weimar on September 5. Here, she joined in Beethoven's 'Geister' Trio, Op.70, No. 1, as well as contributing Henselt's 'Wenn ich ein Vöglein war', Chopin's B minor Mazurka, Liszt's transcriptions of Schubert's 'Ave Maria' and 'Erlkönig', and Thalberg's Fantasie on Rossini's *Moïse* to a curiously mixed programme, overjoyed throughout the whole evening because Robert had come to take her home after what was now quite surely to be her very last public appearance as Clara Wieck.

Back in Leipzig Schumann had one more surprise in store. On September 11, he presented her with a volume of songs, *Myrthen* (Op.24), beautifully bound in red velvet, and inscribed 'To my beloved Clara on the eve of our wedding, from her Robert', including avowals of love like 'Widmung' and 'Du bist wie eine Blume' eloquent enough to tell her that no sacrifice she might make on his behalf could ever be too great.

The little village church of Schönefeld, near Leipzig, was chosen for the ceremony. 'What am I to say about this day?' Clara wrote on the eve of her coming of age. 'We were married at Schönefeld at ten o'clock. First came a chorale, and after that a short address by Wildenhahn, the preacher, a friend of Robert's youth. His words were simple, but heartfelt. My whole self was filled with gratitude to Him who had brought us safely over so many rocks and precipices to meet at last. I prayed fervently that He would preserve my Robert to me for many, many years. Indeed, the thought that I might one day lose him is enough to send me out of my mind. Heaven avert this calamity! I could not bear it.

'Emilie and Elise List took me by surprise after the wedding. We spent the morning in company with Reuter, Wenzel, Herrmann, Becker, Mother and the Lists, at the Carls', the afternoon at Zweinaundorf and the evening at the Carls' again, when Madame List came too.

'There was a little dancing, no excessive gaiety, but every face shone with real satisfaction. The weather was lovely. Even the sun, which had hidden his face for many days, shed his warm beams upon us as we drove to Church, as if to bless our union. It was a day without a jar, and I may thus enter it in this book as the fairest and most momentous of my life.'

SEVEN

Counter-claims 1840–42

'I dare say you have indirectly heard of our marriage – now you hear it directly from one who knows what the happiness of life means', so Schumann wrote to his old friend, Töpken, on September 28, 1840. One of his early presents to his wife was a cookery book, *Neues einfaches Kochbuch für bürgerliche Haushaltungen* (including graphic diagrams of the cuts of edible beasts and fowl) with 'Meiner Hausfrau gewidmet' printed in gold on its shiny red cover. More important was the diary he gave her immediately after the wedding to be kept by them both, week by week in turn, as a record of their musical aspirations, achievements and failures, their personal dreams, satisfactions and doubts. Penalties were planned for whoever failed to produce the prescribed page per week. But over-flowing with musical ideas that he could scarcely fasten down on paper before they dissolved into feeling again, Schumann very soon left the lion's share to Clara. It was she who on December 5, 1840, accordingly recorded: 'We have been married three months today, and they have been the happiest three months of my life. Every day I fall more deeply in love with my Robert, and if I often seem sad, and almost cross, it is but the result of cares which have their origin in my love for him'. Two months later she added: 'We enjoy a happiness such as I never knew before – in spite of moments of despair and depression. ... Father has always laughed at so-called domestic bliss. How I pity those who do not know it! They are only half alive'.

Though totally without regrets about her decision, Clara was nevertheless too caring a daughter and too dedicated an artist to be able to shrug off the past completely. 'If anything can momentarily disturb my content-ment, it is the thought of my Father, for whom I feel the deepest compassion. He cannot witness our happiness, since heaven has denied him a heart, and he cannot understand a joy like ours' was one of her earliest admissions of the continuing pain caused her by the break with Wieck, who after total intractability during the spring of 1841 in an attempted settlement of problems concerning her earnings and belong-ings, with Major Serre at Maxen acting as intermediary, then chose to ignore the birthday greeting she sent him in the summer. As for the counter claims of home and piano that right from the start caused her so many pangs, the obligatory cancellation (for political reasons) of a Russian tour planned with the help of their good friend, Lwoff, quickly brought her conflict to a head. 'Farewell to the virtuoso' she wrote as early as October 1840. 'If only I could persuade Robert to take me to Holland and Belgium so that I might make some use of next winter! It is dreadful to me not to be able to make my talent of any use to him, now while my powers are at their best. . . . I also owe it to my reputation not to retire completely.' Even at home she felt frustrated by restricted opportunities for practice, at once undermining her technique and preventing her from enlarging her repertory in the way to which she had long grown accustomed. Though there were two grand pianos in the apartment, the 'evils of thin walls' was a recurrent moan from them both. Saddened as Schumann was that 'far too often she has to buy my songs at the price of invisibility and silence', and even more by her diary admission that his coldness when in the grip of urgent inspiration sometimes hurt her, he nevertheless always looked to her to make the sacrifice and accepted it with unashamed gratitude.

Consolation for them both was not long in coming. Having 'tingled to be at work on a symphony' ever since unearthing Schubert's 'Great' C major in Vienna, Schumann now at last found the peace of mind in which to turn away from miniatures to larger projects: 1841 brought an uprush of orchestral composition no less intensive than his song-writing of the previous year. For Clara, it was a vindication of her life-long belief in his true stature when on March 31 his first Symphony in B flat, nicknamed the 'Spring' after the spring poem by Adolph Böttger that inspired it, had its première at the Gewandhaus under Mendelssohn's baton. She was doubly happy that despite all domestic complications, she, too, could share in a concert that was such a milestone. Making her first appearance on this august platform as Clara Schumann, she played the Adagio and Rondo from Chopin's F minor Concerto, and solos including Thalberg's *Mosenphantasie* and smaller pieces by Scarlatti, Schumann and Mendelssohn besides joining Mendelssohn in his brand new *Allegro brillant* in A, Op.92, for four hands. There was the additional satisfaction of hearing her own recently composed, turbulent Burns setting, 'Am Strande', as well as songs by Robert, sung by the soprano, Sophie Schloss. As she wrote to her old friend, Emilie List, 'I was received with such persistent applause that I turned red and white, it would not stop even when I seated myself at the piano (I never heard anyone get such a reception . . . not even Thalberg). You can fancy if this gave me courage! I was trembling in every limb with nervousness. I played as I hardly ever remember playing. . . . My husband's symphony won a victory over all cabals and intrigues. . . . I never heard a symphony received with such applause. Mendelssohn conducted it, and all through the concert he was delightful, the greatest pleasure shone from his eyes. The songs, too, were a decided success, and Fräulein Schloss had to repeat the last one'. Schumann himself was no less elated. 'On the 31st concert by the Schumanns' so his diary entry records. 'Happy evening which I shall never forget. My Clara played everything in so masterly a fashion and with such profound understanding, that everyone was delighted. In my artistic life also this has been one of the most important of days. My wife realized this, and rejoiced at the success of my symphony almost more than at her own. With God's help then I will follow this road further. I feel so cheerful now, that I hope to bring to the light of day many a thing which shall rejoice men's hearts'.

Whatever their conflicting musical needs at home, they always managed to reconcile them for a few hours most days in shared study of specially selected classics. Bach's '48' was their initial choice. From preludes and fugues they moved on to the overtures and symphonies of Mozart and Beethoven as preparation for Robert's own orchestral adventures. Nor was their exploration restricted just to musical scores. Having so recently dallied with the idea of writing a thesis on Shakespeare and music to earn a doctor's degree, Schumann was still very much of the opinion that 'No one has ever said anything finer or more significant about music than Shakespeare, and that at a time when it was still in its infancy'. Searching Shakespeare's plays together, every quotation he cherished she undertook to inscribe in a beautiful book. Under his guidance she also tried to deepen her understanding of his beloved Jean Paul, besides, at Mendelssohn's instigation, tackling her old friend Goethe's *Hermann and Dorothea* for the first time. With advancing pregnancy, these fireside intellectual pursuits, shared with just husband and closer, like-minded friends, opened up invaluable new horizons: inevitably, her own tastes, standards and style began to change. As she put it in July, 1841: 'On Sunday afternoon I played some of Beethoven's sonatas, but neither Becker nor Krägen enjoyed them as we enjoy Beethoven sonatas. They have been taught to think more of virtuosity than of real music. A Bach fugue, for example, bores them, they are not capable of discovering the beauty which lies in the different parts taking up the theme, they cannot follow it. . . . The less I play in public, the more I hate all mere technique. Concert pieces, such as Henselt's Etudes, Thalberg's and Liszt's Phantasies etc. etc. I have grown quite to dislike. . . . Nothing of that sort can give lasting pleasure'. In tribute to their own phenomenal wizardry (notably Henselt's), which in secret she knew to be beyond her own, however outstanding, female resources, she did in fact continue to play their operatic Fantasies whenever called upon for fireworks: Thalberg's on Rossini's *Moïse* and *La donna del lago*, Henselt's on Donizetti's *L'elisir d'amore* and Liszt's on the same composer's *Lucia di Lammermoor* were her special favourites. But adding Beethoven's 'Moonlight', 'Waldstein' and D minor (Op.31, No. 2) sonatas to her repertory were the tasks into which she really put her heart at this time.

Summer holidays were cautiously restricted to a short visit to Dresden and a few local excursions to places like Connewitz, of which they never tired. And in the middle of a thunderstorm on the morning of September 1, 1841, after long and difficult labour, Clara gave birth to her first child. Schumann's immediate letter to his mother-in-law, Frau Bargiel, in Berlin tells the whole tale.

Dear Mamma,
    You are the grandmamma of a charming, well-fashioned little girl. There is great rejoicing in our house. But there were also three anxious hours of great suffering for Clara. She is now quite well, quite happy. Court-Physician Jörg, who assisted when Clara was born, has now also assisted with Clara's child. If you could only be with us! You would see happy human beings. Auntie has been a faithful help; she came at four-o-clock in the morning, and at twenty minutes past ten the little creature was born. Her first cry – and we fell into each other's arms, weeping. Clara herself was as though she had been reborn. Goodbye, dear, kind mother of my Clara, grandmother of . . . what shall we call her? Write at once to your 'Happy Children'.

Marie was their eventual choice of name, and the christening took place on Clara's birthday with Mendelssohn,[1] Clara's mother, and Schumann's brother, Karl, and his old Leipzig landlady, Frau Devrient, the god-parents. Young and inexperienced as she was, inevitably Clara worried a lot at first about the child's welfare, not least the problems of finding a wet-nurse. But 'soft and white as alabaster' (as the diary put it), Marie was a contented baby, quickly lulled if ever fretful by Clara's singing or playing. Their joy would have been complete but for Wieck's stony silence when told the glad tidings.

Of the several musical offerings received by Clara on her birthday from her husband, none was more welcome than the score of his new Symphony in D minor. It was not a total surprise. Diary entries reveal that she had 'often heard D minor sounding wildly from afar'. Even so, the speed at which he finished it still amazed her in view of the fact that he had already followed up the 'Spring' Symphony with an orchestral *Overture, Scherzo and Finale* as well as a Phantasie for piano and orchestra (subsequently to grow into the A minor piano concerto). With yet more ideas spilling over into a projected 'little symphony in C minor', Schumann himself, as autumn advanced, wanted nothing more than to stay at home in Leipzig, with his wife and child at his side. But an invitation to Weimar for Clara guaranteeing a performance of his 'Spring' Symphony and some of his songs in the course of her two concerts, the second at the Palace of her old friend, the Grand Duchess, in the end drew him out of his shell.

---

[1] Mendelssohn and Karl Schumann both had to be represented by proxy.

For Clara, it presaged a winter season[1] scarcely less arduous than those
with her father in her teens, with four appearances at the Gewandhaus
between December 6, 1841, and January 10, 1842, demanding very speedy
learning of Mendelssohn's G minor Piano Concerto and Mozart's G
minor Piano Quartet as well as the notorious 'Hexameron' Variations on
Bellini's 'Suoni la tromba' (from *I Puritani*) in which, for a Parisian charity
event organized by Princess Christine de Belgiojoso, Liszt had invited
contributions from Thalberg, Pixis, Herz, Czerny and Chopin to bind
together within his own introduction and grand finale. Sufficiently fond of
the work to arrange it for piano and orchestra as well as for two pianos, he
had proposed to Clara, at their recent meeting in Weimar, that they
should play the slightly shortened latter version together at her Gewandhaus concert on December 6, with a repeat performance at his own
concert on this platform on December 13. Yet in spite of their own
deliriously enthusiastic reception from outsize audiences, Clara was
painfully aware that Robert had not been pleased with her playing, and
worse still, that without Mendelssohn to conduct its première on December 6, her husband's new D minor Symphony had neither been well
presented nor well received (he withdrew it at once for revision, not
publishing it until 1851 as his No. 4). It was all the more galling for her to
have to admit that the astonishing box-office success of both events was
wholly due to Liszt, for already his extravagantly flamboyant life-
style and hubris were beginning to strain their personal affection for him,
just as the audacities in his own works were exhausting their musical
patience. As she observed in December, 1841: 'I cannot call them anything
but hideous – a chaos of the harshest discords, a perpetual murmuring in
the deepest bass and the highest treble at the same time, wearisome
introductions etc. I could almost hate him as a composer.'[2] Bennett's
return visit to Leipzig in January 1842, in the course of which they sledged
to Connewitz, gave them much deeper pleasure.

Platform blandishments during the next three months were to cause far
greater upheavals at No. 5 Inselstrasse. Journeys to Bremen and Hamburg, where between February 23 and March 5, although suffering from a
hurt finger, she gave her first performances of Weber's *Concertstück*, were
arranged without too much heart-searching: though it was not easy to part
from little Marie, initially Clara at least had the willing cooperation and
company of her husband, who managed to secure five weeks' leave of
absence from the *Neue Zeitschrift für Musik* to supervise performances of
his 'Spring' Symphony and some of his songs. While content enough with

[1] She had in fact begun it by joining Mendelssohn and Moscheles in Bach's Concerto
for three pianos at the Gewandhaus on October 14.
[2] She had significantly made no attempt to perform the *Etudes d'exécution transcendante
d'après Paganini* dedicated to her by Liszt in 1840.

their reception in both big cities, their sky was immediately clouded when an invitation arrived from the Court at Oldenburg addressed to Clara alone. Dutifully, she accepted. But as Schumann ruefully observed in the diary 'the thought of my undignified position in such cases prevented me from feeling any pleasure'. This personal slight, together with his acute awareness that in their travels it was Clara who was doing the lion's share of the wage-earning, continued to rankle, so much that having more or less agreed to accompany Clara to Copenhagen (a project they had envisaged for early 1840 but abandoned) he suddenly announced that the *Neue Zeitschrift* could no longer safely be left in strange hands and that they should both return to Leipzig as soon as possible.

The longer Clara pondered on this *volte face*, the harder she found it to accept. While the prospect of disrupting her husband's composition and daily editorial responsibility by forcing him into the role of mere companion on her tours was abhorrent to her, it seemed just as wrong to abuse opportunities that might never come her own way again. The solution that eventually presented itself was a hard one, as a letter to her friend, Emilie List, reveals: 'I thought the matter over, however. I am a woman, I shall not be neglecting anything, I earn nothing at home, why should I not by means of my talent, gain my mite for Robert? Could anyone think ill of me for so doing, or of my husband for going home to his child and his business? I laid my plan before Robert, and it is true that at first he shrank from it, but in the end he agreed, when I represented the matter to him as reasonably as possible. It was certainly a great step for a wife who loves her husband as I do, but I did it for love of him, and for that no sacrifice is too great or too hard for me. In addition to this I now found a nice girl who with the greatest joy offered to come with me; a girl belonging to one of the most highly respected families in Bremen, and with whom my husband knew that I should be safe. We left Hamburg on the same day, Robert for Leipzig, and I, by way of Kiel, for Copenhagen – I shall never forget the day of our parting!'

So much went wrong at the start that there was nothing in the world she would have loved more than to abandon the whole project and rush back home. In Kiel itself, last-minute indisposition compelled her to cancel a recital when the audience had already arrived in the hall, involving her with expenses of 47 marks the very next day. A violent storm, preventing her from sailing for a week, was the next set-back. Returning to Hamburg in search of friends, she then tried to arrange impromptu recitals both in that city and Lübeck to help recoup her Kiel losses, only to find that the imminence of Easter, together with the arrival of an opera company in Lübeck, made all such schemes impractical. Worse still, there were no letters from her husband, who believed her to be already in Denmark. When eventually boarding the 'long-feared but magnificent ship, *Christian the Eighth*', after days when she was often in tears, she confessed 'It felt horrible as we left the land; how I sighed for Robert, for baby, and came near to thinking that I should never again tread on firm land'.

Once ashore, her spirits revived, for her reputation had preceded her. On all sides she found eager audiences and much personal kindness, even if musical standards and taste proved lower than she had expected. Referring to the local musicians as 'mere mechanics', she wrote to tell Robert that because the Copenhagen Orchestra, who had not even yet worked their way through all nine Beethoven symphonies, was so untrained, she had given up the idea of trying to arrange a performance of his 'Spring' Symphony. In her own programmes she included quite a lot of Chopin ('no one has played him hitherto, not even Thalberg') but was wary about introducing her husband's own music to so conservative a public – only one of the *Novelletten* and a transcription of 'Widmung' found a place. Discretion brought its rewards: her two privately promoted concerts at the Theatre Royal on April 3 and 10 and a third at the Hôtel d'Angleterre on April 14, together with three other appearances including one at Court on April 5, earned her some 940 thalers.

Her leisure proved profitable too, with the sculpture of Thorwaldsen affording particular pleasure. Among personal contacts, it was the uprising composer-conductor Niels Gade, at twenty-five only two and a half years her senior, to whom she felt closest, not least because he knew and admired so many of Schumann's own works, though initially she was put off by his appearance ('a little, round-faced, insignificant-looking creature, with good-tempered eyes, whom I should never have credited with such an overture.[1] Another proof that one should not judge people by appearances'). Of writers, it was Hans Andersen, strangely under-estimated by his compatriots, who particularly intrigued her, despite again at first being disconcerted by his looks. Admiring his 'poetic, child-like disposition', she described him to Robert as 'the ugliest man that could be . . . but in spite of this he looks interesting . . . one can only get accustomed to him by degrees . . . but yet, taking him altogether, he looks intellectual'. She also enormously admired the author, Hejberg, and his charming, talented and beautiful actress wife. When told that she resembled Mme Hejberg, Clara, making one of her extremely rare comments on her own appearance, admitted the similarity of figure and features but sadly added in her letter home 'but she is pretty whilst I am ugly'. Besides the intelligentsia, the aristocracy, too, helped to lessen her loneliness. The young Princes of Glücksburg and Hesse sometimes accompanied her on short morning strolls. But it was Queen Caroline Amalie who showed the greatest appreciation after Clara's recital at Court, picking flowers from her own private garden for a personal farewell on the morning of departure, and

[1] *Echoes from Ossian*, which in 1840 won the newly-formed Copenhagen Musical Society's first prize.

proffering a warm invitation to return to Denmark as soon as possible. Clara's reciprocal gesture to the Queen was the dedication of a set of six songs when they eventually appeared in print as her Op.13 the following year.

*

Married life allowed her all too little time for composition. As Schumann eventually admitted in February 1843: 'Clara has written a number of smaller pieces which show a musicianship and a tenderness of invention such as she has never before attained. But children, and a husband who is always living in the realms of imagination, do not go well with composition. She cannot work at it regularly, and I am often disturbed to think how many tender ideas are lost because she cannot work them out'. His own unabating stream of songs throughout the year of their marriage was nevertheless a challenge she could not resist. Determined as ever to measure her strength against his, on Christmas Eve, 1840, she presented him with three settings of his beloved Burns and Heine, of which Burns's 'Am Strande', with its turbulent piano accompaniment in E flat minor to depict the storm-tossed sea and the pangs of separation, obviously pleased them both enough to find a place in their important shared Gewandhaus concert (already mentioned) on March 31, 1841. Of the two Heine settings, a Volkslied ('Es fiel ein Reif in der Frühlingsnacht') and 'Ihr Bildnis' ('Ich stand in dunklen Träumen'), she valued the latter enough eventually to choose it as the first of her set of six songs for the Danish Queen.

Early in 1841 Schumann decided to encourage her more directly by inviting her to join him in a Rückert cycle, with poems selected by himself from that poet's *Liebesfrühling*, just as Mendelssohn had collaborated with his sister Fanny in his cycles of Op.8 and Op.9 a decade before. Whereas his own nine settings were finished in a mere eight days, her own four (of which he only rejected 'Die gute Nacht') cost her much heart-ache and were not ready till his birthday in June. The first of the selected three (subsequently separately listed as her Op.12) is 'Er ist gekommen', in style and spirit akin to 'Am Strande' in its ultimate resolution of minor key unrest into major key calm. For the lovers' fancies of 'Liebst du um Schönheit' and 'Warum willst du andre fragen' she finds a naïve charm not unlike her husband's own in this set. When a printed copy was sent to Rückert the following spring he was sufficiently delighted to express his thanks in what the diary calls a 'master poem'.

Composed at various times between 1840–3, Clara's Op.13 eventually emerged in print as 'Six Songs with piano accompaniment, composed and respectfully dedicated to Her Majesty Caroline Amalie the reigning Queen of Denmark, by Clara Schumann'. All have a deeper romantic glow than those of Op.12. Perhaps because initially written for her husband, No. 1 in E flat, Heine's 'Ihr Bildnis', could almost be mistaken for intimately committed, authentic Schumann in the lyricism of the accompaniment, with an eloquent little prelude and postlude embellished with a characteristically Schumannesque gruppetto just before the cadence. Only the closing 'und ach, ich kanns nicht glauben, dass ich dich verloren hab!' blandly repeating the song's opening phrase betrays a Clara more concerned with musical symmetry than the poetic message. The last of the six, an A flat major setting of Geibel's 'Die stille Lotusblume', comes still closer to Schumann because of a new subtlety in word-painting such as when moving into deep, mysterious flats for the swan's song ('er singt so süss, so leise') and ending on an unresolved dominant seventh in response to the poem's last unanswered question. If No. 2 in G minor, Heine's 'Sie liebten sich beide', with its 'gondola' six-eight, shows her momentarily inclining towards Mendelssohn, it is Schumann's breathless excitement (as typified in 'Frühlingsnacht') that she tries to recapture, albeit more prosaically, in No. 3 in E flat, Geibel's 'Liebes-zauber'. In No. 4 in D flat, Geibel's 'Der Mond kommt still gegangen', and No. 5 in A flat, Rückert's 'Ich hab in deinem Auge', she again seeks to infuse simple lyricism with a quiet inner rapture all Schumann's own. But her accompaniments are essentially those of a pianist composer (a charge which on occasions could be levelled at her husband too): so much of the vocal line is incorporated in them that no great alteration would be necessary to transform the majority of her songs into self-contained piano pieces.

Her own instrument was not entirely neglected during this outburst of song. For Robert's 1841 Christmas present she embarked on her first piano sonata,[1] in the event only managing to complete its opening sonata-form Allegro in G minor and a Scherzo in G major (with a contrasting E minor trio) in time to present to him on the festive day with a plea for indulgence. The brief but soulfully songful Adagio in E flat and the concluding Rondo in G minor were not finished until January 15, 1842. Perhaps because Clara never found time to perfect the somewhat naïvely planned Rondo (the manuscript betrays several uncertainties) or else because the whole work is so strongly influenced by Mendelssohn, it never emerged in print even though probably intended as her Op. 18. This number and Op. 19 are significantly missing from a list of works extending to Op. 23.

---

[1] The manuscript is preserved in the Schumann-Haus at Zwickau.

EIGHT

Reconciliation 1842–44

Leaving Copenhagen on April 18, 1842, Clara briefly visited Kiel to give the concert (the programme was mainly comprised of operatic fantasias by Henselt, Thalberg and Liszt) cancelled on her outward journey, before reaching Magdeburg by boat, where on the 25th, after some initial confusion in finding each other, she was at last reunited with her nervously excited husband. As she put it, 'I did not have long to wait before Robert's arms opened and I flew into them'. The next day's return to No. 5 Inselstrasse was still more joyous: 'A meeting like this makes up for all the yearning pains that went before. Robert, too, seems very happy, and led me home where I found everything decorated with garlands, and in addition Robert has given me a beautiful carpet. But best of all was the look in his dear eyes, which I could enjoy once more, and the rosy cheeks of my little angel, which I could kiss again'. Though busy enough with the *Neue Zeitschrift* and Leipzig's constant stream of musical visitors, Schumann had in fact suffered even sharper pangs of loneliness than she, as diary entries in her absence make very plain. 'It was one of the stupidest things I ever did to let you leave me', he wrote at one point, adding that in his wretchedness he had been unable to compose a single note.

Nevertheless in secret his thoughts had already turned towards chamber music, and more particularly to the string quartet. It was an urge that had laid dormant ever since 1838 when Clara, at the height of her success in Vienna, had slightly damped his ardour by asking if he knew his instruments well enough. Now, she was more than ready to join him in an intensive study of the string quartets of Mozart and Haydn by way of preparation, so that within a month of her return, despite the upheaval of a big charity concert in Hamburg which she organized with David (just as Moscheles had done in London) to raise funds for victims of that city's big fire in early May, Schumann was in the grip of inspiration scarcely less obsessive than when engulfed in songs and orchestral music in the two preceding years. By mid-July he had completed three String Quartets in A minor, F major and A major which he proudly dedicated to Mendelssohn, whose elegantly fluent contrapuntal cunning and structural cohesion had influenced his own style even more than his avowed classical models. Nothing gave Schumann greater pleasure than Mendelssohn's own praise of the first. It was scarcely less gratifying to learn that the eminent critic, Moritz Hauptmann, by whom he had previously been dismissed as a mere eccentric miniaturist, had admitted to finding the quartets 'very cleverly conceived and held together' as well as original and beautiful. As for Clara, for whose twenty-third birthday in September Schumann arranged a special performance in their own home, she was enthusiastic enough to write: 'My admiration for his genius, his intellect, in short for the whole composer, grows with each work. . . . Everything in them is new, and at the same time clear, skilfully worked out, and exactly suited to the strings . . . now for the first time do I begin to take pleasure in chamber music, for hitherto, I must frankly confess, this kind of music has bored me, I could not discover the beauty of it.'

A brief holiday visit in August to Bohemian spas including Marienbad and Königswart (where they were very kindly received by Prince Metternich, who promised his protection if they should ever return to Vienna) rekindled Schumann's zest for work, first a Quintet in E flat for piano and strings completed by the last week of September. Only minor composers had ever essayed this particular instrumental combination before. For Schumann, reunited with his beloved piano, the challenge sparked off a masterpiece, its themes glowing with all the old spontaneous romantic ardour of his youth while disciplined by a mind at the height of its powers. Craftsmanship reaches its peak in the final fugal coda, where, in a manner beloved by Mendelssohn, the work's opening subject is recalled in augmentation with the finale's own main theme as countersubject. Almost before its ink had dried, Schumann followed it with a Piano Quartet in the same key, the Scherzo a lively salute to Mendelssohn's world of elves and sprites, the lyrical slow movement as nostalgically beautiful as any of his Clara-inspired love-songs. Yet though studiously reasoned, the longer flanking movements left no doubt that by now Schumann was exceedingly tired, in fact exhausted to the point of breakdown. In consequence all other projects, including a set of Variations for two pianos, two cellos and horn (eventually revised for two pianos only and introduced to the public by Mendelssohn and Clara at Pauline Viardot's Leipzig concert on August 19, 1843) had to be put aside.

Happily unaware of what this 'weakness of the nerves', as Schumann described it, really presaged, Clara tenderly nursed him back to health. The arrival in Leipzig of Berlioz, whose 'Fantastic' Symphony a few years before had sparked off one of the lengthiest and most perspicaciously analytical articles Schumann had ever written, also helped to rekindle old energy. By January 8, 1843, life was in fact sufficiently back to normal for husband and wife to invite their friends to the small hall of the Gewandhaus for a private morning concert that included Schumann's Piano Quintet (its public première was at Sophie Schloss's farewell concert on February 9) destined to become one of the cornerstones of Clara's repertory. Alone, her outstanding contribution to the programme was Beethoven's A major Sonata, Op.101, the only one of this composer's late sonatas to find a regular place in her recitals throughout her life. As Mendelssohn admired this work enough to salute its opening movement in his own E major Sonata, Op.6, it could well have been at his instigation that she learnt it.

At the end of February Schumann, now quite recovered, embarked on a more ambitious project than anything attempted before, an oratorio, *Paradise and the Peri*, drawn from Thomas Moore's *Lalla Rookh*. And by April he felt able to accept an invitation to teach piano, composition and score-reading at the newly opened Music School in Leipzig for which Mendelssohn had campaigned unremittingly ever since 1840, on learning that a wealthy Leipziger, Herr Blümner, had bequeathed money to the King of Saxony for the founding of a college of art or science. There was good reason why Clara herself could not then join the staff: on April 25 she gave birth to her second child, a daughter christened Elise (with Carl Voigt among the godparents) a fortnight later. It was a much quicker, easier birth than Marie's, and because she had been through it all before she worried far less about nursing the child. Her biggest relief was nevertheless in being able to share the good news with her father, who at the turn of the year had broken his long silence by inviting her to visit him in Dresden, where he had recently moved, with even a hint of possible reconciliation with Schumann too. 'Your husband and I have hard heads, which must be allowed to go their own way, but we have stuff in us. Therefore he cannot be surprised if I wish to see justice done to his industry and to his creative power. Come to Dresden soon, and bring your husband's quintet with you' were the words that restored her to her father's side in the middle of February, 1843, for the first time since her marriage. Though less willing to be patronized on the strength of his increasing recognition, Schumann was aware of what it all meant to Clara. As he wrote to their friend, Verhulst, on June 19, 1843: 'There has been a reconciliation between Clara and her father. I am glad of it for her sake, but the man must be quite devoid of decent feeling to attempt to renew the acquaintance with myself, as he is actually doing. But at last the clouds are lifting, and I am glad on Clara's account'.

The main point of the letter to Verhulst was nevertheless to inform him that 'I finished my *Paradise and the Peri* last Friday: it is my greatest work, and I hope my best. I wrote "Finis" at the end of the score with a heart full of gratitude to Heaven for having sustained my energies while I wrote it'. In the diary he continued 'Except for certain oratorios of Loewe's, which, however, have for the most part a didactic flavour, I know nothing in music that is like it. I do not like to write to speak about my own work; my wish is that it may do some good in the world and assure me of a loving place in the memory of my children'. Despite the constant claims of house and children as well as performances of the Quintet and two-piano Variations involving journeys to Dresden, Clara, having helped considerably in the preparation of the piano score that summer, also played a large part in the rehearsals. On November 23 Schumann even wrote to beg her to return from Dresden 'tomorrow evening. . . . I cannot hold a rehearsal without you, it makes me feel as if I had lost my good genius'. With Livia Frege singing the part of the Peri (the fallen angel exiled from Paradise until returning with the tear of a repentant sinner) and with Schumann making his début as conductor, the Gewandhaus première eventually took place on December 4, with a repeat on the 11th. Except for some uncertain soprano entries (Livia Frege felt that Schumann should have scolded more at rehearsals) the performances went well, winning Schumann 'exceptional applause', a laurel wreath, and the promise of a further performance at a Dresden subscription concert on December 23. Their only serious disappointment was that Mendelssohn had to be away from Leipzig at the time. On learning of the work's success, Wieck's reaction was immediate. Picking up pen on December 15 he wrote

> Dear Schumann,
>   Tempora mutantur et nos mutamur in eis.
>   In the face of Clara and of the world at large we can no longer keep apart from one another. You are moreover the father of a family – what need is there for a lengthy explanation? We were always united where art was concerned – I was even your teacher – my verdict decided your present course in life for you. There is no need for me to assure you of my sympathy with your talent and with your fine and genuine aspirations. In Dresden there joyfully awaits you
> Your father, Fr. Wieck.

This time the hand of friendship was not refused. With his elated wife and children, Schumann arrived in Dresden on December 19, not just for the rehearsals and performance, but all set to stay with the Wiecks over Christmas.

*

Proud and happy as she was as wife, mother, and for the moment as reconciled daughter too, there were still moments of black despair for Clara whenever she thought of her far too often silent piano and her constantly interrupted career, the more so since she was acutely aware that their Leipzig expenditure was far exceeding their income. Mendelssohn had always understood her conflict, and he was one of the first to whom she confided the good news that Schumann had at last agreed to accompany her on her long delayed Russian tour. 'My husband now speaks seriously of our journey, and I am very glad of it' she wrote on

December 9, 1843, 'but I know well whom I have to thank for this. When I think of the morning when I came to you in despair I feel ashamed, and think that I must have seemed childish to you, and how you met all my wishes with a sympathy which made me trust you absolutely.'

Having despatched their two young daughters to Schumann's brother and sister-in-law, Karl and Pauline, in Schneeberg, and found a temporary editor for the *Neue Zeitschrift*, they left on January 26, 1844, with Berlin as a first two-day stop – primarily to renew contact with the Mendelssohns; Felix presented her with his fifth book of *Lieder ohne Worte*, with a personal dedication, while his wife gave her a pair of fur muffetees. Leaving Berlin by flying coach ('the most comfortable in which I ever travelled' as she reported to her father), they reached Königsberg forty-eight hours later, where Clara gave her first two concerts of the tour in an inadequately heated but very well filled theatre. Though having spent half the night packing after the second concert, and getting up at 5 a.m. for the next day's arduous journey to Tilsit, she still had energy and enthusiasm enough to spend most of that evening playing to the family of the postmaster, Nernst, with whom they spent the night. Setting off next morning at 4 a.m., still using the sleigh lent them by the piano manufacturer on whose instruments she had played in Königsberg, they reached the frontier, Tauroggen, in time for an appetizing breakfast at its excellent posting house before taking places booked for them by Nernst (with all customs and passport inspections eased by a letter of introduction from the Russian Consul in Königsberg) in the 'very handsome and comfortable' flying coach to Riga.

Admitting his own reluctance to undertake the Russian visit even before their marriage, Schumann had commented to Keferstein 'Yet I must not let Clara see it. The change will be good for her from the physical point of view, for, slender as she is, she is very healthy, and has the endurance of a man'. The truth of those words, clear enough on the distances already travelled, was doubly proved on arrival in Riga. With no hackney coach or porters available, they commandeered a peasant sleigh, put their boxes aboard and sat on them while 'threading our way with difficulty through the hundreds of peasants' sleighs in the market, and through tiny little alleys' to reach the inn to which they had been recommended, the *City of London*, only to be offered a third floor room so dingy that they rejoined their waiting sleigh and boxes and made their way to the rival inn, the *City of St. Petersburg*. Here the only vacant back room was so dirty that though by now totally exhausted, they dared not sit down. Only after contacting the friend to whom David had given them an introduction were they returned in style to their rightful elegant room at the *City of London*, stupidly booked in his own name. For Clara there was yet worse to come. Delays in arranging her Riga concerts meant that to

fulfill her promises in the much more attractive and artistically appreciative town of Mitau, three hours away, she had constantly to commute
between the two – Sunday in Mitau, Monday and Tuesday in Riga,
Wednesday in Mitau and then on Thursday back to Riga for her farewell.
As box-office concessions she included virtuoso operatic transcriptions
by Liszt, Thalberg or Henselt in each programme. But Beethoven's
'Moonlight', D minor and 'Appassionata' sonatas found a place too,
together with miniatures by Mendelssohn, Chopin, Schumann and a
Scherzo of her own.

To avoid too much discomfort in reaching St Petersburg they took an
extra-diligence giving them not only a guard all the way but also the chance
of a five-day stop at Dorpat en route. Here, they encountered a greatly
helpful Professor von Brocker, who lent them his carriage as well as
making all arrangements for Clara to give three highly successful concerts
– after the last of which she was serenaded by the Fraternitas Rigensis, a
male-voice choir led by a Julius Otto Grimm,[1] in music including her
husband's 'Die träumende See' and 'Die Minnesänger.' With furs and
rugs, Clara herself had been able to stand up to Dorpat's 23° of frost
after two days of travel between 12°–15°. But Schumann himself went
down with a severe chill, prolonging their stay twice as long as they
had intended. As he brooded in bed over *Faust* (no longer as the opera
he so longed to write but rather as an oratorio) she in her turn was
overwhelmed by the kindness of the aristocracy, who on hearing of
her husband's plight, sent in delicacies for lunch every day. Two
gestures touched her enough for detailed description when writing to
her father: 'Yesterday, before the concert, an unknown baroness, who
had heard of Robert's illness, sent jelly, some pastry, and two partridges
just roasted, with the request that we would accept these as we should not
be able to get anything in our bad hotel. On the evening of the concert I
told one lady what uncomfortable, dirty beds we had, and added that my
husband had caught his cold during the night. At 10 o'clock a servant
arrived, bringing two beautiful feather pillows and a magnificent great
counterpane . . .'. Though plainly anxious about the bad road for their
impending journey to St Petersburg, in view of Schumann's indifferent
health, she nevertheless transformed everything into a great adventure in
a special message for Marie: 'We have driven in carriages and sleighs,
across the ice of three rivers, all larger than the Elbe; on the Duna, near
Riga, the peasants hold their wood-market, hundreds of sleighs, laden
with wood, stand in the middle of the river, people walk about as if they
were in a street, and as if it were quite natural, and we, too, drove about for
half-an-hour. There are many wolves in the forests here, they often

---

[1] Then a student of philology, later to re-enter Clara's life as a friend of Brahms.

appear beside the highway and watch the travellers as they pass, quite quietly; so far we have not seen any, but everybody who goes from here to St. Petersburg meets with some, and I am looking forward to seeing some'.

By March 1 Schumann was well enough to leave, and by the 4th they had safely arrived in St Petersburg, relieved to find that contrary to expectations, travel in Russia was really no worse than anywhere else. Here they were warmly welcomed by Clara's old friend, Pauline Garcia, since 1840 the wife of the Parisian impresario, Louis Viardot, and now one of the great stars of the Italian Opera Company that throughout the winter had held the city in thrall. 'I am leaving you Clara Schumann' so Pauline told the press just before her departure at the end of the season. 'Her singing on the piano is better than mine'. Reviewing their stay in a long letter to Wieck (significantly starting 'Dear Father'), on April 1 Schumann explained that although they had arrived marginally too late in view of the imminence of Holy Week, whereas interest in many other distinguished artists, even including Liszt, had waned, for Clara there had been larger audiences at each of her four public concerts. At her orchestral farewell on March 17 she included both Weber's *Concertstück* and Mendelssohn's G minor Concerto as well as solos including a Bach Prelude and Fugue 'by request'. But as always, it was Mendelssohn's 'Frühlingslied' from the fifth book of *Lieder ohne Worte* (her parting present from the composer) that brought the house down. For the Empress, for whom she played in private, she had to repeat it several times.

As for friends, the Emperor's nephew, Prince von Oldenburg and his wife warmly welcomed them at their palace, so did the two Counts Wielhorsky . . . 'distinguished men, and Michael a real artist, the most gifted amateur I ever met – both of them having great influence at Court, and being almost daily about the Emperor and Empress' so Schumann explained to his father-in-law, adding 'Clara, I believe, cherishes a secret passion for Michael, who, by the way, has grandchildren already, i.e. is a man of over 50, though as fresh as a boy in body and soul'. Since Clara had been awarded an honorary diploma degree by the Philharmonic Society, it was particularly gratifying for Schumann that the Wielhorskys, enchanted by a private performance of his Piano Quintet, felt moved to arrange a special orchestral soirée at their home to hear him conduct his 'Spring' Symphony. Of the professional musicians, who were both warm and generous in not taking fees when co-operating ('nothing was expected of us except to have them fetched to the concert'), they found a true ally in Heinrich Romberg, the city's Music Director, but were even more elated to renew contact with their old friend Henselt (and his wife), who had settled in St Petersburg as a teacher. Though now too nervous to perform in public, Henselt still liked to play in private, and once at Prince

Oldenburg's joined Clara in Schumann's Variations for two pianos. More personally, Schumann was overjoyed to discover that an uncle on his mother's side, isolated from the family since becoming regimental doctor at Tver, was still alive and just about to celebrate his seventieth birthday. Leaving St Petersburg on April 2, they even managed to spend Easter at Tver with this Dr Schnabel and his family before arriving in Moscow, their final goal, on April 10.

Here, the public recital season was definitely over: Clara's audiences were disappointingly small. But she was well received by various aristocratic patrons of the arts, and in these circles, at least, won all hearts in her husband's Piano Quintet and Variations for two pianos. For the rest, the pair were content to pass the time as tourists, fitting in a visit to the opera-house to hear Glinka's *Life for the Czar* (which despite national colour Schumann deemed lacking in dramatic development) and to a monastery to attend Vespers and savour the unique timbre of the monks in music dismissed by Clara as 'partly barbaric, partly childish, full of octaves and fifths. Robert slipped away after two hours' martyrdom from this singing (which, however, is celebrated just because of its peculiar sound), and I soon followed him'.

They enjoyed the national costumes of the peasant women, arriving in town in their colourful best for Easter week. As for the Kremlin itself, it sufficiently impressed Schumann, though no artist, to emulate Mendelssohn and take up pencil to draw it. The city also inspired him to write two poems. But the 'Arabian Nights' magic of the Winter Palace in St Petersburg, no less than their general welcome in that city, had moved them still more. So it was a delight to return there, with the light nights and the buds of spring as additional allure, for one last brief reunion with their good friends and patrons before boarding their ship at Kronstadt. Swinemünde and a flying visit to the island of Rügen were the only further stops. Their original intention of extending the trip so as to visit Clara's brother, Alwin, in Reval, then coming back via Helsingfors, Stockholm and Copenhagen was ultimately dismissed in an overwhelming longing for reunion with their children, with whom they returned to Leipzig, having personally collected them from Schneeberg, on May 30. Discreetly offering to reimburse his brother for out-of-pocket expenses a few days later, Schumann wrote happily of the home-coming: 'the children were received triumphantly here by half the Inselstrasse; their little table was covered with flowers and presents. There was much rejoicing among the little ones, and everyone was delighted with their bright looks and nice manners. Marie was never so obedient, good and cheerful as she is now, and we owe that to your affectionate care, next to the protection of Heaven. May she ever remain so!'

*

After the stimulation of the last few months, Clara herself found it none too easy to pick up the threads of domestic life again, with only a little teaching at the Leipzig Music School, together with a private lesson or two, as musical outlet. 'We could not get used to Leipzig again for ever so long, everything seemed so dreary, so empty, in spite of the fact that we were in our old homely surroundings, and had our children again' so she admitted in the diary, obviously speaking more for herself than her husband. Schumann, in fact, was soon absorbed enough in his setting of the last part of Goethe's *Faust*, never attempted by a composer before, to forget everything but the obsessional urgency of the task in hand: he even resigned from the Editorship of the *Neue Zeitschrift*, in favour of Oswald Lorenz, so that nothing should interrupt his flow of thought. It was finished by the end of August, though only 'by the sacrifice of his last strength', causing a breakdown far more critical than anything he had ever experienced before. When a holiday in the Harz mountains failed to help, Clara took him to Dresden, where his condition only worsened after Wieck's well-meant attempts to chivy him back to normality. 'Robert never had a night's sleep, his imagination brought the most horrible pictures before him, and I usually found him bathed in tears in the early morning: he gave up all hope for himself', so Clara sadly recorded as medical help became imperative.

Dr Helbig, the homoeopathic doctor consulted, noted a morbid fear of heights and all metallic substances, medicine and infection, coupled with shivering, faintness, cold feet, headaches, and auricular delusions. 'As he studied every prescription until he found some reason for not taking it, I ordered him cold plunge-baths, which so far improved his health that he was able to return to his usual (only) occupation, composition. As I had made a study of similar cases especially among men who worked immoderately at one thing (for instance accounts etc.) I was led to advise that he should employ himself and distract his mind with something else than music. He first chose natural history, then natural philosophy etc., but abandoned them after a few days, and gave himself up, wherever he might be, to his musical thoughts'.

They had found a pleasant ground-floor flat in Dresden at 35 Waisenhausstrasse. And as Schumann's strength gradually returned in the middle of October so their thoughts increasingly dwelt on the possibility of moving to Dresden for good. For Clara, it had already proved a second home: she had few more congenial friends than the Serres at Maxen, on whose estate they now stayed for a short time as Schumann convalesced. He himself was well aware that 'from a musical point of view Leipzig remains the most important town, and I should advise any youthful talent to go there for one hears so much good music', as he put it in a letter to Dr E. Krüger. But since Mendelssohn's departure to take up a permanent job with the King of Prussia in Berlin, much of the old magic had gone. And though the vacant Gewandhaus conductorship for the 1844–5 season had been offered to as good a friend as Gade, both husband and wife were a little hurt that Schumann himself had not been considered. Flushed with success after his Leipzig conducting début in *Paradise and the Peri*, he was unaware of what Wagner described as his 'peculiar awkwardness in conducting' when the work was repeated in Dresden, just as he failed to appreciate the true extent of his shyness and inability to communicate with his pupils when teaching at the Leipzig Music School.

They returned for a concert in Härtel's Rooms on November 29 at which the thirteen-year-old Joachim took part in Mendelssohn's Octet and Clara joined the visiting composer at the keyboard in two extracts from the *Midsummer Night's Dream*, 'the first at such a pace that I did not know where I was'. On December 5 Clara was back again on the Gewandhaus platform for one of the milestones of her career – her first public performance of Beethoven's 'Emperor' Concerto, 'the hardest concerto I know', she subsequently admitted, on account of its demands on staying power as well as for a 'thoroughly intellectual interpretation'. Three days later they made their official farewell by summoning their friends to another of those special invitation morning concerts in the small hall of the Gewandhaus (as on January 8, 1843) for a mixed programme specifically spotlighting Schumann's E flat major Piano Quartet, as yet unperformed in public. Whereas previously Clara had chosen Beethoven's late A major sonata, Op.101, as her principal solo, this time she played his 'Waldstein'. On December 13 they left for good, Clara admitting to a few private tears in saying goodbye to her birthplace, but with no deep regret.

NINE

Settling in Dresden 1845–47

Only a few days after returning from Russia Schumann had written to Verhulst to say they would seriously consider his suggestion of visiting Holland in January, 1845, and from there continue to England, where Sterndale Bennett was pressing Clara to make her début. But with a third child now expected that March, together with Schumann's indifferent health, all thoughts of touring had to be dismissed. Their immediate problem was adjusting themselves as residents to life in the Saxon capital, which rich as it was in architecture and art treasures, no less than in a beautiful situation on the banks of the Elbe, they soon found curiously hidebound in subservience to the Court, even provincial in spirit, after the stimulating cosmopolitan bustle of Leipzig.

Whatever hopes Clara had entertained of further music-making with her father were quickly dashed on discovering how drastically their sense of values now differed. His determination to keep his name before the public as a teacher, even if it meant bringing out pupils too soon, particularly irked her in the case of her half-sister, Marie, just thirteen. In kindness she had in fact partnered Marie on the platform a year or so before in a four-handed sonata by Moscheles. But she knew Marie was neither technically nor imaginatively ripe for the limelight Wieck already envisaged for her. Marriage, or various other changed circumstances, also slightly separated Clara from various other musical friends of her youth such as Sophie Kaskel, now a Countess. As for the city's rank and file musicians, Clara quickly realized that they were steeped in routine, ignorant of the wider musical world, wary of all things new.

There was nevertheless a warm welcome from their old Leipzig acquaintance, Ferdinand Hiller, always so close to Mendelssohn, who now lived at nearby Pillnitz composing opera with an eye on the Dresden stage. Having invited Clara to join him and Moscheles in Bach's Triple Concerto (Moscheles supplied her with a cadenza while they improvised theirs) at one of the city's none too stimulating established orchestral concerts on January 8, 1845, Hiller lost no time in enlisting Schumann's help in organizing a livelier series of subscription concerts, subsidized by the wealthy Kaskel banking family, in an attempt to rouse music-lovers from an apathy that on one occasion prompted Schumann to confess to his old Leipzig friend, Ferdinand David, 'Here one can get back the old lost longing for music, there is so little to hear'. After an arduous struggle against officialdom the new venture was eventually launched on November 11, 1845. Clara, at the time, was indisposed. The soloist was Joseph Joachim, now almost fourteen and a half, who introduced Dresden to the E minor Violin Concerto Mendelssohn had written for David only the year before. The gesture delighted Schumann, even though, as he told the composer in a letter, he felt that such music was far too good for an audience of mere aristocratic dilettanti.

It was Hiller, too, who introduced the Schumanns to the city's intelligentsia, mainly painters and poets who met regularly at their own various houses, or else at Engel's restaurant in the Postplatz for readings and discussion of burning topics of the day. From a group including the sculptor, Rietschel, the writer, Auerbach, the painter-poet, Reinick, and the painter and illustrator, Ludwig Richter, Clara in her diary singled out the artists Bendemann and Hübner and their wives (who were sisters) as her special favourites 'whom I like better than all the musicians of Dresden put together'.

Inevitably, in such company, it was not long before they came face to face with Richard Wagner, who in response to pressure from Caroline Weber to continue her late husband's championship of German opera in Dresden, had been wrestling with convention as Hofkapellmeister at the bureaucratic Court Theatre since 1843. Because Wagner was as puzzled by Schumann's taciturnity and idolization of Mendelssohn as Schumann was alienated by Wagner's garrulous egotism and defiance of rule, no close sympathy developed between them despite their chance meetings on the banks of the Elbe and walks up to the flanking hills escorted by Wagner's little dog, Peps. Yet in some strange way each respected the other, with Schumann himself always ready to concede the extraordinary potency of Wagner's operas when experienced from the stage. To Clara, however, even the comparatively early Wagner of this period was as repugnant as Meyerbeer had always been to her husband, as a diary entry in November, 1845, makes very clear: 'We went to *Tannhäuser* at last on the 22nd. Robert was greatly interested in the opera, he considers it a great advance on *Rienzi*, with respect both to the instrumentation and the musical ideas. I cannot agree with Robert, this is no music at all to me – though I do not deny that Wagner has great dramatic power. I had better hold my tongue about Wagner, for I cannot speak against my convictions and I do not feel one spark of sympathy for this composer'.

Barely two months after the birth of her third daughter, Julie, on March 11, 1845, Clara had conceived again. So with Schumann's own health still giving considerable cause for concern, once more all hopes of winter touring had to be abandoned. But with a number of concerts in Dresden and Leipzig within the bounds of possibility, she started to practise again in earnest as autumn loomed, with a Concerto by Henselt the first major addition to her repertory to introduce both to Dresden and at the Leipzig Gewandhaus. It was nevertheless more a gesture of friendship than belief in the music itself. Whereas the sparkle of his earlier variations and concert studies had delighted her as a teenager, now she saw only Henselt's paucity of invention – chiefly because her husband had just completed his own first Piano Concerto in A minor by adding an Intermezzo and Finale, with remarkably ingenious thematic metamorphosis to preserve unity, to the single-movement Phantasie for piano and orchestra he had composed in 1841. 'On Wednesday September 3 began to study Robert's concerto' so the diary records. 'What a contrast between this and Henselt's. How rich in invention, how interesting from beginning to end it is; how fresh, and what a beautifully connected whole! I find real pleasure in studying it!' After introducing it to Dresden on December 4, 1845, and at the Leipzig Gewandhaus on January 1, 1846, she then started work on Beethoven's fourth Concerto for the first time. As for Chopin's Barcarolle, she learnt that in 1846 almost before the ink was dry, giving its Leipzig première on November 16.

In her restricted, stay-at-home existence, she had also seized the chance to take up composition again with new vigour. Always eager to share Robert's adventures, she happily joined him once again in an intensive study of Bach, together with Cherubini's treatise, *Counterpoint and Fugue*, and early in 1845 answered his own outpouring of Studies and Fugues for piano and organ or pedal-piano (they hired a pedal-piano in April) with three Preludes and Fugues for piano of her own, published in time for her birthday that year as her Opus 16. The Prelude of No. 1 in G minor includes an imaginative transfer of the melody from treble to tenor voice on its reprise, and the three-part Fugue an ingenious major key inversion of its spirited semi-quaver subject in the middle section. The Prelude of No. 2 in B flat, its opening melody like an unconscious echo of the middle section of Chopin's E minor Etude, Op. 25, No. 5, is possibly a little too romantic to lead inevitably into its closely reasoned four-part Fugue, though both again have an effortless flow. In No. 3 in D minor, on the other hand, the subject of the four-part Fugue is cunningly conjured from the Prelude's own leading theme. The use of pedal basses in both, with a hint of stretto in the coda of the Fugue before the final 'tierce de Picardy', imparts a quality of noble finality to the set as a whole. In the *Quatre Pièces fugitives*, published as her Op. 15, Clara returned to the romantically pianistic world of the character piece. If Schumann's own spirit hovers over No. 1 in F (*Larghetto*) and No. 3 in D (*Andante espressivo*), even down to the gruppettos decorating the melodic line, the sprightlier No. 2 in A minor (*Un poco agitato*) and No. 4 in G (*Scherzo*) reveal with equal clarity how much Clara had learnt from Mendelssohn. As for her second Scherzo in

C minor, published as Opus 14, it points to her third great hero, Chopin, just as surely as its D minor predecessor, so popular in Paris in 1839, had done to Mendelssohn: headed *con fuoco*, its turbulence could well have been sparked off by Chopin's so-called 'Revolutionary' Etude in C minor, Op.10, No.12. The unprepared contrast of the A flat major trio section (*un poco piu tranquillo*) is also as Chopinesque as its chordal texture.

The most remarkable tribute to Clara's industry at this period is nevertheless her G minor Piano Trio, Op.17, completed, after very many alterations,[1] in time for a first rehearsal on October 2, 1846. The diary records her immediate pleasure in her achievement: 'There is nothing greater than the joy of composing something oneself, and then listening to it. There are some pretty passages in the Trio, and I think it is fairly successful as far as form goes'. By November 18 a measure of self-criticism had set in: 'This evening I played Robert's Piano Quartet and my own Trio which seems to me more harmless each time I play it'. But when receiving it in print in September 1847, pride turned to mortification: 'I received the printed copies of my Trio today, but I did not care for it particularly; after Robert's in D minor it sounded effeminate and sentimental'. It was to her credit that she recognized the deeper, darker undertones of her husband's work, in comparison with which her own use of a minor key had yielded no more than plaintive charm. Yet, that said, the Trio remains an outstanding testimonial to Clara's creative potential, well proportioned and free from all procrustean strain in its use of extended forms, and perhaps even more skilful than her husband's first Trio in instrumental interplay, with the piano never allowed to take too much on its own shoulders. The first movement contrasts a lyrical G minor main theme with a chordal second subject which in its syncopation, together with its falling line, could easily be mistaken for Schumann himself. The development, concealing many a stroke of contrapuntal cunning in an effortless flow, is very neatly merged into the recapitulation, which ends with a recall of the first subject emphatically reasserting the home key of G minor. The Minuet in B flat, with its 'Scotch snap' rhythm, has a puckish, Mendelssohnian charm; in its trio, triple time is as effortlessly made to sound like duple as in the finale of Schumann's Piano Concerto recently studied by Clara. The G major Andante grows from a romantically aspiring melody again Schumannesque in the fall of the opening phrase and the expressive gruppetto in the answer, even if lacking the quality of memorability (partly by reason of its conventional harmonization) distinguishing talent from genius. After an agitated central section in minor

---

[1] The manuscript in the Schumann-Haus at Zwickau reveals unusually extensive revision.

keys, the reprise brings charming variations of scoring, with the cello leading the way in compensation for its belated entry at the outset. The G minor Finale, again in sonata-form, shows Clara's craftsmanship at its peak. Not only can the first theme be regarded as a subtle metamorphosis of the opening phrase of the Andante, but in the development section its own rhythm is changed into a stern, quasi-fugal subject which, juxtaposed with the second subject, is explored with a contrapuntal cunning of which Mendelssohn would not have been ashamed even if a little too academic for Schumann. The heightening of tension in the coda is also well controlled.

Joy at the birth of their first son, Emil, on February 8, 1846, was clouded by Schumann's continued ill-health, which having already curtailed a Rhineland holiday the previous summer, now seriously interrupted the new Symphony in C major on which he was working: apart from physical weakness, giddiness and headaches, one of the most disturbing symptoms was a continuous singing in his ears, while every external sound also turned itself into music. His hypochondria increased during convalescence in May at Maxen where from his bedroom window he could see Sonnenstein, a lunatic asylum. Not till a summer seaside holiday[1] on the island of Nordenay, during which they left the children behind in the country near Dresden, did discomfort temporarily abate.

Despite her worries, for Clara there had been one great new enrichment of experience. Even while she was still in bed with Emil in February, her father, always as thrilled by great singing as pianism, had burst into her room uncontrollably excited at his discovery in Weimar of a Swedish soprano called Jenny Lind. When a concert by Lind was announced in Leipzig for April 16, Wieck went on ahead with his young pupil, Minna Schulz, while Clara and her stepmother arrived later, only securing tickets through the good offices of Mendelssohn who was 'nearly torn to pieces in getting them'. Whether in an attempt to restore her self-confidence after child-birth (as he had already done the month before at a private party in Dresden, stopping after playing the first two movements of the 'Appassionata' to insist that only she could manage the finale), or merely to help himself on an evening when he had to accompany Lind as well as play solos, Mendelssohn begged her, the moment she arrived at his house, to share in the solos, 'urging his request so insistently that in the end I allowed myself to be persuaded, which was stupid of me, for it made me painfully excited and destroyed all my power of quiet enjoyment'. She was also a little worried because she had come without an official concert dress. In the event after finishing Beethoven's 'Moonlight' Sonata Mendelssohn came down to where she was sitting in the audience and

[1] She nevertheless gave an exacting solo recital while there.

personally escorted her to the platform to play Nos. 1 and 4 (the 'Bees' Wedding') from his sixth book of *Lieder ohne Worte*, also a Scherzo of his own. Clara's whole-hearted delight in Lind's singing and personality in the end obliterated all else: 'You never hear her howl, or sob, or let her voice tremble, above all there are no bad habits. There is beauty in all she does. Her coloratura is the most beautiful I have ever heard; her voice itself is not large, but it would certainly penetrate throughout any room, for she is all soul'. Discovering her unassuming simplicity as a human being at a grand supper party after the concert was just as moving for Clara. As she put it: 'The recollection of this night will never fade from my mind, and it is doubly dear and valuable to me because I have learned to know Jenny has a sweet and natural character'.

In his own poor health during the spring of 1846 Schumann did not, as in the two preceding years, make his wife pregnant again. So after moving the entire household in early September to lighter, sunnier rooms on the first floor of 20, Grosse Reitbahngasse, Clara seized the chance of a working winter with wide open hands, starting with a visit to Leipzig's Gewandhaus on October 22 to play Beethoven's fourth Concerto for the first time in public with two cadenzas, both stylish and to the point, of her own. Returning on November 16 for a concert including the none too warmly received première of her husband's C major Symphony, she chose Mendelssohn's G minor Concerto, mercifully unaware that never again would she be privileged to play it under the composer's own baton. The real excitement was nevertheless the fulfilment of her long cherished wish to revisit Vienna, the more so since Marie and Elise, now five and three and a half respectively, were deemed grown-up enough to go too. Both parents were proud of their offsprings' behaviour. As Schumann wrote in his *Little Book of Memories*: 'They were very sporting, and we were pleased with the way in which they adapted themselves to the less pleasant incidents of the journey. From Prague onwards we travelled by train: they enjoyed this still more, and shortly before we reached Vienna Lieschen struck up with "Come a birdie a-flying" with humorous variations'.

Remembering that the greatest triumphs of her entire career were scored in Vienna only eight years earlier, Clara had haughtily dismissed[1] an invitation from her old friend, Emilie List, to travel via Augsburg to meet the influential columnist, Kolb, with a view to advance publicity. It was a decision she was bitterly to regret, especially when gathered round the modest little Christmas tree in their rented rooms (costing a ducat a day) they were only able to celebrate the festivity with trifling token gifts

---

[1] Considering her dignity insulted, she had replied no less starchily to the French composer, Felicien David, when on a visit in 1845 he had mistakenly interpreted an invitation to write in her autograph book as a request for a professional testimonial.

for the children. There had been just a few ducats in hand after her first concert on December 10 when besides Beethoven's fourth Concerto she had played Chopin's Barcarolle and miniatures by Schumann, Mendelssohn and Scarlatti. But ticket sales only just covered expenses at the second on December 15, with Schumann's Quintet and Andante and Variations for two pianos (Clara's partner was the sixteen-year-old Anton Rubinstein) the main works alongside Chopin's A flat Polonaise, Op.53, one of her own Scherzos and smaller pieces by Mendelssohn and Henselt. There was still worse to come on January 1, 1847, when Schumann's Piano Concerto and elsewhere warmly acclaimed 'Spring' Symphony (both conducted by himself) drew so small an audience that they were left with a deficit of 100 florins. After this humiliating occasion Clara could no longer contain herself: although in the company of friends she gave vent to her indignation so vehemently that Schumann felt obliged to intervene. 'Calm yourself, dear Clara, in ten years' time all this will have changed' were his prescient words. Their immediate *deus ex machina* was Jenny Lind, who having arrived in Vienna just in time to attend this ill-starred orchestral evening, immediately volunteered to sing at Clara's last concert on January 10. Whereas in the printed programme Clara was pledged to the 'Appassionata' as well as a Prelude and Fugue in A minor by Bach and miniatures by Mendelssohn and Henselt besides her husband's 'Traumeswirren' (from Op.12), Jenny promised only Schumann's 'Der Nussbaum' and Mendelssohn's 'Auf Flügeln des Gesanges' alongside two trifles by von Geraldy and C. A. Mangold. Yet as at every Lind concert each seat could have been sold twice over. Instead of returning in debt, the Schumanns found themselves with 300 thalers in hand to take back home after all expenses for the entire Viennese trip had been paid. Inevitably, remembering 1838, Clara had her secret pangs. As she put it 'I could not get over the bitter feeling that one song of Lind's had done what I, with all my playing, could not do'. But she still knew she had found one of the rarest friends of her life, their sympathy deepened not only by Jenny's spontaneous camaraderie with Marie and Elise but also by Clara's intuitive awareness that the reason Jenny had always sung Mendelssohn's music so beautifully was because 'she loves him no less as a man than as a composer'. Schumann was no less appreciative. 'I have never before met so clear an understanding of music and text at first sight, and simple, natural and deep comprehension of a work at first reading' was his reaction to their first rehearsal of his own songs. Having felt her miscast as Donna Anna in *Don Giovanni* a year before, he was all the more thrilled to discover her true operatic potential in Vienna, even if only in a performance of Donizetti's *Daughter of the Regiment*.

The visit brought a less welcome operative encounter for Schumann when he found himself invited to an artists' club reception at which the

other guest-of-honour was Meyerbeer. For Clara there was a different
moment of shock when she unexpectedly ran into Marie and Elise alone
and totally lost in St Stephen's Square while trying to deliver a letter to Dr
Fischhof – at the misguided request of their day-dreaming father. But
there were more than a few pleasant personal memories, besides those of
Jenny, to carry home in compensation for disappointments at establishment and Court level, not least Eichendorff's arrival at their farewell party
and subsequent affirmation that it was Schumann's music that had given
life to his verse. They were also enormously heartened by the warmth of
their reception at concerts in Brno and Prague on the way home,
celebrated with enough of Clara's much loved champagne to allow her to
forget her shame at a brief lapse of memory in Scarlatti. The children in
their turn particularly enjoyed their meals at Prague's Black Horse Hotel.
Marie was even allowed her first visits to the theatre.

Delighted as she was to be reunited with her two babies, particularly as
little Emil was far from well, Clara could never entirely suppress a feeling
of anti-climax, even boredom, when first back home after a tour. So it was
no real hardship for her to pack their bags again on February 10, after less
than a week, for a visit to Berlin, where the Singakademie had invited
Schumann to direct a performance of his *Paradise and the Peri*. Unfore-
seen difficulties awaited them yet again. The choir's inability to master the
work's unfamiliar idiom, together with the caprices of the soloists first
engaged, in fact taxed Schumann so sorely that he was driven to bed the
day before the concert. It was Clara herself, having surprised everyone by
sitting through most of the rehearsals, who did most of the final work with
last-minute substitutes and others unsure of their way. Even so there were
enough breakdowns in the third part of the première on February 17, all
too flaccidly conducted by its now totally dispirited composer before a
good-sized audience including the King, for Clara to confide to her diary
'I was in agonies, and thought I would sink into the ground'. A much
hoped-for repeat performance with Pauline Viardot (then at the Berlin
Opera) as the Peri brought her the disappointment of a refusal from her
old friend, though in sympathy Pauline did consent to sing at Clara's own
two concerts on March 1 and 17. In her unflinching determination that
Berlin should know Schumann's true worth she chose his Piano Quintet
as the centrepiece of both programmes as well as his Piano Quartet for a
private matinée on March 8, though as so often before, applause for her
own playing exceeded that for the music. It was the unofficial, purely
social side of the visit that at the end sent them home so happy. Apart from
now conceding, in agreement with Robert, that the intelligentsia of Berlin
were much more seriously cultivated and worthwhile than the flighty,
pleasure-loving Viennese, Clara found great personal joy in again being
near her mother – since 1841 a widow. She was also delighted to discover

herself so closely attuned to Mendelssohn's sister, Fanny, now Frau
Hensel, even while recognizing her personal brusqueness, and musically
admiring her so much more as a pianist than as a composer. 'Women
always betray themselves in their compositions, and this is true of myself
as well as of others' was her candid admission in the diary.

TEN

To Stay or Leave? *1847–50*

Having enjoyed the sociability of Berlin enough to toy with the idea of moving there – or at any rate until the distressing news of Fanny Hensel's sudden death, Clara, back in Dresden, was at first more than usually restless. Work again proved the palliative: besides embarking on a four-handed version of her husband's C major Symphony and a short (piano) score of *Faust* she also began a new Concertino in F minor of her own as a present for his birthday. Though possibly intended as her Op.19 (missing, like Op.18, from her list of published works) all that survives of this work is a sketch[1] in short score of the first movement's exposition, in all some 175 bars. After an arresting orchestral call-to-attention, the piano enters with a flourish before taking up the first subject proper, chromatically inflected in a way testifying to her previous year's study of Bach. The second subject in A flat is more Schumannesque in its lyricism, and its continuation brings some charming duetting between keyboard and orchestra before the latter takes over to end the section and merge exposition into development.

By the end of May, 1847, after the usual spring-tide sexual upsurgence, Clara knew she had conceived again. 'What will become of my work?' she asked in the diary. 'But Robert says: "children are blessings", and he is right for there is no happiness without children, and therefore I have determined to face the difficult time that is coming with as cheery a spirit as possible. Whether I shall always be able to do so or not I do not know'. The new pregnancy was to prove more of a blessing than she then guessed, for barely a month later they were mourning the death of their only son, Emil, at the age of sixteen months. As Schumann wrote in his *Little Book of Memories for our Children*: 'Our little Emil died during the night June 21–22 at 2.30 a.m. He was almost always ailing, has had few pleasures in the world. I have only once seen him smile; that was when I took leave of him on the morning before we departed for Vienna. On Wednesday June 23 at 6 p.m. he was buried. You little ones do not yet realize your loss. Since June 1 Emil and Julchen had been in the country, in Schärnitz, half an hour's distance from here. Julchen, who is still delicate, has benefited by the air and fresh milk. But it was not God's will that Emil should survive'.

[1] Preserved in the Schumann-Haus at Zwickau.

July brought just the tonic they needed to override sorrow in the shape of an invitation to Zwickau for a little festival in Schumann's honour, its centrepiece a concert on the 10th at which Schumann conducted his C major Symphony, Clara played his Piano Concerto, and Dr Klitzsch, the town's director of music, conducted the première of Schumann's *Lied beim Abschied zu singen*, a choral piece specially written for the occasion. They were not just welcomed by old friends, like Schumann's justly proud old teacher, Kuntsch, but once or twice found themselves serenaded by the whole town, as when crossing the river Mulde (hymned by Robert in youthful poems) for an open-air concert in front of the Burgkeller. This was particularly gratifying to Clara, so often smitten to the heart by the world's apparent indifference to her husband's achievement. She even enjoyed visits to some of his old flames, now, like herself, wives and mothers.

As her pregnancy advanced in the autumn, Clara increasingly turned to chamber music, particularly enjoying piano trios with the violinist, Franz Schubert, leader of the Dresden orchestra, and his cellist brother, Friedrich. She also replenished the family purse, while unable to give concerts, by taking on more pupils. When trying to induce Moscheles to leave London so as to join the staff of the Leipzig Music School, Mendelssohn had sent him a detailed estimate of likely expenses and earnings, recommending one and a half thalers for private lessons as opposed to the two charged by Clara – in Mendelssohn's opinion an excessive rate for all but the casual visiting foreigner. But such was her renown that by December, 1847, she could record in the diary that she gave two lessons nearly every day, with the eighteen-year-old Otto Goldschmidt, formerly a student of Mendelssohn at the Leipzig Music School, and in five years destined to become the husband of Jenny Lind, among her most talented pupils.

Schumann, temporarily better in health, was meanwhile enjoying a great new surge of creative energy, capping Clara's G minor Piano Trio with two of his own in D minor and F major. The sunnier, more lyrical No. 2 was Clara's favourite, not least because its first movement included a quotation from his love-song, 'Intermezzo', inspired by her in 1840. Still more important was his realization of a long cherished dream in the realm of German opera. After rejecting at least twenty to thirty possible subjects (including an Arthurian parallel to *Lohengrin* dropped in November 1845 on discovering at one of their regular artistic gatherings that Wagner was already working on it) he at last seized on the medieval legend of Genoveva, asking their poet friend, Robert Reinick, to prepare a libretto drawn from Hebbel's starkly dramatic and Tieck's tenderer handling of the tale. Not satisfied with the result he appealed directly to Hebbel, who did them the honour of visiting their house in the summer of 1847 to discuss the project even though declining to take a hand in it himself. So having already composed the overture in his first great flood of enthusiasm for the subject, Schumann spent much of the remainder of that year preparing his own libretto, meanwhile refusing all improvements suggested by Wagner, who quickly realized that Schumann 'simply wanted me to be swayed by himself, deeply resenting any interference with the product of his own ideals, so that henceforth I let matters alone', as he put it in *Mein Leben*.

Hiller's departure in mid-November to become Director of Music in Düsseldorf made them sad. But Mendelssohn's death from a stroke on November 4, only six months after his sister, Fanny, completely overwhelmed them. Neither had ever had a more cherished or idolized musical friend. For Schumann, the bond had been cemented by common admiration for Bach and determination to supervise publication of a complete edition of his music, much of it stored away in manuscript in the Berlin Singakademie. For Clara, now too advanced in pregnancy to accompany Schumann to Leipzig for the memorial service, it was a still more personal loss: no one had ever better understood how deeply she was torn by rival claims of home and career. Nor was grief quickly or easily assuaged. Even the following June, when to celebrate Liszt's unexpected arrival they gave a party in their house, Schumann exploded with anger and walked out because the all too well-wined Liszt dared to praise Meyerbeer while criticizing Mendelssohn as 'too Leipzigish'. Apologizing for his rudeness when approached by Liszt for permission to perform his *Faust* at the Goethe celebrations in Weimar in 1849, Schumann still could not resist the caustic rejoinder 'But, dear friend, might you not find my *Faust* too Leipzigish?'

Immersed as he was during the first six months of 1848 in *Genoveva*, and almost immediately afterwards in incidental music for Byron's *Manfred*, Schumann also found much satisfaction in a mixed Choral Society he had formed in early January, the all-male Choir he had inherited from Hiller having proved too limited to hold his interest. After the birth of her second son, Ludwig, on January 20, Clara herself was an active accompanist at rehearsals as well as helping to prepare scores and parts. By the summer they were already tackling Beethoven's *Missa Solemnis*. What with this and the growing musical interest of their children, whose piano playing she liked to supervise even if entrusting ground-work to their aunt, Marie Wieck, at this period Clara seemed more than usually prepared to accept curtailment of her travels and attune herself to life at home. Even the start of a new pregnancy in October, her sixth, worried her considerably less than the last. She was delighted when for Marie's seventh birthday on September 1 Schumann started to compose his *Album for the Young*. By mid-November his splendid progress with *Manfred* even provided them with another excuse to celebrate with the champagne both loved so well. Her own main musical challenge at this time came in a cycle of Dresden chamber concerts (she shared in a similar series the following winter) with Franz and Friedrich Schubert, the more memorable in that in several of the programmes they were joined by Clara's lifelong operatic idol, the great soprano, Schröder-Devrient, now just forty-four, whose groups of Lieder included several by Schumann.

But as so often before, life was not destined to run smoothly. 'Outwardly we are quieter here, but even Dresden, usually so indolent where politics are concerned, cannot resist the great universal whirlpool' had been her words to a Viennese friend as early as July 1848. The revolutionary spirit was rising, and increasingly both Robert and Clara, sympathizing with democratic principles, found themselves in violent argument with many old friends – even the Bendemanns and Hübners. 'It is sad to see how few really liberal-minded people there are in the educated classes' she wrote in the diary. On May 3, 1849, barely a month after the death of Schumann's beloved brother, Karl, Dresden's own blood-bath began, as they discovered all too painfully the next day when walking in streets barricaded by republicans armed with scythes they saw fourteen dead bodies piled up in a hospital forecourt. Realizing that her husband had neither the physical nor emotional reserves with which to face violence, Clara made a lightning decision when early on Saturday May 5 men called at their house to demand Schumann's enrolment in their own street guard: insisting he was not at home, she immediately snatched up Marie, who was already dressed, and escaped with Schumann by the garden door to the Bohemian station from where they went by train to Mügeln, then on foot to Dohna, and from there to Maxen to take refuge with their old friends, the Serres.

Arriving at 7 p.m. that same evening, Clara was desperately anxious to return at once to fetch Elise, Julie and Ludwig, left behind with the ailing maid, Henriette (feared to be hatching small-pox) and the cook, Mathilde. But as she put it 'I found no one who would accompany me so late. Robert could not come with me, for it was reported that the insurgents were searching the neighbourhood for all men capable of bearing arms, and were compelling them to take part in the battle'. Undaunted, although already seven months pregnant, she at last discovered an estate-agent's daughter and a certain Frau von Berg willing to set out with her at 3 a.m. on the morning of Monday, May 7. 'It was a terrible drive', so her diary records, 'I was anxious lest I should never come out of the city again. . . . We drove to Strehla, and there Frau von Berg went her way, and we went ours across the field to the Reitbahngasse. We entered amidst the continuous thunder of the cannon, and suddenly we saw forty men with scythes coming towards us. At first we did not know what to do, but we plucked up heart and went quietly through (and with us a man we had met in the field). We arrived safely in Reitbahngasse where the doors of all the houses were shut – it was horrible! Dead silence here; in the city incessant firing. I found the children still asleep, tore them at once from their beds, had them dressed, put together a few necessaries, and in an hour we were once more together in the field outside. Henriette, who was ill when I left, I found still suffering, she lay quietly in one place and took no notice of anything. This made me very anxious, especially just now when I needed her so much. In Strehla we got into the carriage again, and before dinner we were back in Maxen, where at last we were all reunited once more; my poor Robert had been spending anxious hours, and was therefore doubly happy now'.

To ease the pressure on the Serres, Clara quickly sent the three youngest children with a nursemaid to lodge with the doctor with whom she and Robert had stayed during his convalescence in 1846 before they all moved to lodgings in nearby Kreischa on May 11. Not only was it more sheltered and beautiful, but it also allowed them to escape from various aristocratic refugees in Maxen who infuriated Clara by referring to the insurrectionists as 'canaille and rabble'. 'The Major is the only liberal-minded person in the whole house', her diary continues, 'and he some-times tells the aristocrats roundly just what he thinks'.

Avidly reading the newspapers, they were in constant awareness of the ensuing turmoil when Prussian troops were called in to support those of the Saxon Court (whose king had now taken refuge in Königstein), of the burning down of the Opera House, and of Wagner's active support for the insurgents until a warrant was issued for his arrest, causing him to flee from the city. As a token gesture of sympathy Schumann even wrote a set of 'Barricade Marches' for piano. But most of his work at this time took the form of gentle song, its escapism surprising Clara enough to com-ment: 'it seems extraordinary to me how the terrible events without have awakened his poetic feeling in so entirely contrary a manner. All the songs breathe the spirit of perfect peace, they seem to me like spring, and laugh like blossoming flowers'. At heart Schumann was in fact at peace, enjoying country life with his children at this benign season as never before. Having already recorded his surprise at finding his very first bird's nest when staying with the Serres in June, 1846, his *Little Book of Memories* now specifically mentions 'the beautiful trees and fields, springs and fountains, the cuckoo, the lilies-of-the-valley, the "Herr Baron's" chil-dren. Julchen especially has benefited from the country air, although she still does not grow. We sent you to the village school at Kreischa, so that you should not be quite idle, and I am glad to be able to say of you elder ones, Marie and Elise, that you seem to like lessons and instruction, and are giving satisfaction to your parents'. But shortly after his birthday, in a sudden fit of depression, Schumann decided they must all return at once. Repugnant as it was to Clara to contemplate life in a city still swarming with Prussians even though hostilities had ceased, she had no alternative but to comply. Only just over a month later, on July 16, 1849, her third son, Ferdinand, was born.

Back in Dresden, Schumann's own thoughts turned at once to the imminent Goethe centenary: preoccupation with a *Requiem für Mignon*, a set of *Wilhelm Meister* songs and further scenes from *Faust* even helped him to forget his irritation at the intrigue delaying the production of *Genoveva* in Leipzig. On the birthday itself, and the day after, he had the satisfaction of having his already completed setting of Goethe's final scene performed in Weimar (under Liszt), in Leipzig (under Rietz) and by his own Choral Union in Dresden – with great success except in Leipzig, where Rietz misjudged certain tempi. 'Robert takes it with an indifference I cannot understand' was Clara's characteristically indignant comment.

November 1849 brought Schumann a new problem in the shape of an invitation from Düsseldorf to succeed Hiller as its Musical Director. Part of him had long secretly hankered for an official appointment – if only for the financial security it would bring Clara and his family. It was primarily for them that in 1844 he had briefly considered a proposition from the Grand Duchess Hélène to found a Conservatoire in St Petersburg. In 1847 he had also written to Nottebohm to enquire about the vacant directorship of the Vienna Conservatoire, and early in 1849 to Dr Härtel in Leipzig after it was rumoured that Rietz was relinquishing the Gewandhaus conductorship. Moreover, he knew how it incensed Clara when, because he had no official connection with the Dresden establishment, they were subjected to indignities such as being refused regular free seats at the Opera by the bureaucratic Intendant, Herr von Lüttichau, on the grounds that such favours were only available to 'those who write for the Dresden stage', and very recently, not being allowed the use of the Frauenkirche for a memorial service for their old friend Chopin, who had died on October 17. As for the city's musical conservatism, and 'the gentlemen of the band, who taste every new composition as though it were a sour apple', all this was increasingly irritating them beyond endurance.

Yet there were practical problems to be considered before making so distant a move. It meant uprooting the elder children from their schools and music lessons. Marie, now enrolled at Fräulein Malinska's Piano School, was already showing considerable talent, surprising Clara on September 13, 1849 by joining Schumann in a splendid performance of the 'Geburtstagmarsch' opening his new volume of piano duets, *Zwölf vierhändige Clavierstücke für kleine und grosse Kinder*. Schumann's long reply to Hiller also revealed his anxiety about the politeness or otherwise of Düsseldorf's orchestral rank and file, about the cost of the move and future lodgings, and last but not least about prospects of work for Clara ('you know her, she cannot be inactive'). In a second letter, only a fortnight later, while admitting a growing inclination to accept, he voiced a far more secret, personal worry: 'The other day I looked for some notices of Düsseldorf in an old geography book, and among the places of note in that town I found mentioned three convents and a madhouse. I have no objection to the former, but it made me quite uncomfortable to read about the latter. I will tell you how that is: A few years ago, as you will remember, we lived at Maxen. I there discovered that the principal view from my windows was on to the Sonnenstein (a lunatic asylum). In the end I perfectly hated the sight of it, and it entirely spoilt my stay there. So I thought the same thing might happen in Düsseldorf. But possibly the notice is altogether incorrect, and the institution may be merely a hospital, such as one finds in every town. I have to be very careful in guarding against all melancholy impressions of this kind. As you are aware, we musicians often dwell on sunny heights, yet when the unhappiness of life comes before our eyes in all its naked ugliness, it hurts all the more. At least that is my case, with my fervid imagination'.

In a third parrying letter to Hiller in January, 1850, Schumann reaffirmed that he could give no definite answer until early April, partly because some 'influential people', as he put it, had just submitted his name for the sub-conductorship of the Dresden theatre (a post which in the event went to Hamburg's former theatre director, Karl August Krebs) but equally because of the coming production of *Genoveva*. Believing that rehearsals were imminent, the Schumanns in fact accepted an invitation to stay with their Leipzig friends, the Brockhauses, in early February – only to find that at the last moment Meyerbeer's *Le Prophète* had been given priority. For Clara there was the added disappointment of a lukewarm reception at the Gewandhaus on February 14 for her husband's new *Concertstück* in G, Op.92. While hastening to attribute it to her own nervousness, she knew she had also recently exasperated him by hurrying the tempo when introducing his new four-handed *Bilder aus Osten* at a soirée with Moscheles, even though provoked into doing so by Moscheles's 'frightful ritardandos'. But all was not in vain: at least they now found themselves free to take up an invitation to Hamburg refused earlier that winter, with a brief stop in Bremen on the way.

As previously in Vienna, so once more an exhausting sequence of chamber and orchestral concerts was crowned by the sudden arrival of Jenny Lind, who not only volunteered to join in Clara's matinée at Altona on March 21 but insisted on prolonging her stay for an additional shared matinée in Hamburg on the 23rd. Though advertised only twenty-four hours in advance, it brought Clara the biggest profit she had ever received in Germany (some 800 thalers after all expenses had been paid) as well as the satisfaction of knowing that this time, unlike Vienna, she had really held her own. 'I was very happy, and not least because I did not come behind Jenny Lind as an artist in the estimation of the public, but awakened like interest and experienced equally enthusiastic applause' she subsequently wrote. 'This inspired me to put forth my intellectual and physical powers to the utmost; I had been very much afraid of the humiliating sensation of being slighted, and I was overjoyed that this was not the case!' For Jenny herself, Clara's enthusiasm was again un-bounded: 'I never loved and admired any woman more than I do her' she confessed in the diary. Like Robert, whose own songs Lind had just sung with such personal involvement, Clara nevertheless had one small re-servation: 'One thing only could we suggest to Jenny Lind: that she should sing only good music, and discard all that stuff (which she has sung in other places) of Meyerbeer's, Bellini's, Donizetti's etc., for she is too good for that'. Before Lind's arrival, Schumann's doggedly unyielding belief in his own ideas had in fact cost Clara what she described as 'paralysis from fright' when at a merry party in an oyster-bar after one of their concerts, he had got up and walked out, calling one of their hosts, Carl Grädener, an impudent fellow after his refusal to drink to Jean Paul in the same toast as J. S. Bach, as Schumann had requested on their shared birthday.

On the return journey an evening spent with Caecile Mendelssohn and her fatherless children was heart-rending, though Clara found some comfort in playing them a lot of Mendelssohn's music. By the end of March they were back in Dresden, now firmly convinced after perform-ances of Schumann's Piano Concerto and Overture to *Genoveva* in Hamburg that they must move as soon as possible to a city where he would have an orchestra of his own. As the diary put it 'Here we may sit still for years with all his treasure buried'.

But first there was *Genoveva* itself, for which they returned to Leipzig, this time to the congenial rural home of the Preussers where they could even eat breakfast in the garden, in readiness for the first rehearsal on May 22. For Clara, no less than Robert, the strain of the next few weeks was acute, betraying itself in vitriolic outbursts in the diary at any real or imagined under-estimation of her husband's stature. There was even one tirade against the 'Mendelssohn-clique' headed by their old ally, David. But as the great day approached and friends began to arrive, so her spirits revived: Spohr, Reinecke, Gade, Hiller, Moscheles, Joachim, Haupt-mann, Kuntsch, Grädener, Ehlert, Liszt, Pauline Schumann and Clara's own mother were among the many ready to lend their moral support. Though the première on June 25 under Schumann's baton was marred by stage accidents in the last two acts, the two remaining performances went better, moving Clara sufficiently, after the second, to write: 'the music filled me with delight. What dramatic feeling, what instrumentation, what

characterization are in it! Here we have once again real, beautiful,
German music that does one's heart good'. After the third performance,
conducted by Rietz, the floodgates of her heart opened to the full: '. . . the
singers were recalled after every act, and at the end they called so loudly
for Robert that he had to thread his way through the labyrinth of passages
which lead to the stage; naturally this took some time, and the longer they
waited, the louder became the cries; at last he appeared in a frock-coat (he
had not even a dress-suit) and was received with a regular storm of
applause. I could have wept for joy to see how he came forward, so simply
and unassumingly; if ever he seemed to me lovable, it was at this moment,
as he stood there, true artist and man!'

While admiring the opera's musical integrity, even many of their truest
friends secretly questioned its dramatic viability, as Wagner had done on
first seeing the libretto. But recognizing only its idealism and purity after
what she regarded as the audacities, vulgarities and superficialities of
contemporary leaders of operatic fashion, Clara was impervious to criticism. So Dresden's indifference to them on their return was all the more
galling, as her diary entry on July 10 makes plain: 'It is really as if the people
here had no blood in their veins, no enthusiasm for anything'. The only
quasi-official recognition of their impending departure came in a farewell
dinner on the Terrace on August 30 offered by Schumann's Choral
Union, an evening clouded by universal awareness of how membership
had dropped in recent months. 'It was very dull' Clara subsequently
recorded, complaining of scraping basses in the room below that disturbed Reinecke's toast and speech, and of the Kuntze Orchestra's
unsuitable choice of music ('a piece of regular Dresden pedantry') to play
in Robert's honour. Only the singing of his own 'Wenn zweie auseinan-
dergehen' and some other old, well-known songs revived their spirits.

But saying goodbye at a private musical party on August 25 to the
Hübners and the Bendemanns did cause Clara pangs. These two families
had been true friends.

ELEVEN

Düsseldorf 1850–54

The deference paid to Schumann on arriving at Düsseldorf, in succession to Mendelssohn, Rietz and Hiller, was for Clara the fulfilment of a life-long dream. Led by Hiller, the concert committee of the city's Allgemeine Musikverein (which had been paying Schumann's salary since the spring in appreciation of his acceptance) escorted them to the leading hotel, the Breidenbacher Hof, where laurel trees had been placed at the entrance and flowers in their rooms. Later that same evening of September 2, having left Dresden early the day before, they were serenaded by the Liedertafel. The following night as they sat at dinner the strains of Mozart's *Don Giovanni* Overture suddenly surprised them from the adjoining room, where the local orchestra had assembled for a similar salute. The city's formal welcome was reserved for Saturday, September 7, when a gala concert of Schumann's music was followed by a supper with toasts (though the diary records with 'extraordinarily little to eat') and a ball. But strenuous house-hunting, at the end of which they had only found a noisy, stop-gap apartment at the corner of Allee- and Graben-strassen, and then unpacking, tired them too much to stay for the ball, and more embarrassingly even caused them to withdraw from the expedition which Hiller and others had planned for the following day to show them the beauties of the neighbourhood.

Schumann's directorial duties, allowing him plenty of free time for composition, consisted of weekly rehearsals with choir and orchestra in preparation for the regular subscription concerts, together with a few extra performances connected with the Roman Catholic Church. Having expressed great satisfaction with the large Choral Union and its fresh-toned sopranos, and found the orchestra 'quite excellent for a small town', he eventually conducted his first public concert on October 24, the programme including his own *Adventlied* cantata, Gade's choral *Comola* and Beethoven's *Die Weihe des Hauses* Overture besides Mendelssohn's G minor Concerto in which to introduce Clara. Their reception was triumphant. 'Robert was received with a threefold flourish of trumpets when he entered' so Clara recorded. 'It was a particular pleasure to me to watch Robert conducting today, perfectly quietly and yet with such energy. . . . I, too, was received with a flourish of trumpets, and was dismissed in like manner, after I had played. I succeeded excellently in everything, and I can never remember such unanimous applause as I had today. It was the first time for many years that I once more publicly played an orchestral piece by heart. Is it possible that youthful powers and youthful freshness should return once more? In spite of what I have done I do not believe it. The boldness needed for playing by heart is an attribute of youth ... since Mendelssohn's departure there has been no such feeling of universal enthusiasm as was felt today by orchestra and chorus'.

Though her last remark was largely wishful thinking, the rest of Clara's self-satisfaction was understandable: the diary reveals how sorely she had been overwhelmed by domestic worries keeping her away from her piano throughout the first weeks of their arrival. The large, exposed windows of their noisy new home, the dilatoriness of workmen, the pretentiousness of her cook (whom she had to dismiss) and the general lack of respect from the lower classes caused her many secret tears, particularly in view of the great expense of the move and her husband's nervous irritation when unable to compose. Their only wholly carefree day had been September 29, when they visited Cologne and its noble cathedral, and afterwards the Belvedere with its glorious view of the Rhine and the Siebengebirge.

As for the Rhinelanders themselves, Clara found them much more spontaneously welcoming and merry than the majority of their old Dresden associates. Through Frau Bendemann's brother, Wilhelm von Schadow, now Director of the Düsseldorf Academy of Fine Arts, they quickly met a lively group of artists including Hildebrandt, Köhler, Carl Sohn and Lessing, all keen amateur musicians, besides Dr Herz and the notary, Euler, in the legal sphere, and most notably Dr Müller, from Königswinter, in the medical. After a supper party on October 21 at the Müllers', when Clara played the 'Appassionata's' finale, she wrote: 'We were very merry; people here, as a rule, are in good spirits when they are together, which I find very pleasant; one is particularly struck by the merry, unrestrained manner of the ladies, which indeed may sometimes overstep the bounds of womanliness and propriety.... Married life here is said to be more like the French – Dr. Müller's wife is a notable exception to all this, I think that we are likely to make good friends.' The easy-going Rhineland temperament was to please her rather less the following year, when she and Robert formed a little chamber choir to sing choral rareties, also a chamber music society to meet once a fortnight in their own home. Likening their new friends to school children, she indignantly noted in the diary that they much preferred to chatter than to work – the good Hildebrandt more than most, so provoking Robert on one occasion that he walked out, always his most spontaneous way of expressing disapproval. Though the choir in fact survived six months, the chamber music project collapsed after only two meetings because of general reluctance to undertake the necessary preparation. Not being able

Clara Wieck, 1832, from the
lithograph by Eduard Fechner

Clara at the time of her marriage,
1840; ascribed to Johann Heinrich
Schramm

Robert and Clara Schumann, 1850, after a daguerreotype taken in Hamburg

Robert Schumann, from a lithograph by Eduard Kaiser

Clara in 1853, from a painting by Sohn

Friedrich Wieck, 1870

Marie (aged 21)

Elise (19)

Julie (22)

Ludwig (18)

Ferdinand (18)

Eugenie (17)

Felix (17)

The seven surviving children of Robert and Clara Schumann

Johannes Brahms, *c.* 1856

Joseph Joachim and Clara
Schumann, 1854, from a drawing
by Adolf von Menzel

Clara in 1878, from the portrait by Franz von Lenbach

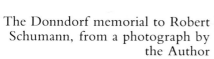

cottage in Baden-Baden,
small oil painting which
s ordered and presented to
humann family

The Donndorf memorial to Robert
Schumann, from a photograph by
the Author

Clara Schumann in London, 1888

to do without chamber music at home, they themselves quickly sought the cooperation of younger professionals, notably the violinist, Wasielewski, invited by Schumann to lead the Düsseldorf orchestra, and the cellist, Reimers, with Clara herself sometimes ceding the piano stool to Julius Tausch. An ex-pupil of the Leipzig Music School like Wasielewski, Tausch had come to Düsseldorf at Mendelssohn's suggestion to teach piano and in time to conduct the Liedertafel and Men's Choral Society. Schumann was even impressed enough by his compositions to recommend him more than once to Breitkopf and Härtel. Clara herself nevertheless took against Tausch from the start, finding him personally unattractive, and his playing rough. Even after the initial gala concert in their honour on September 7 her diary had recorded 'Herr Tausch conducted quite well. If only the man himself were more pleasant; he has something in his face, which I cannot get used to'. The slightest subsequent murmur of criticism about Schumann's own conducting – and as early as March 1851 fears of falling standards were openly voiced in the *Düsseldorfer Zeitung* – was enough to make her suspect Tausch as the source of all evil.

Schumann's amazing burst of creative activity throughout that first winter and spring, including a cello concerto, a 'Rhenish' Symphony (inspired by their memorable visit to Cologne the previous autumn), an overture to *The Bride of Messina* (the first in a series after literary tragedies) and an extended cantata, *The Pilgrimage of the Rose*, together with his warmly acclaimed performance of the *St. John Passion* on Palm Sunday – and also the secret knowledge that they had just conceived another child – swept them along over all reefs and shoals to their summer holiday, described by Clara as 'the most beautiful journey Robert ever took me'. Because they were so happy, they extended it from the originally proposed Rhine tour into an expedition into Switzerland (with a brief stop at Robert's beloved Heidelberg en route) that left indelible memories of Mont Blanc, cow-bells, and the sun breaking through the clouds over Vevey after a storm on the Lake of Geneva – as well as the pleasure of that elegant city's extraordinarily cheap champagne. Only a few days after returning home they left again for Antwerp, where Robert was one of the judges at a male voice choir contest, this time also seizing the chance to explore Brussels and its museums and galleries. Back in Düsseldorf once more, they were immediately enlivened by the arrival of Liszt and his cultured but 'matronly' Princess Wittgenstein (with her fourteen-year-old daughter and governess); they revelled as ever in his wizardry at the piano in the spacious music room (it could seat sixty people) of their much more congenial new apartment, acquired in early July, but found themselves reduced to embarrassed silence by his latest piano compositions.

For Robert's own unceasing flow of ideas in the autumn of 1851, chiefly channelled into a third piano trio, and more important, into two violin and piano sonatas that she could scarcely wait to try over with Wasielewski, Clara's admiration reached new heights. 'How magnificent is a mind like his, with such a power of incessant creative activity, and how fortunate I am that heaven has given me sufficient intelligence and feeling to understand his mind and character. A terrible anxiety often comes over me when I think how much more blessed I am than millions of other wives, and then I ask heaven if I have not too much happiness. What are all the shadows cast by everyday life, compared with the hours of rapture and bliss which come to me through my Robert's love and work?', so she wrote towards the end of October. Just over a month later, on December 1, her seventh child, a daughter named Eugenie, was born. Only three hours before the birth Clara had been with Robert at Professor Schadow's jubilee party, which as Schumann put it in a letter, 'we had not wanted to miss'.

Outside the domestic cocoon, the clouds were gathering. Many members of the Choral Union had failed to return at the start of the new 1851–2 season, while a committee meeting on September 6 proved vexatious enough for Schumann to confess to 'many doubts about the future'. As for Clara, the apathy of the choir's response to masterpieces like Bach's *Mass in B minor* and *St. John Passion*, rehearsed throughout the winter, made her 'boil with rage'. Though she herself had a warm enough welcome when returning to public life on March 4, 1852, for her first concert after Eugenie's birth, by the end of that month she was incensed enough to write 'I would like nothing better than for Robert to withdraw from the Society, for the position is beneath his dignity. If only he could do so at once!' Dispassionate observers were by now well aware that all the singers needed was systematic, vigorous direction, that without disloyalty or malice of any kind they were wholly perplexed by a shy, withdrawn visionary, increasingly hesitant in speech, whose conception of the music as it should be and practical means of realizing it were as far apart as he, personally, was from them as people. But to Clara, recently compelled by domestic responsibilities to withdraw from her self-imposed role of rehearsal accompanist, any thought of Robert being found wanting was inconceivable.

The middle of March in fact brought them a few days' welcome escape to Leipzig and the solace of a particularly enthusiastic reception for Schumann's *Manfred* Overture and the 'Rhenish' Symphony (if less so for the *Pilgrimage of the Rose*) besides much happy music-making for Clara after two years' absence from her birthplace, in company with a variety of old friends including Moscheles, whose G minor Concerto ('a fine thing which by no means deserves to be so soon forgotten') was her choice for her return to the Gewandhaus. But back in Düsseldorf, where Schumann at once flung himself obsessively into the composition of a *Mass* (Op.147) and *Requiem* (Op.148), trouble grew. With symptoms diagnosed as rheumatic, giving rise to the acutest hypochondria and depression, he was compelled to cancel their visit to Weimar for the first complete performance of his incidental music to *Manfred*. When a Rhineland holiday failed to bring lasting improvement, and a concert on August 3 during Düsseldorf's summer choral festival (at which he insisted on conducting his new *Julius Caesar* Overture) reduced him to near breakdown, in desperation they struggled over to Scheveningen to try the sea-bathing recommended by their friend, Dr Müller, who still thought the whole trouble attributable to overwork. While bringing Schumann some small relief, for Clara the shock of cold sea water was traumatic: on September 9 she had a miscarriage. 'My wife has been taken seriously ill' so Schumann wrote that same morning to their old friend and very recent companion, Verhulst. 'I can only tell you the details personally. Come and see us soon – it is always a comfort to see a friend's face. We shall have to remain at least four or five days longer'.

Dutifully, she still kept her promise to play Henselt's Concerto at one of the first autumn subscription concerts of the new 1852–3 season even though Tausch had to conduct in place of her husband. But her reception was lukewarm. Nor was there any show of enthusiasm for Schumann, or the newest in his series of choral cantatas, *Vom Pagen und der Königstochter*, when he was at last deemed strong enough to return to the rostrum on December 2, 1852, or indeed for either husband or wife when on December 30 he conducted the première of Gade's *Frühlingsphantasie* for four soloists, orchestra and piano. Feelings by now were in fact running so strong that immediately after his earlier concert a section of the Choral Union committee proposed that he should resign. Though such impudence led to their own resignation instead, it was nevertheless tacitly agreed that henceforth all choral practices should be taken by Tausch, an excellent choir-trainer, so that Schumann, still under considerable physical strain, could conserve his energy for orchestral rehearsals and public concerts. By this time his occasional aural disturbances were accompanied by the illusion that all tempi were too fast: at one private performance of his Quintet he even beat time on Clara's shoulders to hold her back – in full view of friends. A morbid enthusiasm for table turning and rapping, and various other magnetic dabblings in the occult, was yet further indication of an underlying mental disquiet that even overflowed into letters to Hiller when inviting him to share in the conducting at Düsseldorf's forthcoming 1853 Whitsun Festival. Despite a good reception for Schumann's recently revised D minor Symphony during that event, his new, specially composed *Rheinweinlied* for chorus and orchestra made little impression, and in general the press did little to disguise its preference for Düsseldorf's former music director.

Within the walls of their own home incessant industry and a spirited growing family to cherish and guide was happiness enough. After interim troubles with noisy neighbours when the house with the big music room had to be sold, they eventually found an apartment more pleasing to Clara than any in her married life because her own study was up on the second floor 'where Robert could hear nothing'. On January 9, 1853, she wrote 'Today I began to work again, at last. When I am able to work regularly like this, I feel really in my element; quite a different feeling seems to come over me, I am much freer and lighter, and everything seems to be more bright and cheerful. Music is, after all, a good piece of my life, and when it is wanting I feel as if I had lost all physical and mental elasticity'. Though the only notable additions to her repertory were works by Schumann, she paid quite a few visits to nearby Rhineland platforms including Cologne, Barmen, Elberfeld and Bonn as well as continuing with her teaching, sufficiently satisfying the public to maintain her own self-confidence in the face of increasingly pointed criticism of her playing from her perfectionist husband.

Nothing proved a richer artistic stimulus for her at this time than growing friendship with Joachim, now twenty-two, whose performance of Beethoven's Violin Concerto had been one of the great glories of Düsseldorf's 1853 Festival. After a late summer visit to the Schumanns that year, Joachim made his own feeling for the pair very clear in a letter to a friend: 'Schumann's character, which I have been able to study closely for the first time, seems to me splendid. His slightest words bear witness to his absolutely uncompromising honesty, combined with a charming sympathy, and at the same time he has such a naïve innocence, that, in knowing him more intimately, one cannot but feel at ease with him. His mind is always so full of music that I can bear him no grudge for being unwilling to let outside matters clash with these sounds, although it was owing to this that I, for instance, misunderstood him sometimes at first. There is no conceit in him, but his thoughts are noble. You know the touching manner in which Clara interprets his ideas. It gave me extraordinary delight to play Robert's compositions with her.'

*

It was shortly after the Whitsuntide Festival that with both Joachim's violin and her husband's imminent birthday in mind, Clara again turned to composition. A present for Schumann had to come first, accordingly on May 29 she began work on a set of Variations (published as her Op.20) on an F sharp minor theme which he had composed in 1841 but not published until 1851 as No.4 of his retrospective collection, *Bunte Blätter*, Op.99.

Apart from its ideal simplicity for variation treatment, it embodies the falling five note motto so often used by Schumann to enshrine her image before their marriage, so there was strong personal reason for her choice. In key, her only excursions are from F sharp minor to F sharp major, and at no time is the outline of the theme far out of earshot. In comparison with the freer variations on the same theme written by Brahms the following year, Clara's still betray her allegiance to the older, decorative virtuoso tradition. Nevertheless the figuration is imaginatively pianistic, never mere mechanical patterning. And while No. 6 (a canon at the fifth and octave) shows her as ingenious a contrapuntist as ever, No. 3 in F sharp is marked by unprecedented harmonic daring.[1] The Three Romances for piano, Op. 21, followed at the end of June; they are more personal in style than the Variations and more potent than her previous essays in the genre of the character piece (except, possibly, for the heartfelt G minor Romance, Op. 11, No. 2), although still the music of a devoted wife rather than an original thinker. In No. 1 in A minor, Schumann's influence is apparent in the undercurrent of secret lyrical elation in the middle section in F major, its triplet figuration recalling the first episode of his first *Novellette* in the same key (dear enough to her to play time and time again at the expense of the rest in the set). Midway through there are nevertheless harmonic excursions almost Lisztian in seductive allure. No. 2 in F is an elfin-like march (its chords very precisely notated in semiquavers followed by rests rather than staccato crotchets) stemming from the same world as the Scherzo of Beethoven's 'Spring' Sonata (beloved by Clara and Joachim) and many a Mendelssohnian sprite-land as well as Schumann's own Fughetta, from Op. 32, and 'Soldiers' March'. No. 3 in G minor derives much of its restless agitation from accented passing notes; even its calmer middle section in G major is considerably less predictable in harmony than the Clara of old.

The two piano works were in fact separated by a set of six songs, Op. 23, with words from Hermann Rollett's *Jucunde*. Her diary entry for June 22 reveals her special happiness in returning to this genre after an absence of seven years: 'Today I set the sixth song by Rollett and thus I have collected a volume of songs, which give me pleasure, and have given me many happy hours. There is nothing which surpasses the joy of creation, if only because through it one wins hours of self-forgetfulness, when one lives in a world of sound'. The pretty nature imagery of the verse (by a poet never set by Robert) is charmingly matched by Clara in all but the slightly inflated second ('An einem lichten Morgen') and last ('O Lust') of the set, where she falls back on a demonstrative, patterned accompaniment to support her sturdily expansive, strophic melody. She is much more her

---

[1] The work found a place in several of her recitals in the next few years.

husband's faithful pupil in the winning, conversational charm of No.1 ('Was weinst du, Blümlein, im Morgenschein?'), in the intimate secrets of No.3 ('Geheimes Flüstern hier und dort') significantly written in the more mysterious key of D flat with subtle two-four cross-currents within a triple pulse, in the plaintive economy of No.4 ('Auf einem grünen Hügel') so akin to Schumann's own strophic Volkslieder vein, and in No.5 in D major ('Das ist ein Tag'), a radiant six-eight spring song with fanciful echoes of its huntsman's horn in the accompaniment.

Apart from a solitary setting of 'Das Veilchen', which she composed in ignorance of Mozart's song until subsequently told of it by her husband, the last fruits of Clara's remarkable little surge of creative energy at this time were Three Romances for violin and piano, inspired by and dedicated to her good friend Joachim. The gem of the set, published as her Op.22 after completion on July 3, is the first in D flat, a poetic nocturne with intimately interwoven violin and keyboard parts prompting the marking *Innig* in its heading. Besides echoing her husband in the gruppettos enriching the melodic line, also in the duple cross-currents within a three-eight time signature (as in the third of the Rollett settings in the same key), Clara undisguisedly acknowledges his inspiration by quoting the opening motif of his A minor violin sonata of 1851 at the climax of the more urgent, minor-tinged central section. Yet the music's delicately perfumed fragrance remains all her own. No.2 in G minor, *Allegretto, Mit zartem Vortrage*, opens and closes in more resolute narrative style. The incisively contrasted G major trio has a pretty, spring-like radiance nearer the world of Gade or Bennett than Schumann. In No.3 in B flat, *Leidenschaftlich schnell*, the warm, romantic melody is slightly vitiated by one of Clara's more perfunctory accompaniments, its arpeggiated semiquavers dutifully varied in patterning at the reprise. Nevertheless in the central section in G the pianist is released from the role of mere accompanist to take turns with the violin as melody-maker in a happy theme redeemed from naïvety by passing flirtations with six-eight rhythm within its triple pulse.

*

'For my dear husband, for June 8 1853, a weak attempt once more on the part of his Clara of old' was how she inscribed the manuscript of her F sharp minor Variations. The birthday itself was blissful. Having been serenaded by friends the evening before, they drove out with the children to Benrath for a walk through the woods, and as the diary relates 'it really seemed as if the good God himself meant to serenade Robert, for there was a regular wood-concert of every possible kind of little songster. I should have liked to stay there for hours. We passed the evening very cosily at home, and our hearts were light to think that Robert had spent the day so happily and feeling so well, which was not the case last year. . . . We must leave the future in God's hands. Today I can only be thankful for the good that has come to us'. That same month Schumann wrote piano sonatas for Marie, Elise and Julie, now twelve, ten and eight respectively, whose musical progress meant a lot to him. Every Sunday he would hear them play and afterwards 'go to his great writing-table, pull out the drawer which held his money and give each of us a couple of pennies from a bowl. We thought that the nicest part of playing to him, for it was the only time any money was given us' so Marie, his eldest and closest daughter, subsequently related. They loved it when he teased them, as once in the street when pretending not to know who they were. They also enjoyed games and story-telling with him just before bed, a time of day when after long hours of isolation in his study he was theirs alone.

A strange paralytic seizure on July 30, subsequently dismissed by the doctor as rheumatism, and momentary loss of voice on August 30 after some particularly stimulating music-making with Joachim, were the only clouds in Schumann's sky before the excitements of their thirteenth wedding anniversary on September 12 and Clara's own thirty-fourth birthday the following day. 'Can a wedding day be kept more happily than with a dearly loved and loving husband at one's side, and six happy, well-grown children around us! My heart is full of thankfulness for all these rich blessings' was her immediate reaction. The drive out to Benrath the next afternoon was part of the big birthday surprise: returning home at 5 p.m. she found a splendid new Klems piano covered in flowers in her music room, and around it four singers, with one of her pupils as accompanist, waiting to burst into a special birthday setting by her husband of the self-same poem he had placed on the Härtel piano that was his present to her just before their wedding. The manuscripts of a *Phantasie* for violin and piano composed for Joachim, an overture for his *Faust*, and last but not least, a new *Concert-Allegro mit Introduction* for piano and orchestra (Op.134) were further offerings prompting her diary comment: 'It may sound presumptuous, but am I not truly the happiest wife in the world?'

On realizing at the end of September that in this recent surge of happiness she had conceived again, there were some passing pangs as she reflected on yet more interruptions to her career – not least as regards England and the visit Sterndale Bennett had so long tried to arrange. But conflict was quickly banished by a totally unpredictable turn of events when on September 30 an unknown young pianist-composer of twenty called Johannes Brahms, son of an undistinguished double-bass player in Hamburg, suddenly knocked on their door armed with an introduction from Joachim. 'He played us sonatas, scherzos etc. of his own, all of them showing exuberant imagination, depth of feeling and mastery of form.

Robert says that there was nothing he could tell him to take away or to add'
so the diary records. 'It is really moving to see him sitting at the piano, with
his interesting young face which becomes transfigured when he plays, his
beautiful hands, which overcome the greatest difficulties with perfect ease
(his things are very difficult). He has studied with Marxsen in Hamburg,
but what he played to us is so masterly that one cannot but think that the
good God sent him into the world ready made.' Though no stranger to
exciting new talent in his generous, life-long search for it, Schumann still
found such a potential almost beyond belief. Brahms was invited to stay on
in Düsseldorf all October to meet and make music with their friends;
happiness overflowed when in between concert engagements Joachim
was able to join them too. For Joachim's visit towards the end of October,
both to play with the Düsseldorf orchestra and hear his own recent
overture to *Hamlet*, Schumann even invited Brahms, together with his
pupil, Albert Dietrich, to share in writing a violin and piano sonata for
Joachim and Clara, using Joachim's FAE motto (Frei aber einsam, free
but lonely) as a unifying theme.[1] On October 29 Clara and Joachim also
ventured into public for the first time as a duo, including Beethoven's
'Kreutzer' and Schumann's own D minor Sonata in their warmly applauded programme.

With a new violin concerto for Joachim already simmering in his head,
and excitement about Brahms more or less compelling him, though long
silent as a critic, to write an article introducing his protégé to the world,
Schumann had never been farther removed in spirit from his day to day
Düsseldorf duties. Inevitably, his long-suffering choir now felt they had
made allowances enough. After an appalling performance of a *Mass* by
Hauptmann at the Maximilian Church on October 16 they refused to sing
Mendelssohn's *Erste Walpurgisnacht* under his baton at the subscription
concert on October 27. Even the orchestra's patience was strained beyond
endurance by a disastrous rehearsal of Joachim's difficult *Hamlet* overture, when endless repetitions of certain passages without any precise
indication of what they were trying to correct caused one of the cellists,
still not fully recovered from an illness, to get up and walk out. By
November 6 Dietrich wrote to warn Joachim that breaking point had
come, adding that he feared to leave the Schumanns alone in Düsseldorf
since 'even if they are told in the most considerate manner possible it will
be a crushing blow for both of them'. It fell the very next day, with Clara
shouldering the initial impact. As the diary put it 'On November 7 Herr
Illing and Herr Herz were sent by the committee to tell me that for the
future they wished Robert to conduct only his own things, Herr Tausch

[1] Dietrich contributed the first movement, Brahms the Scherzo and Schumann himself
the slow movement and finale. When asked to guess authorship, Joachim was right every
time.

having promised to undertake the others. This was an infamous intrigue, and an insult to Robert which would compel him to resign his conductorship, as I told the gentlemen then and there, without having spoken to Robert. Apart from the impertinence of such behaviour towards such a man as Robert, it was a breach of contract to which Robert will never consent. I have no words to express how indignant I was, and how bitterly I felt not being able to spare Robert this distress . . . what would I not have given to have been able to leave at once with Robert, but when one has six children that is not so easy'. There was no question for Clara of pleading illness, difficulty of communication, or preoccupation with composition. Her husband could do no wrong: a scapegoat had to be found. 'It seems increasingly evident that Tausch, while apparently passive, really wove the whole intrigue' so she wrote two days later, also recording 'Robert has told the committee of his determination to conduct no more'. Just as at a black moment in 1852 they had enquired about the Kapellmeistership at Sondershausen, so now they looked to Berlin and Vienna, and by November 10 had resolved to move to Vienna. But the immediate escape for which they both craved came through an old, open invitation to Holland. Ignoring the concert on November 10 that would formerly have fallen to Schumann, they left on November 24 with no intention of returning until just before Christmas.

Except for an appearance at Court, after which Clara walked out into the snow without waiting to change her satin slippers because so indignant at her own casual reception – besides the fact that her husband had been asked if he was a musician too – every moment of the tour, embracing Utrecht, the Hague, Rotterdam and Amsterdam, exceeded all expectations. At last there was just as much public enthusiasm for Schumann's own music, mostly conducted by himself, as for her playing – and just at this moment there could have been no greater balm for them both. Elated, Clara knew that she was playing at her best. That Robert recognized it too thrilled her still more, for as she put it 'when he is satisfied I am more pleased than if a whole audience lay at my feet'. After their Rotterdam concert, with Schumann's Piano Concerto and third Symphony the principal attractions, the ever faithful Verhulst even assembled a choir and orchestra to serenade them by torchlight in the cold night air outside their hotel for nearly an hour.

After a pleasant enough family Christmas, when Clara's present to her husband was a full-size portrait of herself by Sohn, they were only too glad that January offered them another escape from Düsseldorf and embarrassing negotiations with the Musikverein, this time to Hanover for Clara to play the 'Emperor' under Joachim's baton at a concert in which the great violinist also conducted Schumann's 'Rhenish' Symphony as well as appearing as soloist in Schumann's *Phantasie* for violin and orchestra. In this city both Clara and Robert were subsequently very warmly received at Court; she particularly enjoyed her second visit when the King wanted to hear little else but her husband's music. 'Glorious musical days' was how Joachim recalled the visit; Clara in her turn made special mention in the diary of one particularly merry evening with Brahms and Julius Otto Grimm (by now a Leipzig-trained pianist-composer who had recently befriended Brahms in that city) in Joachim's apartments, when they consumed a very large quantity of champagne.

Back in Düsseldorf Schumann resumed work on his *Dichtergarten*, an anthology of quotations about music culled from great writers through the ages, sometimes alarming Clara with the persistence of his researches, especially in Greek and Latin literature. Yet apart from their first night in Holland alarmingly disturbed by strange noises in the head, he had recently seemed to draw new physical strength from the warmth of family, friends, and awareness of how his music was spreading, 'especially in Holland and England', as he put it to van Bruyck. So it was all the more shattering for Clara when suddenly on February 10 and 11 he suffered 'so violent an affection of the hearing that he did not close his eyes all night'. Sometimes in the days and nights that followed it was a single note that never stopped, sometimes it turned into chords and the strains of a full orchestra. Sometimes the music was 'more wonderful and played by more exquisite intruments than ever sounded on earth', such as on the night of February 17 when he got out of bed to note down a theme brought him by the angels from Schubert and Mendelssohn (in reality a subconscious echo of the slow movement of his recently completed Violin Concerto). At other times it was a cacophony of hyaenas and demon voices, goading him to such desperation and despair that at night he begged Clara to leave him for fear that he might harm her. In rare moments of calm he composed variations on his 'mystical' theme in E flat, and attempted to write letters setting his financial and musical affairs in order. But on the night of February 28 he knew that his life-long dread had turned to hideous reality, and asked to be taken to an asylum. Coaxed to bed, with a male nurse in charge, he awoke next day in the profoundest melancholy. 'If I so much as touched him, he said "Ah! Clara, I am not worthy of your love". *He* said this, he whom I always look up to with the greatest, the most profound reverence' so she wrote of the most traumatic day of her life. 'He made a fair copy of the variations, and as he was at the last he suddenly left the room and went sighing into his bedroom – I had left the room only for a few minutes, in order to say something to Dr. Hasenclever in the next room, and had left Mariechen sitting with him (for ten days I had never left him alone for a minute). Marie thought he would come back in a minute, but he did not come, but ran out into the most dreadful rain, in nothing but his coat, with no boots and no waistcoat. Bertha suddenly burst in and told me that he had gone – no words can describe my feelings, only I knew that I felt as if my heart had ceased to beat. Dietrich, Hasenclever, and in fact all who were there, ran out to look for him, but could not find him; an hour later two strangers brought him back; where and how they found him I could not learn. . . .' It was not until considerably later that she discovered that in his anguish Schumann had thrown himself into the Rhine, and that fishermen had rescued him.

TWELVE

Anguish 1854–56

Not allowed to see her husband for fear of over-exciting him, even though two male nurses had been called in, Clara stayed at the nearby house of her blind friend, Fräulein Leser, containing herself in 'an agony of longing', as Dietrich put it, while preparations were made for Schumann's removal to Dr Richarz's private asylum at Endenich. 'Oh God', she eventually wrote on March 4, 'the carriage stood at our door. Robert dressed in great haste, got into the carriage with Hasenclever and the two attendants, did not ask for me or for his children, and I sat there at Fräulein Leser's in a dull stupor, and thought that now I must succumb'. Later that night she returned home with her mother, who had come at once from Berlin on hearing the worst. Brahms had also rushed over from Hanover, and with Dietrich was waiting for her at the house; Joachim, amidst his tight-packed concert schedule, arrived the next day.

As the news spread, so the letters of sympathy poured in, inevitably making her 'wounds bleed afresh', not least because of the ominous seriousness of newspaper reports of the breakdown (which in her fervent wishful thinking she deemed exaggerated) though at the same time allowing her to marvel at such widespread sympathy and respect for her beloved. As she put it 'I often say to my mother that if he could know of it it would cure him of his melancholy'. Older acquaintances quick to call with well-meant help and counsel included Ferdinand Hiller, recommending that she should move to Cologne where she could find more pupils. Avé-Lallement arrived from Hamburg with a sum of money to ease any immediate financial embarrassments, while from Leipzig Dr Härtel wrote to suggest a benefit concert for her family. These and other proposals she proudly refused. But when the banker, Paul Mendelssohn, sent her a credit note for 400 thalers saying he felt his dead brother whom she loved so well was urging him to do so, because the offer was so delicately made she decided to accept without actually cashing the note just in case of possible future need: 'Robert may take longer to recover than we now hope . . . in three or four months Robert might be so far recovered that he would have to travel for his health' were the thoughts that swayed her.

Bulletins from Endenich arrived with tantalizing slowness. But it was at least some comfort for Clara to learn from personal callers, like her mother and Brahms, that the doctors were kindly, and that the institution consisted of several smallish buildings in a large garden, with a glorious view of the whole range of the Siebengebirge, in which twice a day Robert was taken for a walk. Any subsequent reports of his pleasure in receiving and picking flowers, eating asparagus and listening to the nightingales, or indeed of any evidence whatsoever of recollection of a former way of life made her heart bound to such an extent that Brahms, apologizing for his presumptuousness, cautioned her to keep her feelings in check when writing to the doctors who were increasingly assessing her as 'overstrung' in their own much more guarded optimism. They were only too well aware of the occasional bouts of returning melancholy and delusions of hearing that caused Schumann to talk wildly, pace up and down his room, or fling himself on his knees and wring his hands. If black news of this kind filtered through to Clara, she was totally inconsolable. At night, unable to sleep, she often seemed to hear her husband sighing in the neighbouring bed. Even the children agitated rather than comforted her. 'Frau Schumann is just as overcome as in the early days – often when she mentions him or plays something of his she breaks into sobs' was how Julius Grimm described her condition when writing to Joachim in April to tell him that his well-meant suggestion of trying Count Franz Szápary's experimental cures by magnetism and auto-suggestion, then very fashionable among Berlin high society, had been totally rejected by the Endenich specialists. Knowing money was imperative, as early as March Clara had struggled to resume her private teaching. But with her next child due in June the effort was often intolerable. 'I am suffering a great deal physically. My nerves are so upset that I should like to lie down continually' was her admission on May 20. At other times the inactivity imposed by her pregnancy irked her still more. In her heart of hearts she longed for the birth to be over so that she could return to the concert platform where an income could be more congenially earned.

Just as for her own reading she turned to Robert's early critical essays and concert notices recently published as an anthology under the collective title, *Music and Musicians*,[1] and more significantly, to their carefully preserved love-letters up to the time of their clandestine engagement, so at the keyboard she constantly sought assuagement in what in the diary she called 'His music'. Sometimes nostalgic memories were too acute and she could no longer continue, as once when playing the D minor Sonata with Joachim. But for the most part it was a comfort to re-explore larger, less familiar works such as *Faust*, the *Requiem*, the *Hermann and Dorothea* Overture and the *Overture, Scherzo and Finale* at the piano with close friends like Dietrich, Julius Otto Grimm and Brahms. It was not until mid-April that she had any desire to start serious practice again in the

---

[1] She gave a copy to Brahms for his twenty-first birthday on May 7, 1854.

repertory-at-large, and only then because Brahms had written a new Piano Trio in B which she wanted to play with Wasielewski and Reimers on their imminent Easter visit.

Of the younger circle so gallantly standing by, there was no one to whom she felt closer than Brahms, who, since more free than the others, never long left her side. She at once allowed him to take over responsibility for the *Haushaltbuch*, in which ever since 1837 Robert had recorded day to day expenses and details of projects begun or finished in the minutest detail, even in later years of their marriage inserting a little secret sign in the margin on the nights when he and Clara made love. She also constantly relied on Brahms as an intermediary with the outside world. Most of all she valued the time he spent playing and reading to her – particularly the E. T. A. Hoffmann he loved no less than Robert. 'He does not say much, but one can see in his face, in his speaking eye, how he grieves with me for the loved one whom he so highly reveres, besides he is so kind in seizing every opportunity of cheering me by means of anything musical. From so young a man I cannot but be doubly conscious of the sacrifice, for a sacrifice it undoubtedly is for anyone to be with me now' was one of her earliest comments. Scarcely a day passed without some reference in her diary to his piano playing (often too free in rhythm for her liking yet more akin to her own style than Liszt's flamboyance) or to his not always immediately communicative yet still remarkable new compositions, including the first draft of what ultimately grew into the D minor Piano Concerto. Like Joachim, she, too, was aware that in Brahms's personal character there was a strain of egotistical uncouthness, an occasional tendency to ride rough-shod over the finer feelings of those of no concern to him, stemming from a plebeian upbringing and the necessity of fending for himself at too early an age. But experiencing only his selfless sympathy at this time, and sharing Robert's belief in his unlimited musical potential, she found her feeling for him warming every day, particularly after a memorable walk in the woods towards the end of May, bringing intimate exchanges of confidences. As she put it in a letter to Joachim on June 9: 'Brahms is writing this with me. I am learning to understand his rare and beautiful character better every day. There is something so fresh and so soothing about him, he is often so childlike and then again so full of the finest feelings. His is a youthful and open nature combined with a manly earnestness of purpose. And as a musician he is still more wonderful. He gives me as much pleasure as he possibly can, as you can imagine, and he does this with a perseverance which is really touching. It often oppresses me to think of how much he is giving me, and of how very, very poorly I can repay it!'

Two days later she was in some way able to repay it: when her son was born on June 11, she asked Brahms to be one of the godparents. Nothing would have pleased her more than for Joachim to join him, but at that moment Joachim's Jewish faith stood in the way of his acceptance. Significantly, he renounced it to become a Christian barely a year later. The baby's own baptism was postponed indefinitely in the hope that it could coincide with Robert's own recovery, but from the very start Clara selected Felix as one of three possible names.

A few days before the birth she was relieved to hear from the mayor of Düsseldorf that it had been decided not to consider Schumann's post vacant for the time being, and that she could rely on receiving his salary until the end of the year. But her great solace was news from Endenich that Robert was 'quiet, with no delusions or nervousness. He did not speak wildly and he asked some questions which showed that he is beginning to remember the past.' When a singer friend, Fräulein Hartmann, returning from Bonn in July, brought her roses and carnations which he had picked in the asylum garden as if for the first time aware of to whom they were going, Brahms subsequently reported to Joachim that 'she danced round the room with joy. I have never seen her in such good spirits and so calm' – and this even though she had just felt obliged to leave her third daughter, Julie, now nine but still the most delicate of the four girls, in the care of her mother, Frau Bargiel, in Berlin.

With an arduous autumn tour ahead, a strength-giving holiday was obligatory. So with Henriette Reichmann, her old ally in Paris in 1839, and a promise that Fräulein Leser would follow, she set off on August 10 for Ostend. Running into Vieuxtemps at this popular resort she was cajoled into giving a concert on August 26 in cooperation with a baritone previously unknown to her, Julius Stockhausen, seven years her junior,[1] who sang three of Schumann's songs beautifully enough to remain one of her lifelong collaborators and friends. For the rest she was only happy when escaping from the crowded sea-shore on solitary walks, and could hardly wait to return to her children and friends on September 6.

Brahms was among the first to greet her, writing to Joachim on September 12 that she looked well and was playing 'with all her old power, but with more intensity, *more than ever* like you. Yesterday she played me my F minor Sonata, just as I had imagined it, but with more nobility, more tranquil enthusiasm and with such a pure, clear rendering and such magnificent tone in the stronger passages: these are all little advantages she has over me'. His excited anticipation of her imminent thirty-fifth birthday overflowed in every paragraph, for as a surprise present he had arranged Schumann's Piano Quintet for four hands as well as surreptitiously weaving the theme of her old *Romance*, Op.3, into the set of variations he was then writing on the same F sharp minor theme of

[1] Both his parents were professional singers.

Robert's used by her the previous year. The birthday also brought Clara the pleasure of hearing Marie and Elise perform four of Schumann's *Bilder aus Osten* duets, after secret coaching from Brahms. His affection for the children always touched her, particularly when in March he had given Marie a little empty book inscribed on the first page 'Poems by Marie Schumann', and on the second 'Let who will and can pour forth, Melodies from every tree, There is room for many birds, In the woods of poetry'. Nevertheless it was the Endenich doctors who totally transformed the anniversary for her by at last granting her permission to write to her husband. As Brahms put it to Joachim: 'She wrote two letters; in one she mentioned the dates (12th and 13th), in the other she did not. But Herr Schumann told the doctor quite of his own accord of the great importance he attached to those two dates. So they gave him the first letter. At midday on the 15th a letter came from the doctor with enclosures. I handed it to Frau Schumann in fear and trembling! Were her letters being returned or was it a reply? She opened the letter, and could hardly stammer 'from my husband'; she could not read it for some time. And then, what unspeakable joy; she looked like the Finale to *Fidelio*, the F major movement in 3/4 time. I can describe it in no other way. One could not weep over it, but it fills one with a deep and joyful awe. I was the first to read the letter after her. Now I am sending you, his dearest friend, the first news and a copy of the letter'. Her own answer to Robert's affectionate albeit loosely strung questions about family and music in its turn elicited a still more lucid reply from him, including the clear wish that their new son should have 'the name of him who will ever be remembered'. So although slightly daunted by the rigours of her forthcoming tour, she could write to Joachim with an almost jubilant heart: 'Oh, dear Joachim, I thought I knew what a splendid thing it is to be an artist, but I only realize it for the first time now that I can turn all my suffering and joy into divine music, so that I often feel quite happy.'

*

Setting out on October 14 she had the company of Brahms and Julius Grimm as far as Hanover for a happy reunion with Joachim and a performance at Court before proceeding with Agnes Schönerstedt as official companion to Leipzig. Here, too, she was heartened by old friends like the Preussers, with whom she stayed, and the Bendemanns, who came over from Dresden, together with students of the Conservatoire and the Paulinerchor who serenaded her, no less than by the audience's warm reception at her two Gewandhaus concerts on October 19 and 23. For concertos throughout the tour she had prepared Beethoven's fourth as well as Robert's in A minor and his D minor *Concert-Allegro*, Op.134. Her solos now significantly included the Andante and Scherzo from Brahms's

F minor Sonata, Op.5, of which the Andante, prefixed by lines from a Sternau love-poem, had always lain particularly close to her heart. Weimar came next, with an all-Schumann programme conducted by Liszt. But neither his own personal gallantry and kindness nor his respect for her husband could modify her growing dislike of the aura of his circle, and still more, of his music. When receiving the B minor Sonata generously dedicated by Liszt to Robert shortly after his breakdown she had cursorily dismissed it, and other works, after a quick run-through by Brahms, as 'really gruesome . . . nothing but noise – there is not a wholesome thought in them; everything is confused; there is no sign of any clear harmonic progression.'

She was as displeased by pettiness in Frankfurt as she was by the stiffness of Hamburg's audiences. But at least Hamburg brought her reunion with Brahms and the chance of meeting his parents ('simple folk, but worthy of all respect. . . . I always enjoy unaffected bourgeois life of this kind'), of seeing his cherished boyhood collection of tin soldiers, and an introduction to his teacher, Marxsen. Altona, Lübeck, Bremen and Breslau finally led to a month's stay in Berlin and the comfort of seeing her mother and her daughter, Julie, again, also various members of the Mendelssohn family, Bettina von Arnim, the Grimms and many other valued friends. Musically, her greatest satisfaction came in a series of soirées with Joachim,[1] and it was with him, after visits to Frankfurt and Potsdam, that she eventually travelled, via Hanover and Leipzig, back to Düsseldorf for Christmas.

It was Joachim, who after a lucid exchange of letters, was now privileged to be Schumann's first personal visitor at the asylum on December 24, finding enough that augured well to rush back that same night to tell Clara the good news and bring Brahms a letter from Schumann using the familiar 'du'. This particularly intrigued Clara, since only very recently Brahms had begged her to address him in this way herself. 'I could not refuse', her diary reports, 'for indeed I do love him like a son'.

Though to Clara's bitter chagrin the doctors still would not allow her to see her husband, Brahms was permitted his first visit on January 11, 1855, finding Schumann well, cheerful and anxious to hear Brahms's recently composed F sharp minor Variations and four Ballades (Op.10). Sharing in Clara's delight at this continued improvement, also in the children's Christmas excitement, in Felix's long-delayed baptism on New Year's Day and a pleasurable excursion to Hanover for a rehearsal of Joachim's new *Heinrichs-Overture* had together made the holiday period a happy one for Brahms, never previously parted from his own family at this season.

[1] As well as Schumann's two Sonatas in A minor and D minor they always particularly enjoyed playing Beethoven's 'Kreutzer' and G major, Op.96, Sonatas at this time.

But watching Clara pack her boxes for another Dutch tour, with other long journeys ahead, suddenly began to hurt. In fact after accompanying her and her companion by steamer on January 15 as far as Emmerich to delay the farewells, only two days later he followed her to Rotterdam. 'He quite frightened me at first, but afterwards I gave myself up to the truest joy' so Clara wrote in her diary of the six days he remained. When the previous summer her friend, Fräulein Leser, had tactfully intimated that in view of his extreme youth she was not sufficiently keeping her distance and preserving her dignity as an artist, she was indignant: she knew Brahms's loyalty to the lonely sufferer at Endenich was as rock-like as her own. But the depth of his devotion to her was now becoming unmistakable, likewise the ache in his heart which he sometimes concealed in rueful humour, as when asking 'why did you not allow me to learn to play the flute so that I could travel with you?', but very often expressed in open longing. On her lonely travels she, too, was becoming increasingly aware of her own need of his moral support: there was no other person in whom she could so completely confide all her musical no less than personal problems, or on whom she could more wholly rely for candid reports on the children's welfare under their faithful housekeeper, Bertha, or more important still, for the latest news from Endenich. It was to Brahms that she wrote at once on receiving a letter from Robert with the chilling words: 'My Clara, I feel as if I were facing some terrible calamity. How dreadful if I should not see you and the children again'. And it was Brahms who at once tried to allay her fears by reminding her that when writing his *Requiem*, Schumann, like Mozart, had often tortured himself – and her – with premonitions of death. But her disquiet unsettled her playing when moving on to Leyden, Utrecht, Amsterdam and the Hague, all so redolent of Robert and their recent shared triumphs.

Back in Berlin by the end of February, after a brief glimpse of Brahms and the children en route, it was Joachim who restored her musical confidence, particularly when they travelled to Danzig for two joint concerts mainly devoted to Beethoven, both sonatas and concertos. 'We had a splendid musical evening yesterday' Joachim wrote to Brahms on March 2. 'Frau Schumann played magnificently (as I have not heard her play for a long time) and taught me to find new beauty in things long familiar to me'. It was no less of a relief to Brahms to hear of Joachim's success in talking Clara out of a projected tour of England that summer. 'Frau Schumann only thinks of what she calls duty', Joachim wrote, 'and as she seems to me to have much too large (not to say false) an idea of this for human nature, I felt obliged, as her sincere friend, to oppose her blind zeal for self-sacrifice with my cold common sense'. But it was already too late to dissuade her from what proved a physically exhausting and artistically unrewarding trip to Pomerania in the snow, taking in Greifswald and

Stralsund before a hazardous extension of the journey by sleigh across the ice of the sound, to the island of Rügen for a soirée in Bergen.[1]

Except for a fortnight's teaching at the Court of Detmold at the end of June and a concert at Ems with Jenny Lind soon after, the spring and summer of 1855 were now entirely her own. She had accepted the invitation to give Princess Friederike piano lessons very reluctantly, only to find her royal pupil to be 'an amateur such as is not often to be found among princesses' and her brother (the reigning prince) and their mother deeply interested in all things musical. There were generous opportunities for playing herself, both with the court orchestra and at soirées – in these Joachim was twice invited to join her – as well as comfortable apartments close to the glorious Teutoburger forest. Showered by so much sympathy and kindness, she left on July 1 in tears. Her concert with Jenny Lind, who had so beautifully sung the part of the Peri in Schumann's oratorio at the recent Düsseldorf Whitsuntide festival, was less agreeable. Not even a profit of 1340 thalers ('enough to bring my family through the summer and leave something over') allowed her to forget that in one of those occasional bursts of imperiousness so wounding to her friends, Jenny Lind, perhaps fearful that Clara might include some Brahms (for whom she herself had no time), requested her to choose 'only simple things which can be understood by people who love beauty'. In the event Clara played Beethoven's 'Waldstein', Mendelssohn's *Variations sérieuses* and miniatures by Schumann, Chopin and Weber while Jenny, including an aria from Haydn's *Creation* as well as a song by Schumann, only pandered to popular taste in four of Chopin's mazurkas 'with Italian words and obbligato piano of Otto Goldschmidt' (since 1852 her husband) and some Swedish folk songs. It could therefore have only been a society audience's obvious preference for the Swedish nightingale that prompted Clara's bitter admission in the diary that 'the whole of last winter, with all its torments, did not extract such a sacrifice as this evening when I was forced to humiliate myself from a sense of duty'.

It was Brahms who once more consoled her, this time collecting her and her companion (both of whom sent their luggage on ahead and used Brahms's knapsack for all immediate needs) for an idyllic, sun-soaked walking tour along the banks of the Rhine, an excursion far more therapeutic in effect than her subsequent official sea-bathing holiday in August, much of it in the company of the singer, Livia Frege, and the Leipzig publisher, Dr Härtel and his wife, though the smaller resort of Düsternbrock, near Kiel, with its beautiful beech-woods, pleased her more than Ostend the previous year.

[1] The only surviving programme for this soirée is in Brahms's handwriting, prompting the question as to whether or not he was with her.

In his letters in March Brahms had started to address her as 'My dearly
beloved Clara'. While she was at Detmold he wrote nearly every day,
elated as ever if he had even the tiniest shred of good cheer for her from
Endenich, yet no longer attempting to disguise the fact that she had
become the centre of his whole life. 'I can no longer exist without you' he
confessed on June 25, ending the same letter 'Please go on loving me as I
shall go on loving you, always and for ever'. They had been studying
counterpoint together since her return from Pomerania. At the start of
April they had travelled to Cologne to hear 'that most gigantic of all
works', Beethoven's *Missa Solemnis*. Towards the end of the month they
went to Hamburg for a performance of Schumann's *Manfred*, drawn the
closer by this time both staying with Brahms's parents. And for his
twenty-second birthday on May 7 Clara wrote him a Romance in B minor
more revealing of her own torn heart than any of her subsequently
destroyed letters to him at this period. 'Its tone is sad, but I was sad when I
wrote it' so the diary records. The falling line of the main theme is in fact a
direct reminiscence of the Andante of his F minor Sonata as it emerges
transformed from A flat major into B flat minor in the fourth movement
entitled 'Rückblick'.

Ex. 5

The central section in G major, still nostalgic despite its dawn of new
hope, is again more Brahmsian than Schumannesque in texture. Signed
'Liebendes Gedanken, Clara', the Romance was the last solo she ever
wrote for the piano; Brahms himself could well have remembered its
concentrated intimacy of expression, in a world apart from the miniatures
of her youth, when writing his own Intermezzi in later life.

The birthday itself was happy. As she put it 'He was very merry, and thoroughly enjoyed it, so that I too seemed to grow younger, for he whirled me along with him and I have not spent so cheerful a day since Robert fell ill, in spite of the fact that I had received a few lines from Robert this morning which made me very uneasy'. There had been hints from the doctors that Schumann's feverish resumption of work on accompaniments for Paganini's Violin Caprices, started in 1853, and several other projects, including a piano duet arrangement of Joachim's *Heinrichs-Overture*, was not the good omen once thought: already the strain was inducing renewed aural hallucinations, melancholy and loss of touch with reality. Yet uneasy as she was, it never for a moment occurred to Clara that the letter to which she referred, dated May 5, 1855, might be her last:

Dear Clara,

I sent you a spring message on May 1st. The following days were very unquiet; you will learn more from the letter which you will receive the day after tomorrow. A shadow flickers across it, but the rest of its contents will please you, my darling.

I did not know it was the birthday of our dear friend. I must make myself wings that my letter may come with the score.[1]

I have enclosed the drawing of Felix Mendelssohn, so that you may put it in the album. A priceless keep-sake.

Farewell, dear heart

Your Robert

It was not till the approach of her own thirty-sixth birthday in September, after a strenuous renewal of music-making (often in company with Princess Friederike who had come to Düsseldorf for more piano lessons), that the truth slowly dawned. Desperate at Robert's four months' silence she had written to beseech just 'one word' – only to receive a letter from the doctor advising her to abandon all hope of a complete recovery. The anniversary itself brought gifts from her friends. Marie and Elise played her Schubert's C major Duo. There was an afternoon excursion up the Grafenburg with all the children. There was an evening music party with Brahms and Joachim at Fräulein Leser's. 'Nothing was lacking that birthday celebrations should have', so the diary records, 'yet without Him, everything was wanting'.

By this time Düsseldorf had appointed Tausch as Schumann's official successor, dashing Clara's secret hope that Brahms might get the job. While happy enough to give him a cosy room of his own in the new flat at 135 Poststrasse to which she had recently moved, not least to have a man in the house during her absence, as during the violent thunderstorms throughout the night of August 24 when he calmed all the terrified

---

[1] Schumann sent Brahms the manuscript of his overture to *The Bride of Messina*.

children on his knee, she was nevertheless worried by his loss of contact with the wider musical world and the mere pittance he was earning by teaching three or four unremarkable local pupils. So it was a great relief when after starting her new autumn tour in Elberfeld and Göttingen, she had opportunity to summon Brahms to Berlin and Danzig to share in some of her recitals with Joachim: he joined her in Schumann's Variations for two pianos and Joachim in Schubert's B minor Duo as well as including Beethoven's G minor Fantasia, Op.77, and his own C major Sonata among his solos. She herself had set out with two new Beethoven works in her repertory, the C minor Variations, first played in Berlin on November 3, and more significantly, the 'Hammerklavier', a sonata then rarely heard from a woman, (although a seventeen-year-old English girl, Arabella Goddard, had recently included it at her London début) which she risked in Leipzig on December 8.[1] For concertos she had principally prepared the 'Emperor', also Robert's G major *Concertstück* Op.92, much more happily received at the Gewandhaus on December 6 than at its première. After further appearances at Rostock and a court soirée at Schwerin she rushed home to join the children and Brahms for a toy-studded Christmas but even before the end of 1855 was on her way to Vienna.

Her great surprise here, after her ill-starred return in 1846, was the warmth of her welcome even though at all five recitals she played only music close to her heart, notably Beethoven (again the 'Hammerklavier'), Schumann and Brahms. At her first concert on January 7 she was recalled fifteen times. Only at a crowded, pretentious soirée given by the Hungarian Countess Banfy did she suffer misgivings about her demanding choice. Confiding her fears to Liszt, he teasingly retorted 'Why not play a couple of bad pieces by Liszt? They would be in place here'. 'You are right, but I cannot do that' was her unsmiling reply, no doubt the more heartfelt because of a letter from Joachim just before Christmas expressing recent disillusionment of his own about Liszt.[2] Moving on to Budapest, she was still more enthusiastically acclaimed in programmes that her Hungarian agent had initially feared far too serious for that city. After Schumann's *Carnaval* she was even given a laurel wreath tied with ribbons in the national colours as a present for her husband. Congenial social activity included several meetings with Joachim's family as well as taking her from court circles to the gypsies, whose exuberant improvisation particularly delighted her. Her diary, in consequence, was singularly free from the carping which even amidst success had crept into observa-

---

[1] It did not remain in her repertory for very long.

[2] 'I shall never be able to meet Liszt again', Joachim had written, 'because I should want to tell him that instead of taking him for a mighty erring spirit striving to return to God, I have suddenly realized that he is a cunning contriver of effects, who has miscalculated'.

tions about her friends in Vienna, where she gave yet another 'extra' recital, followed by two more in Prague, on her way back to Leipzig. Staying in Leipzig with her old friends, the Preussers, who were just about to move to Loschwitz, near Dresden, she insisted on appearing at a farewell matinée at their home with Stockhausen. Best of all was the chance of seeing Marie and Elise again, recently despatched to a boarding school in this city. Laden with sandwiches, fruit and chocolates, supplied by friends, they had joined the train in Düsseldorf under the watchful eye of Brahms, who had written to Joachim to ensure that he would be on the platform with coffee for them when they pulled in at Hanover.

As ever, Brahms's letters had been Clara's life-line while away, keeping her in touch with every aspect of the children's development ('Ferdinand is too lazy, Ludwig is too self-willed, and Felix is even more so. Genchen (Eugenie) is for the moment just a little bit too passionate' was his summing up of the four youngest still at home on February 26, 1856) as well as with all his own latest literary or musical discoveries, ranging from Shakespeare's debt to Plutarch, or of his acquisition of the manuscript of Beethoven's late A flat sonata,[1] to his views on textual accuracy and the performance of ornaments in Bach. One of his most delicate tasks, in view of her pride, was informing her in February that her Leipzig friends, headed by David, had started a subscription fund to cover Schumann's medical costs because they refused to allow her 'to go on toiling and moiling to earn the money required by the dear man during his illness'. But this time his own fervent wish to keep her within easy reach was thwarted. After one further stop-over in Hanover, and a hasty visit to Düsseldorf to see the four younger children, she parted from Johannes ('the most painful I have ever had') on a gloomy, rainy night in early April for her long projected, frequently postponed first visit to England.

*

It was Clara's old friend, Sterndale Bennett, now a composition professor at the Royal Academy of Music[2] just about to begin a new appointment as conductor of the Philharmonic Society, who had at last persuaded her, and it was at Bennett's home at 15 Russell Place, Fitzroy Square, that Clara at first stayed, even within an hour or two of arrival going to the piano and playing for quite a while to Mrs Bennett. A Broadwood grand was installed in the front dining room for her own special use, and the servants were asked to be particularly considerate in view of her own personal anguish – which they all too soon discovered. On the very morning of her début a letter arrived from Brahms telling her, as gently as possible, that

---

[1] It was a present from Avé-Lallement in December 1855.
[2] He became its Principal in 1866.

all thoughts of a change of treatment (he had urged a move to a hydropathic establishment) had been dismissed by the doctors as useless, and that on a recent visit, he had found Schumann barely able to utter a single sentence. 'I could not play a note all day, I could do nothing but weep aloud from morning till night, and then wearied out and depressed I went to the concert. Heaven was gracious, it all went very well, I was quite successful, but I knew that this day, and the many days of tears which followed, would cost me a great part of my health' was her diary comment.

The concerto chosen for her début was Beethoven's 'Emperor': she played it under Bennett's baton at his own first Philharmonic Concert in the Hanover Square Rooms on April 14, 1856. 'A positive sensation, even among those who are moved with difficulty' was the immediate reaction of the *Morning Herald*. *The Times* was a little more specific, praising the slow movement for its expressiveness, and the finale because 'sportive, capricious, and varied with exquisite delicacy and unerring taste', but deeming the first movement 'lacking in breadth, fire and grandeur'. Even her solo after the interval, Mendelssohn's *Variations sérieuses*, was thought occasionally too fast, albeit in the main sufficiently close to the composer's own interpretation to suggest that she had heard him play this work very often. Attending her first solo recital the next day for the Musical Union, London's most fashionable chamber concert series founded by John Ella, *The Times* again qualified its praise of her readings of Beethoven's D minor sonata, Op. 31, No. 2, and a group of Mendelssohn's *Lieder ohne Worte* by describing them as 'different from what has been heard at the hands of other pianists'. And while finding her 'exquisite' in Schumann's 'Des Abends', the piece itself was dismissed as belonging to a school 'that runs counter to our ideas of musical propriety'. When on May 14 she introduced her husband's A minor Piano Concerto under Dr Wylde at a concert of the New Philharmonic Society, founded in 1852 as a challenge to the falling orchestral standards of the older Philharmonic Society, her own performance was warmly applauded in *The Times* for technical mastery and a deep enough personal involvement to suggest that she had composed the work herself. The concerto was nevertheless judged 'laboured and ambitious', with many of its bravura passages 'utterly extravagant'.

Her own initial disappointment and disillusionment were intense. 'They are dreadfully behind the times, or rather they can only see one thing at once. They will not hear of any of the newer composers except Mendelssohn, who is their god. *The Times* always shuffles when there is anything to say about Robert' was her diary observation on her critics – whether or not she knew that *The Times*'s anonymous J. W. Davison was a former friend and devoted disciple of Mendelssohn and the teacher and husband-to-be of England's uprising young pianist, Arabella Goddard,

she did not disclose. As for performing standards, she found them as
slipshod and commercially determined as Joachim had warned her she
would: 'They call it a rehearsal here if a piece is played once through, but
nobody thinks of working at it carefully. It is the artists' own fault; they
allow themselves to be treated as inferiors in English society, since
nothing is too humiliating to be borne if only they make money. How badly
I fit in here! They simply laugh at me when I express my disgust' she
concluded on May 11. When at one private soirée the guests went on
talking as she played, she made her indignation plain by stopping and
letting her hands lie in her lap until everything was quiet, this time eliciting
not laughter but a letter of apology from the hostess, Lady Overstone, the
next day. Even the kind Bennett, who sent one of his servants all over
London in search of lilies-of-the-valley for her to despatch to Schumann
for his birthday, came in for criticism in the diary on account of the
money-earning hack-work indulged in from dawn to dusk which she felt
was robbing him of his old freshness and vigour. As early as May 24
Brahms urged her to postpone the remainder of her commitments if
everything had become too much of a strain, in the same letter confessing
how he longed to join her in England but for the fear that it might be
regarded as improper.

But dutifully she stayed on, discharging nearly thirty public and private
engagements that took her to Liverpool, Manchester and Dublin as well
as many different London venues – not forgetting Buckingham Palace,
where remembering the royal taste for Mendelssohn she contributed the
Variations sérieuses to a mixed programme from several different artists.
For the rest, joining the fine Italian cellist, Piatti, and the Czech violinist,
Ernst (both had adopted England as their home) in piano trios gave her
particular pleasure. On various other occasions she collaborated with
artists including Pauline Viardot, Emma Busby, an aspiring pianist from
Camberwell with whom she for a while lodged (in Moscheles's four-
handed 'Homage to Handel'), Bennett and even the formidable young
Arabella Goddard herself (at a farewell jamboree on July 2) in Schumann's Variations for two pianos. At her second appearance for London's
Philharmonic Society, as also for that of Dublin, she chose Mendelssohn's D minor Concerto. She also helped Bennett to prepare Schumann's *Paradise and the Peri* for a Philharmonic concert on June 23,
modestly singing in the chorus herself (to the cynical amusement of quite
a few of the more sophisticated) while Jenny Lind as the Peri filled the hall
to overflowing with an illustrious audience including the Queen, Prince
Albert and several other European crowned heads and grandees. When
the time came to leave, some of her initial dislike of the country had
softened. 'The Englishman is cold, difficult to approach . . . but when
once he is warm he is so for ever and is capable of any friendship', so she

eventually wrote, even admitting to her diary that she had 'grown very fond of some people'.

She was met at Antwerp on July 4 by Brahms. Because he had never previously seen the wide open sea they spent the next day together in Ostend, but by July 6 were back in Düsseldorf. Already in London she had been forewarned of her husband's rapidly deteriorating condition: paying him a forty-sixth birthday visit Brahms had found himself practically ignored as Schumann, for much of the time confined to bed with swollen ankles, pored over the atlas he had recently requested, stringing place names together in alphabetical order. By July 14 she was desperate enough to go to Bonn in person to beseech Dr Richarz to let her see her husband, a request refused on this occasion, and even again after receiving a telegram summoning her to the asylum on July 23 when the end was deemed imminent. Eventually she could bear the separation no longer. Returning with Brahms on the 27th she now demanded one last reunion, and was granted it between 6 and 7 in the evening. 'He smiled, and put his arm round me with a great effort, for he can no longer control his limbs. I shall never forget it. Not all the treasures in the world could equal this embrace' she wrote in the diary. 'Two and a half years ago you were torn from me without any farewell, though your heart must have been full, and now I lay silent at your feet hardly daring to breathe; only now and then I received a look, clouded as it were, but unspeakably gentle. Everything about him was holy to me, even the air which he, my noble husband, breathed with me. He seemed to speak much with spirits, and would suffer no one to be near him for long, or he became restless, but it was almost impossible to understand him any longer. Only once I understood "My" – "Clara" he would no doubt have added, for he looked at me affectionately; and then once again "I know" – "You" probably'.

The next day, spent going in and out of his room with Brahms, brought her the comfort of giving him the wine and jelly which alone had sustained him for weeks, especially when he sucked the wine from her finger in real haste with the happiest expression, for 'ah, he knew that it was I'. But twitching limbs and often vehement speech were heart-breaking enough evidence of his suffering for her to 'pray God to release him because I loved him so dearly'.

Release came the following evening, July 29. She was not with him at the time, but saw him half an hour later. The diary tells all else: 'I stood by the body of my passionately loved husband, and was calm. All my feelings were absorbed in thankfulness to God that he was at last set free, and as I knelt by his bed I was filled with awe, it was as if his holy spirit was hovering over me – Ah! if only he had taken me with him. I saw him for the last time today – I laid some flowers on his head – my love, he has taken with him. . . . The funeral was at 7 o'clock on Thursday, the 31st. I was in the little chapel at the churchyard. I heard the funeral music. Now he was lowered into the grave. Yet I had a clear sense that it was not he, but his body only – his spirit was with me – I never prayed more fervently than at that hour. God give me strength to live without him. Johannes and Joachim went before the coffin, which was carried as a mark of respect by members of the Concordiagesellschaft, who once serenaded him in Düsseldorf. The Mayors went with them, and Hiller came from Cologne, but there were no other friends. I had not let it be known, because I did not wish a number of strangers to come. His dearest friends went in front, and I came (unnoticed) behind, and it was best thus; he would have liked it so. And so, with his departure, all my happiness is over. A new life is beginning for me'.[1]

[1] Recent researchers such as Eliot Slater, Alfred Meyer and Eric Sams have rejected earlier psychotic diagnoses of Schumann's breakdown in favour of tertiary syphilis, or general paresis, contracted, albeit treated and ostensibly cured, during student days. Dr Richarz himself, in an appendix prepared for Wasielewski's biography of Schumann (1857), summarized the illness as a progressive organic disease which "first took root in early youth, gradually increasing with the growth of the man, and not resulting in madness for a long time". His eventual autopsy revealed distended blood vessels, ossification of the base of the brain and degeneration of covering tissues, which, with considerable atrophy of the whole brain itself, he guardedly attributed to the stress of over-work impairing the nutrition and metabolism of the brain.

THIRTEEN

A New Start 1856–63

'You must not imagine her [Frau Schumann] as oppressed by sentimental grief; she has a healthy impulse to work and a warm love of music which will always raise her above ordinary people throughout her life' so wrote Joachim to Gisela von Arnim (for whom he then cherished a hopeless passion) exactly ten days after Schumann's death. Clara's immediate need was nevertheless for escape. Knowing that Marie and Elise were being excellently cared for by the Preussers at Loschwitz and Julie by her grandmother in Berlin, also that the two youngest were happy enough at home with the loyal Bertha, she set out on August 14 with Ludwig and Ferdinand, together with Brahms and his none too strong twenty-five-year-old sister, Elise, for a holiday in Switzerland. She had conscientiously sent Frau Brahms a detailed list of the underwear and dresses that Elise, who had not travelled before, should bring, recommending only barest essentials to avoid heavy luggage and laundering expense. 'She will need only one hat, in preference a dark straw. She probably has a warm shawl for the journey. Don't buy her any gloves. I can give her some if she does not mind wearing washed ones. I think this is all. How glad I shall be if Elise benefits by this summer!' were her final words. Gersau, on Lake Lucerne, was their main centre. They also visited Lake Constance, the Rhine and Heidelberg.

The journey brought home the boys' urgent need of masculine supervision. Accordingly one of her first tasks on returning, discharged with a heavy heart, was to board them out in the home of a private tutor called Herchenbach. Three days later, on October 21, Brahms left too, to take up residence again with his parents in Hamburg. 'I went to the station with him – as I came back I felt as if I were returning from a funeral' was her bare diary comment. But a letter to Joachim, on September 28, sheds just a little more light on the parting. Confessing that the courage to go on living sometimes deserted her she continued: 'When you saw me at Bonn I was composed and calm to a degree I could never have believed possible, but I was entirely dominated by the thought of his peace; all sorrow vanished in gratitude that God had released him. But that could not last, and now I feel my loss more bitterly every day.' In the same letter she warned Joachim not to stay too long in Berlin with the Arnims: 'Are you not exposing yourself to unnecessary pain? . . . You wish to steel your heart to renounce a love, but you are feeding it daily. Do not exact too much from yourself, lest that noble, generous heart should succumb'. She could well have felt it her duty similarly to warn Brahms, fourteen years her junior. Even if not, as unfocused past fantasies gradually crystallized into present realities, both must have realized the total impossibility of trespassing in realms made all the more sacred by death. Already in a letter written to Clara on December 4, 1855, Brahms had hinted at renunciation to come: 'You have taught me and are every day teaching me evermore to recognize and to marvel at what love, attachment and self-denial are'. The unchallengeable proof of the intensity of his own conflict was his D minor Piano Concerto, tried over with Clara on two pianos immediately on completion, just before his departure, also the first two movements of a Piano Quartet, which on its emergence as his Op.60 in C minor some twenty years later, he admitted to his publisher had been conceived by a man akin to Goethe's Werther.

With a family of seven to support single-handed, Clara's return to the platform could not be long delayed. Between October 28 and November 5 she played in Frankfurt, Karlsruhe, Darmstadt and Göttingen (on the last occasion with Joachim) and by the end of November had sufficiently taken the bit between her teeth to return to Copenhagen, at the invitation of Gade, for a series of solo, chamber and orchestral engagements, with Schumann's Op.54 in A minor her chosen concerto. Though England had yet to be won over, her standing in Europe at this time had been summarized by Hanslick with exceptionally perceptive fairness after her first two concerts in Vienna early that year: 'She could be called the greatest living pianist rather than merely the greatest female pianist, were the range of her physical strength not limited by her sex. . . . Only he who can draw the full tone from an instrument can project the full impression, be it in the tempest of an allegro or in the long-drawn cantilena of an adagio. . . . I remember, for instance, Rubinstein or Dreyschock, whose more powerful touch, compared with Clara Schumann's, got them more compelling effects'. That admitted, he was quick to hail her as one of the most salutary programme-builders before the public, the first to stand above 'insipid trifles of virtuosity to preach the gospel of the austere German masters. And yet she did not grow stale in the one-sidedness of a single school. She made Schubert, Chopin, Schumann, and above all, Henselt available to the public at a time when the dawn of their fame had hardly risen above the musical horizon'. He also commended her unswerving determination to subordinate her own personality to the intention of the composer. 'To give a clear expression to each work in its characteristic musical style and, within this style, to its purely musical proportions and distinctions, is ever her main task. She seems to play rather to satisfy a single connoisseur than to excite a multitude of average listeners'. Of her technique he wrote 'In one or another aspect of virtuosity she may be surpassed by other players, but no other pianist stands quite as she does at the radial point of these different technical directions, focusing their respective virtues on the pure harmony of beauty. . . . If one were to express a preference for one aspect of her so excellently developed technique, it would be for the dazzling facility with which she plays delicate fast movements. She succeeds best with tender, light, graciously moving pieces'. The subtlety of her accentuation (not an 'affectation of subjective emotion' but rather a 'careful elucidation of rhythmical or harmonic contrasts') and her extreme restraint in the use of rubato were further factors differentiating her, in his eyes, from the common virtuoso run.

By January 1, 1857, she was back at the Leipzig Gewandhaus playing Mozart's D minor Concerto K.466, with cadenzas attributed in her diary to Brahms, for the first time. And before a reluctant return to England from April 21 to early July (with the average Englishman's inability to discriminate between good and bad performances and Rubinstein's untoward outbursts of keyboard violence her main diary grumbles) she had already given concerts, some of them with Joachim, in Hanover, Göttingen, Elberfeld, Barmen, Cologne and Dresden as well as Leipzig. Even on holiday by the Rhine at Oberwesel and St Goarshausen in July and August, after taking a cure at Wiesbaden, she seized the chance to learn Beethoven's Op.109 and Op.110 sonatas ('the A flat major, which used to seem to me chaotic in places, has now become quite clear'[1]) before completing her working year with visits to Dresden, Leipzig, Augsburg and Munich as well as Zurich (where she re-encountered Wagner, and played Schumann's *Etudes symphoniques* to him at his request), Berne, Basel and Winterthur. Recitals with Joachim, in a growing repertory of sonatas by Bach, Haydn, Mozart and Beethoven, were always a particular joy, such as one in Dresden in November when, as the diary put it, he played 'more beautifully and wonderfully than ever. His music often sounds like that of the spheres. I never listen to him without feeling myself really uplifted'.

After snatching a brief Christmas break with Emilie List and her sister, Frau von Pacher, both of whom now lived in Munich, she was up and away again early in 1858 to Nuremberg, Fürth, Erlangen, Karlsruhe and Stuttgart and from there on to Switzerland (where fees for visiting celebrities were as high as living and professional standards for Swiss musicians themselves were low), this time taking in Guebwiller, Geneva, Lausanne, Vevey, Zofingen, St Gallen and Schaffhausen as well as Basel

---

[1] Despite her assertion she never played this sonata in public. Nor did she risk the E major sonata, Op.109, until the 1870's, and then only rarely.

and Winterthur. Only then was there time to visit Ludwig and Ferdinand, since May, 1857, boarding at Stoy's school in Jena, and subsequently to organize some kind of family life in the light and spacious flat in Berlin to which she had moved from Düsseldorf at the end of September, 1857, installing her old friend, Elisabeth Werner, as housekeeper-governess so that Marie and Elise could live at home again.

Basically strong as she was, thanks to her father's insistence on fresh air and exercise in childhood, the strain of such a schedule inevitably now began to take its toll. In Munich towards the end of November, 1857, she had suddenly felt acute pain in her left arm,[1] diagnosed as 'rheumatic inflammation caused partly by overwork and partly by catching cold', followed by an attack of neuralgia affecting arms, neck and breast so violently that the doctor was compelled to prescribe opium for relief. Obligatory cancellation of concerts exacerbated her distress, so much so that Joachim was even moved to offer financial aid. Melancholia in her loneliness on tour was also a constant hazard, sometimes enough so to prompt Brahms to remonstrate at length: 'My dear Clara, you really must try hard to keep your melancholy within bounds and see that it does not last too long' he wrote on October 11, 1857, soon after embarking on a new three-month contract at the Court of Detmold. 'The more you endeavour to go through times of sorrow calmly and accustom yourself to do so, the more you will enjoy the happier times that are sure to follow. Why do you suppose that man was given the divine gift of hope? . . . You must seriously try to alter, my dearest Clara. . . . Passions are not natural to mankind, they are always exceptions or excrescences. The man in whom they overstep the limits should regard himself as an invalid and seek a medicine for his life and for his health. Consider yourself for the moment, my dear Clara, as a serious invalid and without necessarily being anxious, but on the contrary, with calm and perseverance, try to look after yourself'. Not long afterwards he seriously advised her to consider the offer of a salaried teaching post at the Stuttgart Conservatoire to avoid the strain of so much travelling – unaware, as yet, that nothing made her more determined to take on still more concerts than any outside suggestion that she should stop.

The summer of 1858 put heavier strains on their personal relationship, starting in June with his reproach, indignantly repudiated by her, that she too hastily and insistently forced her enthusiasm for his music on others. She was still more piqued when he intimated that he would prefer to stay at home to compose rather than join her on holiday at Göttingen (where the recently married Julius Otto Grimm now lived and worked) as with Joachim he had done the previous year at St Goarshausen. Though not

---

[1] As early as the autumn of 1841 there had been diary references to pain in her fingers.

yet six, Eugenie always remembered being dipped in the Rhine by her mother, as if in symbolic baptism, during that hot summer of 1857 – just as she never forgot a game of hide-and-seek in Göttingen in 1858 when Clara, dressed in a white muslin dress with black sprigs and a broad black sash, tripped and fell headlong as she rushed from concealment in a thick green asparagus bed towards the tree which was 'home'. The accident proved prophetic. After morning work and afternoon relaxation with the children, evenings were nearly always spent in communal music-making, for which they were sometimes joined by a 'not bad' local string quartet or choral group, and still more often by the Grimms's friend, Agathe Siebold, daughter of a professor at the University with a contralto voice likened by Joachim to the tone of an Amati violin. When Brahms eventually arrived he was nonplussed to find himself in the company of this high-spirited girl of his own age, eager to sing his newest songs, sharing his love of the open air, and obviously strongly drawn to him at sight. Sensing that the attraction was mutual and much encouraged by the Grimms, Clara was woman enough to find the situation unbearable. After sending the children back to Berlin she made her own escape to Düsseldorf. The full trauma of the experience is plain from her letter to her old friend, Emilie List, written from Budapest in mid-November: 'Do not lay it to my charge that I have been silent so long; I have had a bad summer, and in September, when I spent four weeks in Düsseldorf with Frl. Leser, my nerves were still in such a wretched condition that I could do nothing. But since the beginning of November I have felt a little stronger, and so you see me once more on my wanderings'. Writing from Vienna on December 9 to Joachim (unable to get leave of absence from the King of Hanover to join her in projected recitals) she confessed to a total breakdown of self-confidence: 'Just imagine, I cannot give a single concert at which I do not play one piece after the other in an agony of terror because my memory threatens to fail me, and this fear torments me for days beforehand. After my last concert in Pest I completely lost my head in two pieces, and my thoughts were so confused that I had to summon my last atom of strength to prevent myself from stopping altogether. After experiences like these you can imagine the state of mind I was in when I gave my concert here. After the first piece I had such a fit of crying that it was a long time before I was myself again. But I think it would be better if you were with me; apart from the artistic benefit it would be balm to my heart, which is so terribly lonely. Ah, my dear Joachim, my art must soon come to an end, for even if my physical strength should suffice, my mind is weakened and my heart seems broken. If only I knew that I would find my Robert again!'

As if to distance herself from Brahms and developments she deemed inevitable, she remained in Vienna until the end of February, 1859, giving at least three private lessons most mornings before getting down to her own practice and personal engagements. She was much comforted to discover how Schumann's music had begun to capture popular imagination. By now she frequently played *Carnaval*, nearly always including a special introductory note in the printed programme to explain its curious genesis, yet invariably omitting 'Estrella' (a portrait of her erstwhile rival, Ernestine von Fricken) as well as 'Eusebius' and 'Florestan' (Schumann's own two Davidsbund pseudonyms) and 'Coquette' and 'Réplique'. On February 12 she gave one of her as yet rare performances of the G minor sonata, Op.22. But she still had doubts about *Kreisleriana*: 'They seem so unsuitable for a concert. However, I must give way, for Spina tells me I shall attract bigger crowds if I play them. But I shall have to make a selection; it would never do to play them all'. (At her concert in Vienna on January 2, 1859, she in fact only omitted numbers 3 and 6 from the eight pieces. As time went on she far more often restricted her selection just to five pieces, and later to four, never on any occasion including No. 3, even though rivals such as Anton Rubinstein risked the whole work.)

Though too busy for much theatre or gallery going, she nevertheless found time to renew acquaintance with Meyerbeer's *Les Huguenots* ('quite immoral music') and to see *Lohengrin* for the first time. 'Full of romanticism and thrilling situations' she wrote of the latter, 'so much so that even the musician himself at times forgets the horrible music. Nevertheless on the whole I like *Lohengrin* better than *Tannhäuser*, in which Wagner goes through the whole gamut of abominations. They told me in Prague about the music of *Tristan and Isolde*. Apparently it is even worse than what has gone before, if that were possible'.

Despite strained personal relations, she had recently introduced Brahms's new Hungarian Dances to both Budapest and Vienna (perversely with more success in Austria); and no one was more genuinely shocked than she that Leipzigers had dared to hiss his D minor Concerto when he introduced it to that city on January 27, 1859. He in his turn still took it as a matter of course that his every new work should first go to her for criticism, a challenge to which she always responded with time-consuming thoroughness and honesty even if her judgement often reflected her own exaggerated respect for orthodoxy. When she returned to Berlin, via Prague, to spend Easter with her children, Brahms even joined them for a week before she left again on April 25 for England.

Her major engagement this visit was Beethoven's fourth Concerto for the Philharmonic Society on June 27. To please her father she had brought her half-sister, Marie, across the channel too, partnering her in Schumann's Variations for two pianos at the Queen's Rooms on May 7 to introduce her to London. (In Germany they frequently played together.) She also shared in three matinées with Joachim and their mutual friend, Stockhausen. But despite this baritone's acutely sensitive mood and word painting in Lieder (not yet widely appreciated in London) and Joachim's phenomenal popularity with the English, box-office receipts were slender. Joachim's own incessant activity gave her more than a few qualms, no least his frequent appearances with Arabella Goddard (who, still only 23 had already introduced all Beethoven's late piano sonatas to London), and perhaps even more his growing intimacy with Arabella's erstwhile teacher and very recent husband, none other than *The Times* critic, J. W. Davison still mercilessly biased against Schumann. Nevertheless, discovery of the green English countryside and its parks and trees proved balm enough. As for Windsor Castle, the sight of it made her feel she had lived through the whole of Shakespeare.

Stays in Düsseldorf (where her old friend Eduard Bendemann had recently been made Director of the Academy), Kreuznach, Wildbad and then Honnef and Mehlem with Marie and Elise (who needed eye treatment in Kreuznach) brought much-needed summer relaxation. But the increasing expense of the children's education and upkeep (with yet another move from Jena to Dr Breusing's school in Bonn for Ferdinand and the unsettled Ludwig) prompted a hectic winter's work principally in Aix la Chapelle, Cologne, Bonn, Bremen, Düsseldorf and Celle before a brief family reunion at Christmas, and then in 1860 on to Hanover, Cassel Braunschweig and Düsseldorf before a further Dutch tour, with Elise a. companion, taking in Utrecht (where this time torchlight serenade organized by students in her honour aroused nothing but reflections on the hollowness of fame), Amsterdam, Rotterdam and the Hague. Her melancholy, always so much more easily roused than joy, was considerably increased in Holland by renewed pain in one of her fingers. She was also much distressed by news of the death of Schröder-Devrient (whose Leonore in Beethoven's *Fidelio* had been one of the greatest operatic experiences of her life), all the more by reason of the fact that her own recent, sharp condemnation of this great singer's wish, despite declining powers, to return to the platform in further shared recitals, such as they had given in Dresden and Leipzig in the winter of 1848–9, had completely estranged them. From Holland she travelled to Vienna, now with Marie for a series of concerts in March and April in the course of which she not only introduced Schumann's *Faschingsschwank aus Wien* and ten numbers from the *Davidsbündlertänze* (as with *Kreisleriana* she favoured a selection rather than risking the complete work) but on March 8 also took part in the first public performance of her own G minor Piano Trio.

Back in Germany, a pleasant reunion with her father after a concert in Leipzig was quickly eclipsed by relief in rapprochement with Brahms, by now aware that he neither loved Agathe enough to sacrifice his own freedom – nor to risk any further loosening of links with the cherished past. He did not escape Clara's reproaches for hurting the girl by allowing the affair to go so far. But resolving to try and feign indifference to his occasional fits of ill-humour she gladly accepted his invitation to Hamburg for his twenty-seventh birthday; at the end of her stay she left with a golden memory of a steamer excursion with his cherished, recently-formed Ladies' Choir to Blankenese, where on arrival they 'sought out the most beautiful trees in the garden and sang under them, Johannes sitting on a branch to conduct'. As a further gesture to both Brahms and Joachim at this time she also offered to sign the manifesto they had prepared in condemnation of the principles of the so-called New German School of Liszt and Wagner, though in the event its unintended premature publication in the *Berlin Echo* totally wrecked its efficacy.

The summer of 1860 brought respite in Düsseldorf and Bonn with Brahms, Joachim, Stockhausen and her sympathetic half-brother, Woldemar Bargiel (a composer and professor at the Cologne Conservatoire whose keyboard miniatures she sometimes played) before she was joined by all the children at Kreuznach, selected for its remedial waters. The cost of her treatment here was almost covered by her recital at the start of the visit, for which Marie, Elise and Julie insisted on selling the tickets themselves rather than allow the local music shop to claim commission. Eugenie always remembered this particular holiday for the sweltering day Stockhausen joined them for a row on the Nahe dressed in a thick fur coat 'to keep out the heat'. Clara herself had the odd experience of suddenly finding a diamond, mislaid for a week, nestling in a bowl of sugar from which she was then helping herself. 'Afterwards I had to think of all the ways in which I could possibly have lost it a second time!!!!' was her uncommonly jocular comment to Brahms. Saying goodbye to her two youngest children was a greater wrench than ever, particularly Felix, who, now six, was already strongly drawn to the violin. She was deeply touched when at Christmas of that year Joachim wrote to offer his Guarnerius (silent since 1850 when he had acquired a Stradivarius) to the 'little fiddler' he would so much like to have had as his godchild.

It was with Joachim that she had started that autumn season, warning him in advance that she was 'sticking' in every piece in sheer fright at the thought of facing the public again. 'It is nothing new to me that you have completely forgotten how to play the piano; I have heard that too often from you before, and I satisfied myself of the truth of it at Kreuznach, when you played the Bach Suites and the Beethoven sonatas! That comes of walking over Eberburg and Rheingrafenstein instead of diligently practising finger exercises!' was his teasing reply, adding 'incidentally the same thing happens to me at the beginning of *every* winter; I can never understand how I shall ever be able to stand in front of so many people without sinking through the ground with shame if I think of it *beforehand*. And for that reason one must not think of it; it goes all right at the time,

because the music makes one forget all that nonsense!' The arduousness
of her schedule for the start of 1861, including one or more visits to
Barmen, Cologne, Hamburg, Altona, Hanover, Osnabrück, Detmold
and Düsseldorf and then on to Belgium for concerts in Antwerp, Liege,
Mons, Bruges, Ghent and Brussels, nevertheless sufficiently alarmed
Brahms for him again to beg her to spare herself such excessive strain.
Her reply from Detmold in February was merely to remind him of the
cost of feeding, clothing and educating seven children. Necessity was
in fact constantly sharpening the commercial instincts implanted long ago
by her father. That same letter to Brahms ended in amused indignation at
underpayment for appearances at the Detmold Court, the more since a
bracelet given her by the Princess was so hideous that she could only
assume it to be one discarded in youth. When subsequently asked by
Stockhausen if she would like to play to the Grand Duchess Hélène of
Russia in Baden-Baden her retort was for what fee, since, as she added, 'I
am not after any honours at the hands of these grandees'. But in May she
immediately declined a second offer of a handsomely paid American tour
so as not to be too far from the children. Besides the constant worry of
Julie's delicate health, Ludwig's mental backwardness and bursts of
recalcitrance had even compelled her to send him off to a country parson
for personal tutoring and supervision while Ferdinand proceeded nor-
mally to the Joachimsthaler College in Berlin.

After a lonely, melancholic month at Spa, in Belgium, seeking treatment for rheumatism, and then a summer holiday with an assortment of
family and musical friends divided between Kreuznach and Switzerland,
the autumn of 1861 brought a surprise offer from the King of Hanover
(who earlier that year had sent her 1000 thalers for past performances with
Joachim) of a resident post at the Court, to teach the princesses, for an
initial period of six months. But despite a frequently expressed wish to be
able to settle in the same city as Brahms or Joachim, her refusal was just as
firm as in the context of Stuttgart a few years before. 'I cannot yet accept
such a position, I am conscious of too much power and vigour, too much
capability for performing in public' was how she justified her decision on
November 3 to Marie, who, considerably more mature than her mere
twenty years, had just assumed responsibility for the new Berlin flat and
the younger children in succession to Elisabeth Werner.

Having tried out Mozart's A major and G major Concertos[1] while in
Detmold (in response to Brahms's enthusiasm for these works) and learnt
Mozart's C minor Concerto, K.491, to perform for the first time at
Hanover on November 23, she now followed up Brahms's own Hungarian
Dances and Ballades, Op.10, with his brand new Handel Variations,

---

[1] Presumably K.414 and K.453

Op.24 (written in secret for her birthday), his G minor Piano Quartet, Op.25, and last but not least, his D minor Piano Concerto. With Bremen, Hanover, Oldenburg, Hamburg and Leipzig her main ports of call on this new winter season, nothing gave her deeper satisfaction than playing the D minor Concerto for the first time under his own baton in Hamburg on December 3 even though the public 'understood nothing and felt nothing'. The Variations, on the other hand, were warmly applauded both in Hamburg ('Johannes, however, hurt me very much by his indifference') and when she repeated them in Leipzig before returning to Berlin for a family Christmas.

1862 started strenuously with engagements taking her from Düsseldorf, Cologne, Bonn, Frankfurt and Karlsruhe to Switzerland, where she was joined in some recitals by Stockhausen. That in Zurich on February 22 was notable for their first public performance together of Schumann's *Dichterliebe* cycle complete, given, as on many subsequent occasions, in two parts separated by a group of piano solos (on this night she chose three numbers from *Kreisleriana*). At Basel on February 24 Stockhausen's delight in Schumann's songs even led him to make a selection from the *Frauenliebe und -Leben* cycle. The tour was nevertheless overshadowed by yet more pains in her right arm thought by her to be rheumatic, the result of leaning out of a window on this arm. The possibility that weighty works by Brahms might have strained muscles already assessed by both Hanslick and Davison as not of the strongest had not yet occurred to her, though she admitted to Marie that his Handel Variations were 'frightfully difficult'. Her displeasure with her old friend at this moment was of a different kind: when writing to him at the end of January she made no secret of her bitter disappointment that he had failed to join her in Cologne for the first performance ever of her husband's *Faust* in its entirety, under Hiller, which she attended with her arm in a sling. Whatever the effort, she rarely missed any revivals of Schumann's major rarities, such as his *Mass* at Aix la Chapelle in July, 1861, when her earlier qualms about allowing its publication were at once overcome.

The climax of the season was a hastily planned visit, with Marie, to Paris, where for most of March and April they stayed in a hotel as guests of Mme Erard, who also presented Clara with a splendid new piano. Soirées (with Schumann's works now in special demand) and private lessons augmented her income to such an extent that she was delightedly able to dismiss all thoughts of going on to London where, as she put it, 'they hold me in no higher esteem than any mechanic'. After playing the 'Emperor' at the Conservatoire on April 6 she could even write to Brahms: 'Except in Vienna I have never had such a reception anywhere'.

Visiting Rossini (whom at 70 she found eccentric but amusing) and his wife ('something of a vixen') proved among the highlights of her tight-packed social round, so did reunion with her old friend Pauline Viardot, who at forty-one, with Paris at her feet after recent performances of Gluck's *Orphée* and *Alceste* (the latter seen by Clara) was already contemplating semi-retirement in Baden-Baden to escape the imperial régime of Napoleon III so repugnant to her liberal-thinking, French impresario husband. But that they lived in different worlds became clearer than ever to Clara after dining in their sparkling, sophisticated home. As she wrote in the diary: 'There is always a sense of restlessness. Callers drop in every minute, or she suddenly remembers that she has a letter to write, and then one sits for hours without having got any pleasure from her or from others. A life like that would not suit me'. Old ties nevertheless triumphed. She was delighted to have Pauline (who at one time had taken piano lessons from Liszt) as her partner in a public performance of Schumann's Variations for two pianos (they had previously played it together in Pest in November, 1858). And it was with Pauline that Clara went on from Paris to Brussels to appear at a highly remunerative, fashionable soirée, in the house of a certain Mme Orloff, again with the Variations in their programme.

On her return, a sudden urge to see her father prompted another surprise visit to Dresden. 'He is untirable, a veritable teaching genius' so she wrote after hearing some of his pupils. 'I am so glad to be with my father, he is in such good spirits and I am so fond of him that my heart always leaps for joy when I see him although our characters are not at all in harmony'. The summer holiday in its turn brought happy reunions with the children and a succession of old friends in Kreuznach, Münster am Stein (both had thermal waters), Switzerland – and most important of all, in the Viardots' much praised Baden-Baden. For Clara, this visit was a revelation. Why maintain a Berlin flat that she scarcely ever saw in the winter, and in the summer wander from resort to resort, with her family rarely complete because of the expense, when she could have a summer home of her own near Pauline? Seeing a property that attracted her she immediately made an offer. By early November, Lichtenthal No. 14 was hers, purchased for 14,000 florins, though another hectic winter of travel, including Frankfurt, Hamburg, Hanover, Leipzig, Dresden and Breslau before a Berlin Christmas and then a cold and stormy migraine-and-cramp-ridden tour of Holland, still stood between her and her haven.

February, 1863, brought the warming news of Joachim's engagement to Amalie Weiss, an opera singer of 23 'with a contralto voice which you only need to hear in order to know the depth and purity of her nature' as he put it to Clara just four months before their June wedding. By then Clara herself had already enjoyed the first month of a new mode of life which for the next decade was to bring her more solace than anything experienced since her husband's breakdown.

FOURTEEN

At Home and Abroad: 1863–73

1. 'Mother Klara' in Baden

At that time Baden-Baden was a highly fashionable spa. Apart from its famous remedial waters for both bathing and drinking, it could boast legally authorized roulette at the Casino, lively music-making at the elegantly decorated Kurhaus and abundant shooting and hunting in the beautiful adjoining Black Forest countryside to lure an unending succession of the wealthy, distinguished and aristocratic – including many of Europe's crowned heads. Situated in the outlying district of Lichtenthal close to pine-wooded hills, Clara's home was separated only by its own shady garden and the little river Oos from the stately, tree-lined avenue where the elegant took their daily promenades. Originally a farmhouse with an attached barn, it looked unprepossessing enough from its village approach the other side for the children at first to nickname it 'the kennel'. But conversion had made its interior surprisingly spacious, with bedrooms for all, and living rooms able to accommodate three grand pianos – like her father Clara mistrusted uprights. There was always an Erard or Broadwood in the light and airy grey-and-gold-flecked drawing room with its plaster casts of the Apollo of Belvedere and the Venus of Milo, its life-size Sohn painting of Clara (her Christmas present to Robert in 1853) and its row of windows overlooking the vine-covered verandah where above all else she liked to sit with the children or friends and watch the world go by. Dry rot in the dining room caused momentary panic early in 1865. Otherwise it wound itself round her heart as 'the most beautiful little spot in the world'.

Right from the start everything was strictly organized, with the older girls, who arrived ahead in April, 1863, to take charge of furniture installation, sharing all lighter domestic duties harmful to Clara's hands. Marie also supervised the cook, Josephine, and their frugal but wholesome meals, besides making most of the children's clothes (often out of material brought back by their mother from London) and keeping an eye on the large wardrobe room where 'innumerable pretty summer dresses, freshly washed and starched' always hung. Clara loved them to look nice, not least when, as so often, all dressed alike. Marie, Elise and Julie, taught by her personally, were also expected to take charge of the younger ones at

the piano until they were advanced enough for her own help. 'Make use of
minutes' was her constant admonition to them all, whether in music or
their general studies, their afternoon needlework (she herself liked to
crochet bedspreads until fear of stiffening her muscles compelled her to
stop), or on their walks – often taken *en famille* after her daily influx of
4 p.m. coffee guests had left.

Outdoor breakfast in the arbour was one of Clara's special pleasures, and
she loved to remain there talking to old friends like Fräulein Leser and her
companion, who soon became regular lodgers at the retired clergyman's
house next door, or dealing with her copious correspondence, until the
time came to practise. Though always allowing herself a period of
complete rest after the strains of the winter, she rarely relaxed for long.
Eugenie subsequently recalled what they used to hear: 'Scales rolled and
swelled like a tidal sea, legato and staccato; in octaves, thirds, sixths,
tenths and double thirds; sometimes in one hand only while the other
played accompanying chords. Then arpeggios of all kinds, octaves,
shakes, everything prestissimo and without the slightest break, exquisite
modulations leading from key to key. The most wonderful feature of this
practising was that although the principle on which it was based was
always the same, it was new every day, and seemed drawn ever fresh from
a mysterious wellspring. . . . We often pressed Mamma to write down the
sequence of an hour's exercises, but she always said it was impossible to
retain exactly this kind of free fantasia'. After following exercises with
Czerny's *Toccata*, Op.92, always a special favourite of her father's as a
piece to be conquered and played daily to instil confidence, she invariably
turned to Bach, and then to Schumann's *Toccata* and Studies by Chopin,
mostly all from memory, before approaching new works to be learnt. 'We
never disturbed Mamma without good cause when she was at the piano,
but we knew that we might come in at any time, and that she even liked it.
She always gave us a kind glance whenever we entered the room. I used to
wonder at the time that she could go on playing so unconcernedly while
she talked to us of other things. While she played scales she would often
read letters open on the desk in front of her'.

While revering their mother as a famous pianist, it was nevertheless not
for musical reasons that Lichtenthal No.14 came to mean so much to all
the children. They had accepted her return to the platform without
question, not only understanding her abhorrence of charity and determination to support them all single-handed, but intuitively realizing that
concert-giving was her lifeline. Yet boarded out in their separate schools
or families, or looked after by strangers in this or that temporarily rented
home, they all in their different ways had secretly yearned to be together
again as a family, under the shelter of a warm maternal wing.

For the capable, thoughtful, good-humoured Marie, a splendid pianist and musician whose occasional bursts of 'furor teutonicus' (as Eugenie described it) were short-lived, the sense of deprivation had not been too acute. She could still recall happy days with her father, and because the eldest had also remained more intimately in touch with her mother, both as help-mate in the home and travelling companion, than the rest. By 1863 Clara could confide in her as in a sister, and her gratitude for such a relationship knew no bounds. Elise, impulsively resourceful, high-spirited and frank, likewise had sunny childhood memories to sustain her as well as a healthy self-confidence and spirit of independence. Resolving in the autumn of 1865, when still only 22, to set up as a piano teacher in Frankfurt, within a year she had more pupils than she could take. Clara overflowed with pride when on October 31, 1865, Elise joined her in that city in a public performance of Schumann's Variations for two pianos: 'I could not overcome my emotion when I thought what a fine début this was for Elise to play a duet by her father with me at a concert with Joachim. If only he had been able to witness it, how lovingly his eyes would have rested on her'. To be able to describe her at this time as 'dependable, and true as steel', was a joy. For in the letter Clara had written to all the children at the time of their father's death she had felt obliged to single out Elise, at the age of 13, as the one who most needed to try to improve her behaviour.

Even in earliest childhood as sensitive as she was frail, Julie had always needed the intimate care that Clara, after Schumann's death, had rarely been free to provide. From her grandmother she had gone from one friend to another, in the winter of 1862–3 even being sent off to Nice, followed by long stays in Divonne, Venice and elsewhere, because of her cough, her anaemia and general physical inability to stand up to any undue emotional stress. Her delight in the new family home showed itself in countless little loving acts like making her mother's morning chocolate, or putting fresh flowers by family portraits on special anniversaries – as also in unpredictable outbursts of irrepressible gaiety such as making rude faces at staring Italian operatic celebrities in the house across the road. Confessing that Julie's enthusiasms often made her feel like a girl again herself, Clara seized the chance to try and improve her French with Julie on her return from France. But they grew closest in the summer of 1869 while Julie awaited the public announcement of her engagement to Count Victor Radicati di Marmorito, an Italian Catholic widower with two young daughters and many family problems to resolve before re-marriage was possible. 'As merry and dear as ever' so Clara described her that May. 'There is a charm about her that is irresistible and at the same time she has depth of feeling which draws one to her'. No one was more affected by the eventual announcement of the betrothal than Brahms, who to Clara seemed 'quite altered . . . he seldom comes to the house and speaks only in monosyllables when he does come. And he treats Julie in the same manner, though he always used to be so specially nice to her. Did he really love her?' Six months after Julie's marriage at the Catholic Church in Lichtenthal that September,[1] Clara was overjoyed when Broadwoods in London gave her a boudoir grand to send to Julie in Turin; she forewarned Julie of its arrival by asking an artist friend to paint a little picture of a piano being carried through the air by four Muses, which she posted with a special little birthday poem written by Marie.

Of all the children, the most deeply affected, silent sufferer in isolation had always been Ludwig, in 1863 already fifteen, and more like his mother in features and colouring than any of the others. In his dark brown eyes, with their expression of sweetness and faithfulness, Eugenie prophetically recognized 'a deep pathos such as I have never seen in any human being'. Passionately devoted to his family, he nevertheless sometimes seemed to them as if possessed by a strange evil spirit making him 'blind and deaf to every warning, to all our love and entreaties' as Eugenie put it. By 1865, after he had left his country parson for a further unsettled spell at the Karlsruhe Grammar School, Clara decided to apprentice him to a bookseller in that city, where his uncontrollable oddities frequently upset his motherly landlady, Frau Wills. Unpunctuality and lack of application soon lost him this job – and others secured through kind friends in both Berlin and Leipzig. Ignoring Raimund Härtel's warning in May 1868 that Ludwig's mind was affected, Clara lavished hours on him in Baden that summer to encourage his sudden new enthusiasm for music even though aware that he had no ear, no sense of rhythm, and no creative originality; when the holiday was over she sent him to Dresden to continue his studies under the watchful eye of her father. Not till May, 1870, did she broken-heartedly concede that he was unmanageable enough to need the care of an asylum. 'I have not felt such pain as this since Robert's tragedy' she wrote, confessing that nights were always the worst for her since 'I used to see the poor boy before me for hours together, looking at me with his good, honest eyes which I never knew how to resist'.

Ferdinand, in contrast, was the perfect schoolboy son, who having celebrated his fourteenth birthday during that first Lichtenthal summer, could write to Eugenie from his school in Berlin that he was 'getting on splendidly . . . almost always top of my form. I had another prize on the anniversary of the Battle of Leipzig, October 18; that is my third'. Leaving with flying colours in 1866 he was at once apprenticed (through the influence of the Mendelssohn family) to Plaut's bank in Berlin, where to Clara's deep satisfaction, his industry and correctness were as unfailing as his love for his family, notably little Eugenie and Felix among his brothers

---

[1] On the wedding eve there was a merry gathering of friends, with music-making including Haydn's Toy Symphony.

and sisters, but above all for his mother. Music, particularly playing the piano, was his main hobby, and being allowed to go from school in Bonn to Clara's Cologne concert on February 19, 1861 – the very first time he had ever heard her in public – had proved unforgettable. Though unreservedly bemoaning their constant separation, he lived only to shield her from all heartache and anxiety.

At the end of their first, idyllic Baden summer, Eugenie, nearly twelve, was despatched to a strongly recommended but inhumanly spartan boarding school near Frankfurt, where she frequently cried herself to sleep. The headmistress, Fräulein Hillebrand, allowed her only one week's holiday with her family in the summer of 1864, and the following year no more than a month. Not till 1866 did Clara realize the full extent of her misery, at once moving her to a smaller, kinder, Fröbel-principled school near Wolfenbüttel until she was ready to become a piano student, under Clara's old pupil, Ernst Rudorff, at Joachim's newly established Berlin College of Music in 1869. Because of long separation both mother and daughter felt a certain constraint in each other's company until Eugenie's later teens, though Clara, always so sad when small requested luxuries had to be refused, regularly wrote her long, loving letters at school to help her overcome temperamental problems, such as brusqueness and impatience, growing from early unhappiness. 'Real religious feeling seems to me to consist chiefly in constant, constant work at ourselves, to make ourselves better and better, to live as much as possible for the good and benefit of others, to be kind to everyone with whom we come in contact' was her counsel to Eugenie at sixteen.

Like Eugenie, in the autumn of 1863 the nine-years-old Felix was sent off as a boarder for the first time, though with his brother, Ferdinand, to keep an eye on him at Berlin's Joachimsthaler College, his strain was not so great. Struggle as she always did to show no favouritism, Clara's pride and joy in her 'much beloved Lix' knew no bounds. The other children recognized it but felt no resentment because he was their own idol too. His good looks and charm, his intuitive response to music and literature and his general maturity of perception, even his inclination to extravagance of imagery in letter-writing (sometimes eliciting a gentle reproof from his mother) no less than of expenditure on dress, all these characteristics increasingly made him a reincarnation of his father as a teenager. Bent on joining Eugenie at the Berlin College of Music in the mistaken belief that he could become a second Joachim, he at first resisted his mother's insistence on a full-time classical grounding at school. But once embarked on legal studies at his father's old University in Heidelberg, he knew that Clara had been right in persuading him to keep music as a hobby; as time went on, literature and poetry in fact came to matter to him much more. As he once put it

'Twould become me ill
To live on my father's fame.
Myself to make me a name,
That is my will'.

Even as a schoolboy, begging in fear and trembling, after recent self-indulgence, for the railway fare to come back for yet another cherished Baden summer, he saw into his mother's soul with adult understanding. 'You never talk about religion, do not often go to church or observe outward forms of that kind, but what need for that?' he wrote at fifteen. 'It is in actions that true character reveals itself, and as far as my small understanding can measure your actions they inspire me with deep admiration, respect, love, and the zeal to show myself worthy of such a mother'. But as with Julie, so with her youngest son Clara had one constant, nagging, secret anxiety: she was acutely aware of his very delicate health.

The children always remembered Lichtenthal 14 as full of visitors. By September, 1867, the strain of entertaining at meals had in fact become excessive enough for Clara to resolve 'to play at my own house every Wednesday. It will enable me to repay many social obligations which I cannot do by inviting people in return – too many people are coming here'. Of closer friends, no one's presence was more taken for granted than Brahms. Lodging at the nearby 'Bär' hotel on shorter visits, or on prolonged stays often taking rooms with a Frau Becker whose house was out in the hills where he so much loved to walk in the woods at crack of dawn to watch the sunrise, he nearly always joined Clara for afternoon coffee on the balcony, and frequently returned later for his evening meal in the certain knowledge that he would find a place set for him at table on her right. In 1867 and 1868 he nevertheless sometimes found that privilege withdrawn. When deeply immersed in work – and already a symphony in C minor was fermenting in his mind – he took too little account of her hyper-sensitivity, her over-readiness to take offence at a difficult time of her life, particularly with his well-meant urgings to reduce her concert activity; this always led to ructions with the children, who hated to see their mother hurt. She in her turn often made things worse by failing to appreciate when he was teasing her, as he often did, or with incessant admonishments to find a nice, well-to-do young wife to warm and soften him. But respect for his achievement almost always overrode dissent, and never more so than on Good Friday, 1868, when his German Requiem had its first performance in Bremen. To her recent claim (after converting Brussels to Robert's Concerto) that despite the appalling strain of travel she was playing with greater technical and spiritual mastery than ever, he, horrified at her toil, had replied that her supposed strength could well be mere 'self deception and habit', so incensing her that it was only the cajolings of friends that persuaded her to make the journey to Bremen at all. But once there, an intuitive awareness that it was the great turning point in Brahms's career was all that mattered. As she put it: 'The *Requiem* has taken hold of me as no sacred music ever did before. . . . As I saw Johannes standing there, baton in hand, I could not help thinking of my dear Robert's prophecy, "Let him but once grasp the magic wand and work with orchestra and chorus", which is fulfilled today. . . . It was a joy such as I have not felt for a long time. After the performance there was a supper in the Rathskeller, at which everyone was jubilant – it was like a music festival. . . . Reinthaler made a speech about Johannes which so moved me that (unfortunately!!!) I burst into tears'.

She was no less moved by Brahms's *Alto Rhapsody*, written as outlet for indefinable, unassuaged longings at the time of Julie's wedding the following year. His every new chamber work of course went into her repertory almost before its ink was dry, with the Horn Trio of 1866, conceived in the Baden woods, a special favourite. She herself had played an important part in what in 1864 emerged as his F minor Piano Quintet, Op.34,[1] by persuading him that he had sacrificed too much when recasting the original string quintet version as a sonata for two pianos – tried out by her in Baden in 1863 with Anton Rubinstein and Hermann Levi and later with Brahms himself. That the second movement of his G minor Piano Quartet, allegedly inspired by memories of her, was eventually published with the title 'Intermezzo' instead of the original 'Scherzo' was also her doing, though he wisely ignored her over-academic strictures about the first movement's excess of dominant tonality, just as he did her request to compress his Paganini Variations of 1863 (which in their 'curious ramifications and piquant turns' she thought too complex for the general public) from two books into one, also her condemnation of the second subject in the finale of the F minor Piano Quintet as having no 'real swing'.

Another frequent visitor to Lichtenthal No.14 was Hermann Levi, conductor of the nearby Karlsruhe Court Theatre, whose opera company regularly performed at Baden's Kurhaus during the season. Only two years older than Marie, he was a great favourite with the younger children by reason of *joie-de-vivre* that often found outlet in schoolboy pranks, such as hiding in one of Clara's empty travelling trunks and suddenly bursting into Beethoven's 'O Freunde' (from the Choral Symphony) to startle Brahms, or making his large St Bernard dog, Scamp, tipsy on champagne – often brought by him to their house for special celebrations.

---

[1] It was prompting from Clara that led the admiring dedicatee, Princess Anna of Hesse, to express her thanks by presenting Brahms with the manuscript of Mozart's G minor symphony.

Levi's kindness to Ludwig in Karlsruhe particularly touched Clara's heart. The serious-minded engraver, Julius Allgeyer, often accompanied Brahms and Levi, also the painter, Anselm Feuerbach, whose modest, almost childlike manner, Clara found immediately appealing. Renting a summer villa in Baden, the celebrated Anton Rubinstein (in 1863 still only thirty-three) constantly came and went, thrilling and horrifying Clara in turn with his consummate artistry and unpredictable storming. Old friends like Joachim and Stockhausen with their respective wives, the Florentine and Becker String Quartets, the sardonically disappointed composer Theodor Kirchner (a lesser Schumann disciple then working in Switzerland whose keyboard miniatures Clara did so much to popularize), and the pianist-composer Jakob Rosenhain and his wife (nicknamed 'the Lilliputians' by Julie and 'the Hebrews from the Falkensteg' by the locals) who had made Baden their permanent home, were among others always assured of an especially warm welcome. With favourite visitors there were excursions to such local beauty spots as the Old Castle, the Yburg, Ebersteinschloss and Gernsbach that the children never forgot.

Relations with the Viardots were always cordial. Never a summer passed without at least one Baden concert bringing Pauline and Clara together on the same platform. But even more keenly than in Paris Clara now realized that her girlhood friend lived in a very different, cosmopolitan world. The distinguished Russian writer, Turgenev, had built a villa near the Viardots' own very spacious home; adoring Pauline ever since teaching her Russian when he was 25 and she only 22 (though already four years married to a man twenty-one years her senior) Turgenev was never far from her side. Not just Pauline's three talented daughters and young son Paul but a constant stream of pupils from all over Europe kept the household vibrant with youthful activity ('in her house everything is as merry as if there were no sorrow in the world' so Clara wrote), while her own fame, intelligence, elegance and charm combined to make even Baden's visiting international royalty feel it an honour to be invited to her parties.

Strive as she always did to control baser feeling, Clara was human enough to be piqued at the time of Pauline's official house-warmings at the end of October, 1864. As she put it to Brahms: 'Madame Viardot consecrated her Palace of Arts (as she calls it) the other day, and to the first ceremony she invited high society (the Queen of Prussia etc.) when she naturally did not want me; and afterwards she had a reception for the populace for which I was considered good enough'. Contributing a Beethoven sonata to a mixed entertainment ending with Pauline's own tasteless arrangement of the Bach-Gounod prelude for organ, harp, violins and three women's voices 'bawling unisono', Clara left the house 'bristling with indignation' and went off on her winter travels without saying goodbye. She was all the more sore because of the splendid organ 'the Viardot woman' (who could not yet play the pedals) had been able to afford for her music-room. 'Oh why can't I have such an organ? How sacred it would be to me!' she continued to Brahms. 'And if you came and played on it for me, what music for the gods we should have then! I have often wondered whether I ought not to go to America, where I should immediately earn enough to purchase such an organ'.

At heart Clara was nevertheless too honest, too loyal, too good, to remain bitter for long. Her very genuine admiration for Pauline's extraordinary versatility reached its peak in 1867 after hearing three little operettas composed by Pauline to librettos by Turgenev, *Trop de Femmes*, *L'Ogre* and *Le Dernier Sorcier*, for her children and her pupils to perform either in his miniature garden theatre or her converted music-room. 'I have heard each of them three times, and always with equal pleasure' she wrote to Brahms that October. 'It is all so cleverly written, so dainty, so light, so finished, and with all that so full of humour – it really is wonderful. The libretti are by Turgenev, who is also taking part. And she has not yet copied it out properly; she just plays from loose sheets. And how she has taught them! The children are fascinating and the boy (Paul) really has a genius for comedy. Throughout the accompaniments one divines the instrumentation – in short, I found fresh confirmation of what I have already said, that she is the most gifted woman I have ever known. When I saw her sitting at the piano and managing everything with such perfect ease, my heart melted within me, and I could have clasped her in my arms'.

Opportunities for doing so were to prove all too brief. Though so bitterly opposed to the Second Empire and Napoleon III, the Viardots were still French in nationality: when in the summer of 1870, after long-gathering storm-clouds, the Franco-Prussian war eventually broke, their conflict was sufficiently acute to drive them to seek refuge in London that autumn. It was a dark summer for Clara, too, for just having consigned Ludwig to an asylum she learned in July of Ferdinand's call-up for army training. Alarmed because Baden-Baden was so near the border, and by a breakdown in transport that prevented Brahms from keeping his promise to come and shield them from dreaded invaders (particularly the Algerians) Clara at first thought of evacuating to a safer spot. But concern that her beloved home, if empty, might be commandeered as a billet finally persuaded her to stay, albeit with all her personal valuables, and even her choicest wines, hidden away in the cellar, while with other Baden ladies she spent her days making bandages and comforts for the wounded. Once the battle for Strasbourg began, gunfire shook her walls. From high vantage points such as the Old Castle they could even see some of the fighting, causing her heart to bleed for Germans and French alike as she envisaged what lay in wait for her own son, sent into action soon after the great victory of Metz. But pride in the King of Prussia and his each successive triumph, most of all at Sedan, overflowed on every page of her diary. Like friends and neighbours who had remained, she decorated her house with flags. And when Strasbourg eventually surrendered on September 29, she allowed Levi to take her and the children who were at home by train to see that scarred city, once again, after one hundred and eighty-nine years, in rejoicing German hands. Though proud of their pure Saxon blood – and Clara herself always retained a slight Saxon accent – the Schumanns primarily thought of themselves as Germans. When ultimate victory was won in early 1871, their belief in a new united fatherland shone as brightly as Brahms's own in his *Triumphlied*, given its first performance with Stockhausen as soloist at Levi's farewell concert in Karlsruhe (he had just been appointed to the Munich Court Theatre) in June 1872. 'The deepest and grandest piece of church music since Bach' was her immediate reaction. Stockhausen was the baritone soloist; her own contribution to the programme was Schumann's Concerto, also Brahms's arrangement of the Gavotte from Gluck's *Paris and Helena*, always one of the miniatures she liked to play most. 'It was a most successful concert and left us all in the most exalted frame of mind. There was a banquet after it . . . we were very merry. Of course I took Marie and Eugenie, and I sent for Felix from Heidelberg', so her diary entry concludes.

August of that same year brought Clara a visit from her beloved Julie, already the mother of two sons and now pregnant again. But from their first kiss Clara knew that although blissfully happy in her marriage, Julie, always her frailest child, was creating new life at the cost of her own. Attempts to persuade her to remain quietly where she was instead of returning south proved unavailing. November 10 brought the dreaded news of Julie's death. 'Ah! what a loss for all of us! She was everything – daughter, sister, wife and mother in the truest sense of the words. . . . How magnificently her character had developed! What a treasure she was to her husband, of whom my heart bleeds to think', so Clara wrote to Woldemar, explaining how none the less she had felt it obligatory to carry on with her work. 'It was difficult, but art has always been my most faithful comrade, and is so still; it finds a vent for the soul's anguish and gives balm to the heart. And if I look round me and see what rich treasures are left to me in my other children, I cannot but cast my eyes towards heaven with a grateful heart, and find strength and courage to endure everything.'

It was to keep the others as near her as possible in their different, maturing needs that early in 1873 she began to consider the possibility of giving up Baden to make a permanent home for them in Berlin. But it was far too much of a wrench for any quick decision. The last ten summers had allowed her to fulfill herself as a mother in a way she knew could never come again.

2. In the world at large

.At the end of September, 1863, there had been tears from Clara and her eldest daughter when the time came to leave Lichtenthal No. 14. 'It looked so dreary and desolate with closed shutters' so Marie wrote to Eugenie at her new school. But the expense of that first happy summer had compelled Clara to withdraw 1000 thalers from her capital. Her immediate concern was to replace it, prompting an even more strenuous winter concert schedule than before. 'The deluge of work with which I have been flooded is really almost too much', she wrote to Brahms in mid-October when apologizing for her delayed acknowledgement of a parcel of his works. 'My correspondence about concerts is endless, while in addition I have to practise diligently. Unfortunately my conscientiousness is, I might say, increasing so painfully that I always feel with every piece I approach as if I were just beginning to practise it properly'. Having already attended an exhausting three-day festival in Munich, she was at that moment staying with friends in Düsseldorf preparing for concerts in centres including Aix la Chapelle, Frankfurt, Hamburg, Lübeck, Hanover, Braunschweig, Munster, Wismar, Schwerin, Rostock, Guströv, Detmold and Leipzig. A fortnight's rest in Düsseldorf over Christmas was all that she could fit in before her still more taxing project for early 1864 – a return visit to Russia, preceded by appearances in Hanover (where Joachim's masterly conducting of Beethoven's ninth symphony profoundly moved her), Hamburg (where an unthinking comment from Brahms, now living and working in Vienna, on her good fortune in visiting his home town twice in one winter prompted the acid retort 'Now I come to Hamburg for the sake of my music and stay here as long as necessary; I used to come for your sake and stay as long as possible. You have not forgotten that, have you?'), Berlin (where she stayed with the Mendelssohns and saw both Ferdinand and the far from well Felix) and Königsberg before reaching the German-speaking Livonian towns of Riga and Mitau.

The twenty-four-hour journey from Königsberg to Riga exhausted her. There was absolutely nowhere to stay en route, only 'miserable villages or just groups of houses' so Marie, accompanying her mother, wrote to Eugenie on February 18, 1864, admitting that their hearts had been wrung by the appalling poverty they had witnessed on the way. Though not too rushed before moving on in early March to snow-bound St Petersburg, where the Neva was frozen solid as a road, Clara still felt far from well. 'Nevertheless I got through my concerts with remarkable strength and endurance' she wrote to Brahms from that city on March 10. 'How I manage to get up my enthusiasm again and again I am sure I don't know. But it always gives me great pleasure to find so many devoted admirers of Robert everywhere, and I may say that Robert's things are among those with which I obtain my biggest successes. Thus a week ago today I played Robert's Concerto at the Conservatoire concert and had such enthusiastic applause as I seldom experience. And the same thing happened with the *Etudes symphoniques* at my second chamber-music matinée today'. *Carnaval,* still with her customary omissions including 'Estrella', was also a regular favourite. The average Russian audience she perceptively assessed as intuitively rather than learnedly musical, 'sensitive to much that they do not understand'. Though initially slightly worried about the more or less obligatory hiring (for any artist of standing) of a notoriously expensive theatre seating 3000, she came through this ordeal on March 22 with a profit of 800 roubles, and cleared 700 roubles at her farewell soirée, from which many had to be turned away, as well as playing for the city's greatest artistic patron, the Grand Duchess Hélène (at whose vast palace she and Marie stayed after leaving the pleasant but inconveniently distant home of relations of her brother Alwin Wieck), once with the Emperor and Empress in the audience too.

In mid-April she moved on to Moscow. Arriving at 9 a.m. after a twenty-four-hour journey she was rushed to a rehearsal at 11 a.m. for a concert that same night. Three more followed in less than a week. But the more favourable climate, water and air, together with the solicitude of the half-German family with whom she and Marie lodged, and perhaps, too, the inspiration of Easter night itself experienced in the Kremlin, all these things helped to restore some of her old energy. She was also much touched when the orchestra offered its services without payment for one of her concerts (besides Schumann's Concerto she had also prepared Beethoven's No. 4 and 'Emperor' Concertos for the tour). In this city she met Nicholas Rubinstein, pianist brother of Anton, whose friendly help had so heartened her in St Petersburg. Nicholas's 'thumping' and excessive reliance on both loud and soft pedals displeased her as much as the unfeeling playing of Bülow, also touring Russia at this time without her own box-office success. Lovable rather than admirable was her ultimate verdict on both the Rubinstein brothers, who to her earnest German mind lacked 'sacred seriousness' of dedication. Nothing could blind her to the shocking condition of Russia's poor, though the gradual suppression of serfdom gave her new hope, still more the idealism of the

Czar himself: 'He is really admirable, for in my opinion more courage is required for such reforms than any general would need on the field of battle'. The forty-eight-hour return journey from St Petersburg direct to Berlin was an appalling strain. But resting at Düsseldorf before her Baden summer she realized that takings had sufficiently exceeded anything she could then have earned in Germany to make it all very worth while – this she confided to Brahms, to whom she had by now started to give highly business-like advice (no doubt originating from Mendelssohn's brother and other of her banker friends) as to how best to invest his own first appreciable capital.

Even during that second family summer at Lichtenthal 14 her thoughts turned at once to the new season and the establishment of some kind of pattern in her travels, with more extensive tours reserved for the New Year in the wake of German engagements leading up to, and immediately following, Christmas. Slipping in Berlin's Tiergarten and damaging her right wrist involved many cancellations (including a visit to Vienna) at the start of 1865. But after treatment including the same *Tierbäder* tried by Robert some thirty years before, she recovered sufficiently to appear in Dresden, Leipzig, Zwickau, Naumberg and Prague before setting out in mid-April with her daughter, Marie, and her half-sister, Marie Wieck, for a new assault on London, whose comparatively unappreciative audiences she had deserted for the last five years.

Knowing that in Britain Joachim was already an idol, she had taken the precaution of sounding him about English prospects as early as August, 1864 – not long before he and his wife delighted her by producing their first son on the eve of her own birthday. 'I can give you no better advice than to ask Mr. Grove for his opinion; he is independent enough not to be obliged to consider the pianists over there, and yet his tastes and position as secretary (of the Crystal Palace concerts) make him thoroughly conversant with all the circumstances' was Joachim's reply, for he knew how the average promoter had to keep in with favourites available throughout the whole year like Charles Hallé, Pauer, and most of all, Arabella Goddard, now married to the powerful anti-Schumannite, J. W Davison, of *The Times*. By this time Joachim had come to regard Grove, just 11 years his senior, as one of his dearest friends, a distinguished scholar with 'so true and deep a love of art, such a German absorption in music, that a visit to his simple, hospitable home is delightful'. Joachim also knew that England had no more staunch champion of Schumann: 'whenever anything of Schumann's is being played, there he is with a company of believers, and joins with them in clapping until he is worn out!'

On arrival, staying in pleasant rooms in Orme Square near the Joachims themselves, Clara soon met Mr Grove and discovered the strength of his sympathy for herself. For the first time in England she recognized a genuine interest in her husband's music, not only when she made her first appearance at the Crystal Palace on June 1 in the piano Concerto under the resident German conductor, August Manns (she had already played it on May 29 for the Philharmonic Society under Bennett) but on many other occasions too – not forgetting one of Chappell's Popular Concerts exclusively devoted to Schumann's chamber and keyboard works (even though Davison was on the advisory board) with the *Etudes symphoniques* her principal contribution. Her own playing was also greeted far more enthusiastically than ever before in London. Often in company with the Joachims, both frequent collaborators in her own concerts, she met a much wider cross-section of London's musical establishment (including the John Chappells, the Benedicts and the Macfarrens) than previously, in relaxed, personal surroundings as well as enjoying many pleasant hours with old friends like Moscheles's relations, the Bensons, and the Beneckes. On one night she found herself, with Joachim and a vocalist, involved in a Newspaper Press Fund dinner at Freemasons' Hall, during which she had to sit through no less than thirteen toasts. But only John Ella, 'who invariably gushes to me in the most tender billets-doux', came in for criticism, as 'a curiosity, an absurd figure' (his sudden arrival in Baden the following summer proved no small embarrassment) although she knew very well that there was no more élite audience in London than that for his Musical Union chamber concerts in which she, Joachim and Piatti so frequently appeared. Never on leaving England had she felt more satisfied, or more anxious to return.

Heavy engagements in Germany, Austria and Budapest in fact kept her in Europe throughout 1866, a year necessitating treatment for a liver disorder as well as bringing her new worries about the muscles of her right hand. In Vienna she was even compelled to remove Brahms's hefty Handel and 'Hexen' (as she nicknamed the Paganini set) Variations from her programmes. But by mid-January, 1867, she was up and away again for England, with Joachim as well as Marie for travelling companions. This time sights were set on conquest of the provinces, with Edinburgh, Glasgow, Manchester, Leeds, Bradford, Birmingham, Rugby,[1] Bath, Clifton and Torquay the chosen centres. Their promoter, John Chappell, had assembled a little group for the tour, with Ries, Piatti and Zerbini (a viola player also prepared to undertake piano accompaniments) to make up a quartet with Joachim, and Louisa Pyne (a well-known soprano and promoter of English opera who had several times appeared with Clara at

---

[1] Staying as guests of a housemaster at Rugby School (where Jenny Lind's son was a pupil) Clara and Marie were invited to watch a football match, prompting Marie to write to Eugenie: 'English people seem to think a great deal of these games. Last night the youth who is best at games was introduced to us, just as in our country the pupil who is best at his work would be specially mentioned'.

Philharmonic Society concerts) to provide vocal relief. Clara herself not only contributed miniatures by Schumann, Chopin and Mendelssohn to each programme, but also always joined Joachim and Piatti in Mendelssohn's C minor Piano Trio, or Beethoven's 'Archduke' or G major, Op.1, No.2, Trios. For longer journeys, as Marie wrote to Fraulein Leser, 'we had a saloon, comfortably furnished with armchairs and sofas, and attached to it a compartment for the gentlemen communicating with ours by a door'. With foot warmers for additional comfort in transit, and on arrival first-class hotels and meals personally supervised by an accompanying representative from Chappells, Marie was well content. But long hours of travel on concert days themselves, in trains that seemed dangerously fast, proved a great strain for Clara. As Marie continued: 'Mamma cannot reconcile herself to our present way of life and is frequently depressed, though she exercises great self-control. . . . She no longer has the elasticity for a tour of this sort, in order to feel at home everywhere and take things as they come. Joachim, to whom she speaks most freely, usually says she is wrong, because he does not feel as she does, and this makes her still more unhappy'. Edinburgh's[1] castles and monuments thrilled her, and so did a reception in London just as enthusiastic as the previous year – notably Beethoven's 'Emperor' at the Crystal Palace and fourth Concerto for the Philharmonic Society. But she was exhausted enough to decline most social invitations, as also a request to stay on for the musical 'season'. After visiting friends in Brussels and Düsseldorf, and Ferdinand, Felix and her mother in Berlin, and then having treatment in Karlsbad for her liver, she was back again in Baden by mid-June for another cherished family summer.

In Brussels Clara was always the warmly welcomed house-guest of Hubert and Christine Kufferath; Hubert, a former pupil of Mendelssohn, had settled in Brussels in 1844 as composition professor at its Conservatoire. Her return to London in 1868 brought her comparable good fortune in an introduction to Arthur Burnand, a middle-aged bachelor as handsome as he was wealthy (he was a Lloyds underwriter), and his sister, whose elegant home at 14 Hyde Park Gate, S.W.7, was a well-known rendezvous for all artists and music-lovers. When back in London in 1869, Clara and Marie were the Burnands' guests until finding rooms of their own. In 1870, as on Clara's returns in 1871, 72 and 73, there was no question of her staying anywhere else, bringing her previously undreamed-of domestic comfort (even down to the provision of her favourite kind of mattress) as well as bracing walks by the Serpentine in between her provincial engagements. In 1871 Eugenie was invited as well as Marie; the following year it was the turn of Felix. 'Luxurious by German standards'

---

[1] She returned to this city, as also to Torquay and Bath, for recitals of her own.

was how Eugenie summarized it all, adding 'but in England these comforts did not mean a snobbish display of wealth but were the usual surroundings of the upper classes. ... Nothing seemed to give Mr. Burnand greater pleasure than to show Marie and me the sights of London. Carriages and servants were always at our disposal'. On nearly every visit Clara gave a private soirée, with various supporting artists, in the Burnands' music room, charging a guinea for tickets. Of the many Sunday night dinner parties held in her honour, one in 1871 was unforgettable for a performance of Haydn's Toy Symphony, she at the piano feigning indignation at Joachim's every wrong entry with his cuckoo. A less happy memory of that same year was when thieves broke into the Burnands' house and made off with a lot of Clara's jewels, money and personal mementos. But she was comforted by messages of sympathy all the more touching to her since English feeling was so patently with the French in the Franco-Prussian war. From Jenny Lind-Goldschmidt (domiciled in England since 1856) whom she had recently visited at her Wimbledon home she even received the present of a brooch given her by the Queen of Sweden. In Clara's opinion Jenny's voice had by now almost gone, though many notes had a veiled quality still very moving. It was on this same 1871 visit that Clara had to struggle to keep back tears on discovering her old friend, Pauline Viardot, teaching third-rate pupils in shabby London lodgings, nevertheless following this admission to Brahms with the knowing comment: 'it is a good thing she did not suspect anything; she would certainly have laughed in my face'.

Besides the unfailing warmth of the Burnands' welcome and the discovery of many other friends as cultured as they were sympathetic (including the distinguished surgeon, Sir Henry Thompson, and his wife, to whom Clara subsequently sent a manuscript of one of Schumann's songs as a token of esteem), it was the great new enthusiasm of the British public itself that gradually turned her annual visits – and from 1867 to 1873 she never missed a year – from money-earning routine into pleasure. 'They greet me as if they love me', she wrote, and in that knowledge was ready to stifle her old secret disquiet at the commercial rather than artistic considerations conditioning English concert life. By now she could choose where and what she played. In 1868 she introduced Schumann's G major *Concertstück* to London for the first time at a Philharmonic Society concert. Other off-beat adventure included participation with Hiller, on his visit in 1871, in his four-handed *Operetta without words* (its movements variously entitled 'Air of the Maidens', 'Chorus of Hunters', 'Scolding Song', 'Drinking Song' etc.) and joining Joachim and Piatti in 1873 in the first London performance of her own G minor Piano Trio. As always she was indefatigable in propagation of Brahms, particularly his chamber works, though several times she had to drop his bigger sets of solo variations from her programmes because they so tired her wrists – for the same reason she had to stand back and allow his D minor Piano Concerto to be introduced to London's Philharmonic Society in June 1873 by Alfred Jaell. Out of consideration for her old Parisian friend, Mme Erard, whose firm had been hard hit by the war, she eventually insisted on alternating between Broadwoods and Erards at all concerts despite their marked difference of touch. Looking back on that particular run of English seasons in later life, it was a summons to Buckingham Palace towards the end of April, 1872, that she could never forget. 'Mme Neruda, Frl. Regan and some gentlemen also took part in it. . . . 700 people were invited (it took place from 5 to 7 p.m.) and about 100 were in the hall, the greater number standing behind empty seats' so she wrote in her diary at the time. 'The Queen did not greet us at all, she sat half turned towards our room, talked incessantly, heard only the closing measure of each programme number and then applauded faintly. Above the music one could also hear the mumblings of the other six hundred persons scattered through adjoining salons. The most incredible thing happened during the inter-mission; the Queen rose to have her tea, and in the meantime the royal band blared a folk medley, followed by two bagpipers (in kilts!) who cut loose in the next room. I was speechless, unaware at first of what this could be, until Mme Neruda explained that this was the Queen's favourite music! . . . Beside myself, I was ready to leave right then. But the second part now began and the Queen was half seated when it must have occurred to her that we ought to be spoken to. So she came forward and looking at us in a lump said 'very nice playing', after which she returned to her chair . . . when it was all over she did not utter a word of thanks. Never in my life has such a thing happened to me. This Queen is not going to see me under her roof again; of that I am sure! . . . A dinner had been prepared for us in the anteroom where we left our coats. But I declined'.

Besides playing in England, Russia, Belgium, Austria and Hungary in this particular decade, Clara also followed up an 1863 trip to Holland with two further visits to that country in 1869 and 1871. Whether at home or abroad, every year brought some further addition to her repertoire from Schumann's own works, not least the great C major *Phantasie* so intim-ately expressing his love and longing in dark days when they were forbidden to meet, which she played for the first time in public on December 15, 1866, in Leipzig and repeated frequently until it began to over-tire her muscles. At the instigation of Brahms, she also unearthed Schumann's Variations for two pianos as originally scored for additional horn and two cellos to play with him in Vienna on November 28, 1868, but for this response was unenthusiastic. 'One must not look for too much appreciation from the public for anything so new and original . . . if we do it again next year, things will be very different' so her diary philosophically records. The previous month in Bremen she had played Beethoven's third Concerto in C minor for the first time, as she put it 'with real delight. I made a cadenza for it, which I really do not think is bad. The concerto was very hackneyed at one time, and that is why I did not study it; now, one seldom hears it'.[1] Schubert also found an increasingly generous place in her repertory as this decade progressed, not least his Sonatas in A minor, Op.42, G major, Op.78, and notably the last in B flat, Op.posth, which she played publicly for the first time in Vienna on February 1, 1866.

Apart from solo engagements, she was always more than happy when opportunity arose to collaborate with Stockhausen, nearly always ready and willing to accompany him in Beethoven's *An die ferne Geliebte* and Schubert's *Die schöne Müllerin* cycles as well as her husband's songs: besides the *Dichterliebe* he now often sang the Eichendorff *Liederkreis* cycle and a selection from *Myrthen* as well as many other separate favourites. Between 1871–3 she also appeared quite often with Joachim's singer wife, Amalie (by this time the mother of three children), who, having studied with Stockhausen, had acquired much of his own fastidious concern for word-painting in Lieder so much admired by Clara. The *Frauenliebe und-Leben* cycle (though nearly always only the first five of the eight songs) often found its way into their programmes, so did a selection from the *Dichterliebe*. In Bremen on November 7, 1871, they also included a Mozart Recitative and Rondo with piano obbligato (presumably 'Ch'io mi scordi di te' ', K.505, transposed for contralto).

Nevertheless there was still no one on the platform to whom she felt more closely attuned than Joachim himself.[2] Neither ever forgot how each struck sparks from the other in a performance of Haydn's 'Hungarian' Trio in G at one of London's Popular Concerts in February 1869: 'the audience was electrified' so Clara's diary records. Towards the end of that year they were heard in Berlin in Mozart's E minor and Beethoven's C minor, Op.30, and 'Kreutzer' Sonatas by Amy Fay, a young American studying piano in Europe, who wrote home to her family that it would have been worthwhile crossing the Atlantic just for that experience alone since each inspired the other to play with so much fire. Having got her tickets with difficulty since demand was so great, Amy Fay also had plenty to say about Clara as a soloist. Grouping her with Anton Rubinstein, Bülow and Tausig as Europe's four leading pianists now that Liszt, Thalberg and Henselt had retired from the concert platform, Amy Fay assessed her style as objective in comparison with Rubinstein: 'she gives you the most exquisite pleasure with every note she touches, and has a wonderful

---

[1] Beethoven's first two concertos never found a place in her repertory.
[2] By 1870 she had secretly sensed, and told Brahms, that he was not entirely happy in his marriage.

conception and variety in playing, but she seldom whirls you off your feet'.
Chopin's B flat minor Scherzo, though splendid, most notably lacked the
requisite boldness for this young American, though Impromptus from
Schubert's Op.90 and Op.142 she considered 'tossed off to perfection with
the greatest grace and smoothness', while Clara's Bach (by this time her
repertoire included several transcriptions of organ Preludes and Fugues
as well as some from the '48' and the Chromatic Fantasia and Fugue)
struck her as the noblest she had ever heard. As for Clara's appearance on
the platform, Amy Fay's impression was of 'a large, very German-looking
woman, with dark hair and superb neck and arms. At the last concert she
was dressed in black velvet, low bodice and short sleeves, and when she
struck powerful chords, those large white arms came down with a certain
splendour'.

Like the arms, so Clara's hands, too, were large for a woman, with an
uncommonly long little finger and thumb as well as great breadth of
palm.[1] But very few people in the world at large knew the ever increasing
pain, still basically attributed to rheumatism though aggravated by two or
three unlucky falls, she was now suffering in hands and arms alike, which
costly visits to spas like Kreuznach, Karlsbad and St Moritz to drink and
bathe in iron and oxidized waters did little to alleviate. Much of her
correspondence now had to be dictated (though she always tried to write
to Brahms by hand) and more than a few concerts cancelled. At the start of
1871 she was equally worried by an attack of aural catarrh causing slight
deafness as well as treble notes to sound too high and the bass wholly
confused. All these things doubled her platform nervousness. This she
knew was partly the result of a compelling need to play from memory,
since otherwise 'I always feel as if I were cramped and could not spread
the wings which still possess some power of soaring'. But increasingly in
artists' rooms there were tears.

To her friends it was clear that winter travel was taxing her to an extent
which not even relaxed Baden summers could redress. In November 1871,
at a time when she was sharing a lot of concerts with Amalie, Joachim tried
to help by offering her a staff post at Berlin's new Music School of which,
since its foundation in 1868, he had been Director. Her daughter, Marie,
the Bendemanns and many others pressed her to accept. Even she
realized that Berlin had obvious advantages as a family centre at this point
in the children's lives. But just as, when a teenager, the performer in her
had once or twice been prepared to postpone marriage, and even as a young
wife and mother to relegate domesticity to second place, so at this moment
the truth of her words to Brahms during their altercation of 1868 became

---

[1]   According to Adelina de Lara, a subsequent pupil, Clara's wide stretch enabled her to
run up scales in tenths as others did in octaves.

doubly clear: 'the practice of my art is an important part of my ego; it is the very breath of my nostrils.' Since an outright no to Joachim was as impossible as acceptance, she compromised by proposing outrageous conditions – a salary of 4,000 thalers for life, five months' annual holiday, complete freedom in choice of pupils, both in and outside the school, liberty to accept concert engagements anywhere at any time provided missed lessons were made up, and last but not least equal musical status in the school with Joachim. She knew such terms were wholly unacceptable: her relief when they were rejected knew no bounds.

1872, in consequence, allowed her little respite from travel, with the deaths of her mother, Frau Bargiel, in the spring and her beloved Julie in November crushing her spirit still more. But the start of 1873, just after she had undertaken a further series of concerts with Amalie Joachim, brought unexpected financial relief. While in Leipzig to play Schumann's *Concertstück* in G at the Gewandhaus she was approached by her old friend, Carl Voigt, who felt the time had come to present her with Rhenish railway stock to the value of 30,000 thalers, the capital having grown from money subscribed in secret to a Schumann Fund by well-wishers over the years. The gift was made with such tact and delicacy that despite her age-old pride she was able to accept it without embarrassment, indeed with infinite gratitude as a tribute to Robert. But on learning a few months later that certain musicians in Graz had organized a charity concert in aid of the Schumann Fund she gave vent to another of those outbursts of indignation now recognized by her friends as uncontrollable, with Brahms once more having to sustain the initial impact. 'I am beside myself with fury over this disgusting advertisement in the Graz Gazette' she wrote from London on April 22, 1873. 'I, who, thanks to the strength that has been vouchsafed me, have been able honourably to keep myself and my children from want all these years, who throughout the whole of last winter was still working with the utmost energy and success, and who, owing to the gift from the Schumann Fund, was able to look a little less anxiously into the future – I am now to allow other artists to give concerts for me, and to this end to suffer the publication of such mendacious advertisements for the collection of more money! It is an indignity. . . . I must be vindicated. . . . Then steps must be taken to prevent so much as a farthing of the receipts from coming to me – they can be given to some institution or to a poor musician'.

It was Schumann who was to dominate her thoughts for the rest of that summer, first in a commission from a Paris publisher to transcribe thirty of his songs for solo piano, a task she approached in the belief, supported by Levi, that they should be kept as close to the original as possible rather than wholly recomposed as solo piano music in the way recommended by Brahms. But an invitation from Joachim to take part in a festival in Bonn that August designed to raise funds for a grander graveyard memorial than she herself in 1856 had been able to erect preoccupied her even more. Preparations posed many problems. Brahms was hurt to the quick that limited rehearsal time made it impossible to include his own *Requiem*, as originally proposed by Clara. She in her turn was sternly rebuked by Levi[1] for so unreasonably censoring Brahms (as so often before for different reasons) for his admission of disappointment. Meanwhile Joachim, the festival's conductor-director, wanted only artistic perfection – and peace in which to achieve it. In the end, goodwill triumphed. Surrounded by most of her family (even Ferdinand, who, recently released from the wars, turned up with his new bride on the second day of their honeymoon) and by many of her closest friends and colleagues, Clara experienced a happiness which at the time not even her temperamental leaning towards introspective melancholy could cloud. Between an opening concert shared by Schumann's fourth Symphony and *Paradise and the Peri* (with Stockhausen and Amalie Joachim among the soloists) and a concluding chamber concert in which she took part in the Piano Quintet alongside Joachim and played the two-piano Variations with Ernst Rudorff (her former pupil who had taught Eugenie at the Berlin Music School) Joachim had devised a central, second night programme which, while including the *Manfred* Overture, the *Nachtlied* and a section of *Faust* with Stockhausen in the title role, focused the main spotlight on herself as soloist in the Piano Concerto. Even at the morning rehearsal there was a flourish of trumpets to greet her; at the concert itself Jenny Lind-Goldschmidt rose to her feet in the audience as Clara appeared, and everyone else in the house immediately followed suit. 'At last Mamma was allowed to seat herself at the piano. She looked so beautiful – like a young girl, a bride, a child. Her dress was lovely, and the effect was heightened by a rose in her hair' Eugenie wrote to Fräulein Leser. 'She was not at all nervous, and Brahms himself said that he had never heard the concerto so well played. When it was over a tremendous storm of applause broke out again, there was a flourish of trumpets, and Mamma was overwhelmed with flowers, at least 150 bouquets must have come flying towards her. It was lovely, Fräulein Leser, and I cannot tell you how much we enjoyed it'. It was gratifying to Clara to learn that after all expenses had been paid, 4000 thalers remained in hand for the tombstone, and that Donndorf, a pupil of their old Dresden friend, Rietschel, had been commissioned to

---

[1] On June 27, 1873, Levi wrote to Joachim: 'I am not a good mediator and do not want to go into details, but I could not help giving Frau Schumann a lecture or two on her behaviour towards Brahms, and I wish you had been there to hear some of them. She showed me a letter from Brahms which I was expected to consider inconsiderate, cold and unkind, which, with the best will in the world, I was not able to do. He is just himself; either he was not worthy of your friendship ten years ago, or else he is just as worthy of it now.'

design it. There was also the balm of knowing that Brahms, initially surly, had melted enough during the festival to invite her, just before leaving, to try over with him some brand new Variations for two pianos, very much to her liking, on a theme attributed to Haydn. It was not until subsequently writing to express her gratitude to Joachim (whom she rewarded with the manuscript of the *Nachtlied*) that she confessed to secret awareness of the irony that so much honour should be bestowed on her while her beloved lay under the soil outside. 'It is so hard not to have the consolation of faith at such moments' was her most self-revealing afterthought.

Glowing August memories in some way helped her through the trauma of leaving Lichtenthal 14, which though not sold, she had by the late autumn decided to relinquish as a family headquarters in favour of a congenial flat already at her disposal in Berlin. But there was another blow to come before the move was made. Still smarting from the deaths of her faithful old cook, Josephine, and her mother and Julie in quick succession in 1871–2, she heard that on October 6, 1873, at the age of 88, her father had died. As the years passed she had grown more and more aware of their differences of outlook; ever since childhood she had been irked by his way of boasting about her achievement and his own method. He was still inordinately self-satisfied when visited by Amy Fay in February, 1872, at Dresden, where sitting on his chair as if it were a throne in his large but frugally furnished music room, he put a class of girls – taught by him free of charge every evening – through their solfeggio singing and extemporisation as if he alone held the key to the entire musical universe. But whatever their conflicts, Clara's love never wavered, a love which, as she put it, 'all my life long has been heightened by gratitude. How many years he dedicated to me, to the exclusion of all else, what an excellent influence he had over me in making me understand the beauty of a practical, active life, how many wise rules of conduct he gave me . . .'. Her subsequent discovery that through great self-denial in all personal luxuries he had left quite a lot of money, and remembered her very generously, made her pangs all the sharper.

FIFTEEN

Berlin Trials 1873–79

Before taking up residence at No. 11, Unter den Zelten on November 9, 1873, Clara had to play in Frankfurt and Mannheim as well as travelling to Munich to hear Levi conduct *Manfred*; by the end of the month bags were packed yet again for concerts in Bremen, Hamburg, Schwerin and Leipzig (for Brahms's D minor concerto) besides a visit to her stepmother in Dresden.

'Cosy and charming' was how Eugenie described the new flat, which looked out on the trees of Berlin's Tiergarten. The Joachims and their four children lived immediately opposite; the Stockhausens had also settled in the same city. The newly married Ferdinand by now had his own home. But at their mother's side Marie and Eugenie enjoyed unprecedented opportunities for music-making with friends and pupils as well as improving their harmony with their Uncle Woldemar on his appointment to the staff of the Berlin Music School in 1874. Most important of all, the whole family could rally round Felix, slowly recovering from serious inflammation of the lungs after sharply deteriorating health in Heidelberg. It was primarily so that he could be cared for at home while continuing his studies that Clara had made the move in the first place.

That all was not set fair, despite outwardly propitious circumstances, was nevertheless clear from her letters to Brahms within a week or two of arrival. 'Everything is commonplace in Berlin, except what comes from Joachim' she complained as soon as November 24, enlarging on this on December 12 with the observation that 'the theatre is only so-and-so, the Singakademie is conventional, the symphony concerts are incredibly dull etc. etc.' In the context of where to settle, she had always been liable to build castles-in-the-air, only to find disillusionment just round the corner – Baden-Baden had proved the one great exception. But this time there was a basic physical cause underlying her unease: returning to Brahms's D minor Concerto, which she very dearly loved and rightly felt still needed her advocacy, had seriously strained her right arm. Even before the end of the year pain caused her to propose major modifications in her projected 1874 English tour.

There were momentary gleams of sunshine. Brahms's Christmas

present, a setting of Felix's poem 'Meine Liebe ist grün',[1] brought great joy, not least when they performed it at a party as a surprise for Felix and watched his reactions on realizing the words were his own. A visit to Leipzig in the New Year to attend a special 'Brahms Week' organized by a group of his admirers, in co-operation with the Gewandhaus, proved even more of a tonic. But by now her muscles were badly enough strained to compel her to close her piano completely. Saying goodbye to Joachim on his departure for England on February 10, instead of travelling with him, was a particular wrench.

A still more ominous threat to happiness was learning from the doctors, on her return from Leipzig, that one of Felix's lungs was incurably diseased. As she put it to Brahms: 'I must confess that I feel more desolate than I ever have before in my life. In all my trials hitherto I have had my Art as a faithful helpmeet at my side. But now that has gone, and with it I feel as if I had lost the mainstay of my life. What makes me most miserable is that with all this depression I cannot be a source of good cheer to my children. For, try as I may day and night to be brighter, how is it possible with this fresh terrible anxiety about Felix? . . . Can you imagine what a mother feels, when one son is buried alive, the other, who is so highly gifted, in failing health and possibly never to be seen well and sound again, and another dear child, also exceptionally gifted, stricken down in the midst of a happy life and already buried! And how many more troubles have I had! If you could put yourself in my place you would not think less of me for occasionally allowing my heart to unburden itself in the hearing of a sympathetic friend'.

Even as a twelve-year-old recitalist in Weimar there was something in Clara's face that had prompted a certain Frédéric Goret, hearing her quite by chance, to observe: 'Pauvre enfant! elle a un air de malheur et de souffrances qui m'a affligé; mais elle doit peut-être une partie de son beau talent à cette disposition à la mélancholie: en examinant de près les attributs des Muses en y trouverait presque toujours quelques traces de larmes'. Brahms himself knew Clara's tears only too well; suspecting a strain of self-pity wholly alien to his own stoicism he often begged her to try to develop a more philosophical disposition. But her last letter he recognized as a genuine *cri de coeur*. 'God grant that you may be spared any further cares, for you have surely had enough for one life' he wrote in reply, overcoming a growing dislike of laying bare his heart in words, as opposed to music, by adding 'Let this deep love of mine be a comfort to you, for I love you more than myself, and more than anybody or anything on earth'.

---

[1] Op.63, No.5. During the next few years he also set Felix's 'Wenn um den Hollunder and 'Versunken' as his Op.63, No.6 and Op.86, No.5.

As soon as Felix, wrapped in furs, had been despatched to the cleaner air of Montreux, Clara herself started treatment with a hefty masseuse who, demanding beer and sandwiches on top of a substantial fee for each daily hour's visit, exhausted the patience of Marie and Eugenie with her wiles to gain their mother's now too easily stirred sympathy and affection. Further treatment at Teplitz between May 21–June 30 brought no improvement either, nor did a return (via Büdesheim to call on Elise) to her still unsold house at Baden, where, apart from a brief stay by the Lake of Geneva with Count Marmorito, she remained until early October, turning down yet another remunerative offer from America while there.

By January 1875, after a compassionate visit to the blind Rosalie Leser, prostrate with grief in Düsseldorf at the death of her lifelong companion and help, Elise Junge, Clara realized it was time for more drastic action: with Marie to uphold her as ever, she entered the Baaschs' nursing home at Kiel for treatment under Dr Esmarch (married to the Princess of Schleswig-Holstein). Aware of a psychological as well as physical problem, Dr Esmarch supplemented massage and water douches with an order to practise an hour a day whatever the pain: this she was able to do at the nearby home of some congenial acquaintances, the Litzmanns.[1] By March Dr Esmarch even decreed that she must give a concert. With the young soprano, Marie Fillunger (an intimate friend of Eugenie's) contributing Lieder by Mendelssohn, Schubert, Schumann and Brahms, this eventually took place on March 18, bringing Clara not only flowers and greetings from innumerable well-wishers but also the deep personal satisfaction of knowing that she had got through Beethoven's 'Waldstein', Nos. 1, 2, 5, 6 and 8 from Schumann's *Kreisleriana* and miniatures by him and Schubert, Chopin, Mendelssohn, and Brahms-Gluck effortlessly enough to put her eighteen months' silence behind her. But saying goodbye to Kiel, where she had been surprisingly happy, was not easy, and she was more than delighted that the first two-day Schleswig-Holstein Music Festival under Joachim's direction that June gave her an excuse to return to play Schumann's Concerto before starting her holiday proper with a visit to Brahms at his summer hide-out of Ziegelhausen, and then joining Felix at the resort of Klosters. For a week they had the company of Count Marmorito and his children, notably Clara's eldest grandson, Duaddo, sufficiently like Julie in imagination and fragile grace to awaken many poignant memories. Her heart had already been wrung when just before returning to Kiel she went to the asylum at Colditz to see Ludwig, who in surprisingly lucid recent letters had begged her to come. Hugging her, he desperately pleaded to be taken home, insisting he was now quite

---

[1] Their son, Berthold, was to become her most distinguished biographer.

better. But with her own return to the platform now an imminent certainty, this was a responsibility she felt unable to face.

Having already in early April travelled to Leipzig for a revival of *Genoveva* (whose ending she was at last compelled to recognize as ineffective), in September, accompanied by Marie, Eugenie and Felix, she was back in Munich for further performances of *Manfred* under Levi, still a close friend despite his recent conversion to Wagner ('I bless the day on which my eyes were opened, dimly at first through the *Meistersinger*, and completely and finally through *Tristan*' was his subsequent admission to Joachim). Out of personal regard for Levi, Clara felt duty bound to attend his performance of *Tristan* on September 8, the night after *Manfred*. The experience proved traumatic. 'It is the most repulsive thing I ever saw or heard in my life' was her diary comment. 'To have to sit through a whole evening watching and listening to such love-lunacy till every feeling of decency was outraged, and to see not only the audience but the musicians delighted with it was – I may well say – the saddest experience of my whole artistic career. I held out till the end, as I wanted to have heard it all. Neither of them does anything but sleep and sing during the 2nd act, and the whole of act 3 – quite 40 minutes – Tristan occupies in dying – and they call that dramatic!! Levi says Wagner is a better musician than Gluck! Are they all fools or am I a fool? The subject seems to me so wretched; a love-madness brought about by a potion – how is it possible to take the slightest interest in the lovers? It is not emotion, it is a disease, and they tear their hearts out of their bodies while the music expresses it all in the most repulsive manner. I could go on lamenting over it for ever, and exclaiming against it'. The much publicized first complete *Ring* at Bayreuth the following summer provided her with generous opportunity. 'There are but few people strong enough to withstand this intoxicating influence' she observed at the time, no doubt recalling with pride how Joachim had upheld her disinclination to take part in the 1870 Vienna Beethoven Festival if Wagner was conducting, though now confessing to secret dismay in her diary at Brahms's growing reluctance to join in her railings.[1]

Before leaving Munich in September 1875 Clara made amends to Levi by partnering Joachim in Schumann's D minor Sonata as well as playing extracts from *Kreisleriana* at a matinée organized for the benefit of the orchestra. And after a few more weeks' holiday in the Rhineland she returned to Berlin in mid-October, only too thankful that she had rejected a renewed offer of a teaching post at the Berlin Music School as she

[1] With closer friends, such as the Herzogenbergs, Brahms increasingly shared a little affectionate mirth at her prejudices, such as when they saw she was scheduled to take part in Beethoven's Choral Fantasy at a Dresden concert that also included Wagner's *Feuerzaube*.

eagerly prepared for engagements in Leipzig, Frankfurt, Cologne and Bonn. Assurances on all sides that she had never played better were even encouraging enough to send her off in 1876 to Chemnitz and Dresden, and then via Düsseldorf and Utrecht to London, almost as if her recent troubles had never been. 'I have hardly ever felt so fresh and enthusiastic' she wrote to Brahms from London in early April, having already played Beethoven's fourth Concerto and solos by Chopin and Hiller at the opening concert of the Philharmonic Society on March 23. Only the illness of Miss Burnand damped her spirits. It was more for the pleasure of seeing old friends than for the necessity of treatment that she in fact returned to Kiel for three weeks that June before a relaxed, wandering summer akin to that of the preceding year, with a visit to Felix, holding his own in Swiss mountain air though coughing too much, its focal point. Back in Baden, where this time she and the girls stayed with their old next-door neighbours since their own house was let, she enjoyed the bonus of music-making with Brahms, also irresistibly lured to these much loved haunts, who played her his recently completed first Symphony shortly due for its première in Vienna.

That she was still in excellent shape when embarking on her German round that autumn was confirmed by an English traveller, Alexander Ewing (composer of 'Jerusalem the Golden') who wrote home 'I heard Mme Schumann yesterday play unsurpassably Nos. 2, 5, 4 and 8 of her husband's *Kreisleriana*. The Concert Room was thronged to the roof, and contained Royalty in the first row. She is in great form, quite recovered apparently. It is a thing altogether unparalleled in its way to hear her play his things. It is quite as if he were in the midst of us – as doubtless he is'. Hearing Anton Rubinstein in the same work not long afterwards, Ewing found more to admire in the Russian's *cantabile*, also in the fact that he offered the work complete. But he still felt that Clara 'played the best'. Her Dutch tour in early 1877 included a gratifying private appearance for the Queen, who to Clara's great delight admitted that she, too, could not bear Wagner. From Holland she proceeded to England, playing Schumann's Concerto for the Philharmonic Society on March 8 as well as enjoying the satisfaction of a performance of his *Faust (Part III)* at their concert a fortnight later. Miss Burnand's very recent death nevertheless cast a heavy shadow over this visit: showered with kindness as ever by her old host, Arthur, and his brother Theophilus (who in the circumstances had lent them his bachelor flat) Clara and Marie spent many a sad evening alone. Having already heard Brahms's C minor Symphony at the Leipzig Gewandhaus that January (and withdrawn all but a few of her initial doubts) she did not stay on for its London première on April 16 even though at the same Philharmonic concert Paul Viardot, son of her old singer friend, was making his début in Mendelssohn's Violin Concerto.

Back in Berlin, any hopes of relaxation she might have cherished were immediately dispelled by an invitation from Novellos in London to edit a new edition of Schumann's piano works complete, granting them world copyright, for a fee of 1,000 thalers. This she would have accepted at once had she not provisionally agreed to edit not just the piano music but Schumann's entire output for Breitkopf and Härtel at some future date – despite their past parsimony over royalties. It was to Brahms that she repeatedly turned for advice as to how to resolve the problem, eventually agreeing with him that the German publishing house, with its more ambitious project, must come first. In gratitude for his astute intervention on her financial behalf she at once offered him at least half the fee if he would accept responsibility for the orchestral and ensemble works.

Personal links between them that spring were still more closely forged by Clara's growing regard for Brahms's Leipzig friends, Heinrich Herzogenberg, president of the Leipzig Bachverein, and his radiant young wife, Elisabet, whose exceptional musical ear and facility prompted Clara to write, after their visit to Berlin in May, 1877: 'It was a real joy to play [on two pianos] with Frau Herzogenberg. How gifted she is, and how much she knows! How well she reads and with what enthusiasm! . . . And how charmingly she sings, too; her voice without being exactly beautiful, is so full of feeling, she enters so completely into the spirit of the music. . . .' As time went on Clara was often piqued to discover that such was Brahms's regard for Elisabet's spontaneous musical discernment (he had briefly given her piano lessons before her marriage) that his newest manuscripts only arrived for her own more academic appraisal after Elisabet had already seen them – as in fact happened with his songs of Opp.69, 70, 71 and 72 that April. But Clara's 'touchiness' in this context, as Brahms subsequently described it, still lay dormant. In fact the two ladies' unanimity over these songs, totally without collusion, must have given him considerable food for thought – not just in the stars they awarded to 'Des Liebsten Schwur' and 'Mädchenfluch' from Op.69, 'Im Garten am Seegestade' and 'Lerchengesang' from Op.70, 'An den Mond' and 'Geheimnis' from Op.71 and 'Alte Liebe' and 'Sommerfäden' from Op.72, but also in what they liked least – though he of course published them all, regardless. For Clara at this time he had a special personal present in the form of a keyboard arrangement for left hand only of Bach's unaccompanied violin Chaconne – in his opinion the only alternative way of conveying its special sense of challenge.

The remainder of 1877 brought a swift alternation of the sunshine and cloud now the warp and woof of Clara's life. The death of her little grandson, Duaddo, in July was immediately followed by happy news of the ever independent Elise's engagement to Louis Sommerhoff, a reliable enough American business man to ease the wrench of speeding them to

New York soon after their marriage in Büdesheim that November. Her anxiety over Felix's indetermination in his studies in Zurich in its turn was offset by irrepressible pride in his fast burgeoning poetic gifts, though both were eclipsed during a cold, late summer in Baden by a drastic deterioration in his health, prompting his immediate departure to the warmer climate of Sicily. Though now able to pick and choose engagements so as to go only to places she liked, or where she had close friends, Clara herself had a heavy winter's work in mind, with projected visits to Hamburg, Schwerin, several Swiss centres, and in the New Year to Holland, as well as some shared recitals in Berlin and elsewhere with Amalie Joachim. In fact as she contemplated the coming season in Baden that September her only complaint was that she had nothing freshly written to play: 'I wish there were more new things, I find that a great privation. I am so fond of studying new works, it stimulates me and renews my youth'. Liszt, who could have filled the gap, was of course as repugnant to her as Wagner: a chance opportunity of hearing him on her way home from London the previous year had provoked as vehement an outcry against his B.A.C.H. Fantasia for two pianos as his lady-killing platform coquetries. In fact it was only Brahms (currently preparing a piano duet version of his recently completed second Symphony in D for her Christmas present) who could provide the same kind of stimulation she had previously found in Chopin and Schumann himself, and ironically it was Brahms who now once more brought her to grief: in a letter to him from Schwerin on October 24 she complained of renewed pains in her arm induced by a return to his D minor Concerto, which she at last sadly realized she could never play again. Compelled to dictate all but the most intimate of her incessant stream of letters, by the end of the year she had cancelled concerts in Leipzig, as well as the projected Dutch tour.

Though a modified schedule was possible as the new year progressed, it was no doubt this renewed warning that caused her to stop and think far more seriously than ever before when during her visit to Frankfurt in February, 1878, Joseph Raff, Director of that city's Hoch Conservatoire, offered her a staff appointment. In her dislike of Berlin (shared by the girls) she had already toyed with lesser blandishments from Düsseldorf and Leipzig. But on the threshold of her sixtieth year, with no certainty that Dr Esmarch could repeat earlier miracles, it scarcely seemed the moment to allow lack of personal sympathy for Raff to outweigh Frankfurt's many advantages, both as a musical centre and as a springboard for the places she loved best – the Rhineland, the Black Forest, Bavaria and Switzerland. By April, her decision applauded by both Levi and Brahms, she had drawn up a contract agreeing to give nine lessons a week (one and a half hours a day) for eight months of the year, to have four months' holiday plus the right to absent herself for shorter concert tours provided lessons were made up, to teach not at the school but in her own home, and to have the help of an assistant using her own method. Though work was not to start until the autumn, she and the girls found a pleasant, openly situated house in Frankfurt that Easter; Eugenie and her friend, Marie Fillunger, organized the furniture removal at the end of May.

A concert in Wiesbaden, followed by visits to Kiel and to Düsseldorf' fifty-fifth Whitsuntide festival to hear performances of Schumann' *Faust*, Brahms's second Symphony (much more to her own and the general public's liking than its predecessor) and a violin concerto by Viotti superbly played by Joachim, conveniently cut short Clara's Berlin farewells. Already every moment of her spare time, as subsequently during her holiday at Wildbad-Gastein, was devoted to preparation of the piano works for the Breitkopf and Härtel complete Schumann edition, a task she found much more exacting than anticipated (and of which she might have despaired but for unstinting help from Brahms), in part by reason of printers' mistakes in early editions when checked with her husband's manuscripts, and also in some degree because of Schumann' own revisions and the responsibility of deciding which to regard as his 'definitive' version (her solution was frequently to include both, as notably with the *Etudes symphoniques*, which Schumann subsequently issued with small alterations as *Etudes en forme de variations*, and the *Davidsbündler-tänze*, later to emerge with a few verbal suppressions, but with metronome marks added, as the *Davidsbündler*). Her biggest initial concern was to check, or supply, metronome markings; she had questioned some of Schumann's in correspondence with Brahms as early as April 1861. In the event the complexity of this particular task overwhelmed her. As she wrote to Brahms on May 7, 1878: '*Carnaval* and *Fantasiestücke* have gone to Härtel's at last, after I had worried over them for days getting the metronome marks right. I bought a watch with a second hand and "the end of the song" is that I gave it up. You were right, it is wearisome work, and one ends by despairing of oneself. Anyone who understands the things will take them right, and those who do not understand them are not worth troubling about . . .'. Both *Carnaval* and the Op.12 *Fantasiestücke* emerged in the Complete Edition without metronome markings, just as Schumann had left them, and so did much else. It was not until 1887, when preparing an 'Instructive Edition' of the piano works for Breitkopf and Härtel, that she made many changes in his speeds as well as inserting her own for everything he had left unmarked.

Back in Munich in August, where for Levi's sake she forced herself to give *Tannhäuser* a second try ('the libretto is good, often so interesting that one even forgets the music, and those are the best parts'), she sat for the great artist, Franz von Lenbach, to gratify the children's wish for a really good portrait ('a remarkable first sitting, nothing but being "on view"

rithout canvas or palette – it was very funny. He wanted to study my face
efore beginning. He thinks he will want only one day for the picture,
ither it will succeed at once or not at all'). But her composure was almost
t once shattered by new agony in her arm, this time relieved only by
norphia, and still worse, by alarming news from Felix. Since he had
ecently been seen by the great surgeon, Theodor Billroth, on tour in Italy
ith Brahms, Clara had even dared to hope that Billroth was not merely
revaricating when saying that a cure, however slow, was not beyond the
ealms of possibility. So to learn that he was ill enough to have gone to
Count Marmorito in Turin, who advised an immediate return home, was
shock surpassed only by actual reunion with Felix in Munich on August
4, now creeping along like an old man unable to get his breath, and with
ncessant coughing only intermittently relieved in sleep by chloral. When
evi, as unfailing in help and advice as he had been with Ludwig a decade
efore, had to leave on August 26, Clara, and the girls took Felix to Baden,
here they found rooms at the Bär hotel until arrangements could be
nade for Eugenie to take him to a sanatorium at Falkenstein, near
rankfurt, while Marie went back to put the finishing touches to their new
ome. Clara herself was persuaded by the girls to go to Büdesheim (where
ne received news from New York that Elise had given birth to a son) to
eek strength and poise for the autumn's strenuous professional de-
nands.

A concert in celebration of the Hamburg Philharmonic Orchestra's
ubilee at the beginning of October marked the start of her new season.
hough considering herself one of Mozart's greatest champions, she
evertheless had a passionate altercation with Avé when he proposed this
omposer for what she saw as a 'city father' rather than specialist
udience; in the event she played the D minor Concerto, K.466, with
reat success, admitting to Brahms that she had borrowed a couple of
assages from him for her own newly composed, much-praised
adenzas.[1]

The great event for which she had long tried to steel her courage was
ill some three weeks distant – a concert at the Leipzig Gewandhaus to
ommemorate her first appearance there, exactly fifty years before.
he Frankfurt Conservatoire, aware of what was afoot, decided on a
reliminary salute of its own to its distinguished new staff member: on
October 20 she found herself escorted by Raff, along a flower-
rewn path, to a garland-crowned chair to enjoy, after speeches and
ne presentation of a laurel wreath, a special concert of her own com-
ositions performed by teachers and students of the school. Back at
ome, friends had organized a party at which she was showered with

[1] See Chapter 13, page 142, and Chapter 17, page 201.

presents, including from her family a slate clock 'exquisitely painted afte
Raphael, and with all the children's names and some charming verses o
Felix's engraved under the dial'.

By the 22nd she was in Leipzig, delighting everyone the next day by nc
only rehearsing Schumann's Concerto but also playing her solos (Schu
mann's B major *Romance*, Op.28 and B minor *Novellette*, Op.99) for th
benefit of the Leipzig Conservatoire students, most of whom she knev
would not be able to get into the actual concert. The 24th itself brough
non-stop celebration, from a morning of 'magnificent presents, addres
ses, flowers, wreaths, telegrams' to a splendid party at the Freges', wit
the Paulinerchor to serenade her as she arrived, after the concert.[1] Ethe
Smyth, then a twenty-year-old student in Leipzig, was overwhelmed b
the events of both days: 'The woman surely never played as she did la
Wednesday at the rehearsal, and above all last Thursday in the concer
... The Saal was beautifully decorated with trophies, and all round th
room laurel wreaths with 1828–1878 therein, really very pretty. One mo
successful idea was selling little bouquets on the stairs, to be thrown a
Frau Schumann as soon as she appeared. When she entered, from ever
corner of the room showered flowers. She did not in the least expect i
whichever way she looked she was smothered in them. I never saw anyon
look so delighted in my life; round the piano they lay a foot thick and sh
and Reinecke really had to dig a pathway and a clear space round the stoo
She played too exquisitely, such fire and pathos, and looked so beautiful a
the same time in dark red velvet with a long satin train'. A magnificent gol
laurel wreath, with names of composers played by her in the course of he
career on each of its leaves, was her present from the orchestra, presente
by Reinecke at the very end. 'And so I went to bed with a very gratefu
heart because God had allowed me to enjoy this day in the full possessio
of my artistic powers' was her own final diary comment.

Two things alone chilled the glow. Realizing that Brahms had distar
engagements as well as being totally submerged in his Violin Concerto, o
October 8 she had written to say that unless he could combine the journe
with some useful objective she would rather he did not come just on he
account. But that he took her at her word hurt her to the quick. As sh
wrote again on November 4: 'the fact that, although you were on you
travels, and the principal concert in Dresden was over, you did not se
your way to come – and secretly I did not give up hope till Thursday – wa
quite incomprehensible to me. Neither could I understand that amid s

---

[1] With the Concerto as its centrepiece, the programme, (including her own sor
'Warum willst du andre fragen' as well as five by Schumann sung by Frau Schultzen vo
Asten) began with the Overture to *Genoveva* and ended with Schumann's secon
Symphony, for which she sat in the audience.

many hearty congratulations, which came to me from friends and strangers alike, I had to go without yours, and it pained me very much'.[1]

Infinitely worse was the knowledge that while she rejoiced, Felix, the most beloved of her children, lay dying. By mid-October the doctors at Falkenstein, unable to do anything more, insisted that he should return home; he rejoined the family in Frankfurt on November 1. The devoted Eugenie, to whom he had always been closest, never long left his side. There was a decorated tree for what all knew would be his last Christmas. But his suffering was cruel and incessant, exhausting everyone the more in realization of their total inability to help. With the New Year Clara resumed a heavy work schedule, albeit with a bleeding heart, even accepting engagements as far away as Basel[2] and Zurich because, as she put it: 'In times of trial work is the one thing which keeps the soul erect. Then again, work of this sort is part of my vocation as an artist, and this is so much part of my life itself that I cannot imagine myself following the same sort of daily round as ordinary people. I knew, too, that my Felix liked it when I was in request on account of my art'. Rather than break an old promise, on returning she also played Schumann's Concerto and his 'Traumeswirren', also miniatures by Mendelssohn and Chopin, at a Museum concert on February 14, subsequently marvelling in the diary how she got through it without missing a single note since constantly haunted by a vision of her emaciated son, gasping for breath. On the night of February 15–16, after a fearful struggle, Felix died – in the arms of his sister, Marie, 'she who is always sacrificing herself, so full of love, she wished to spare me this'. When his body was taken away, Clara's anguish was sharpened by the bitterest remorse that on the 14th it had been the call of music she had felt it her duty to answer. Yet there was assuagement in the knowledge that he was now at rest. As if aware that fate could bring her no more dastardly blow, barely a week later she could write to Brahms: 'But I am calm, only terribly sad'.

[1] On October 18 Elisabet Herzogenberg had even been moved to write to warn him of the pain his absence would cause Clara.
[2] At her second concert in Basel on January 29 she included 'Eusebius' in *Carnaval*, as she had never done before, or was ever to do again in public, insofar as can be gleaned from surviving printed programmes.

SIXTEEN

The Frankfurt Teacher and Editor 1879–88

It was work that kept her soul erect in the immediate future. 'In one way the days are too short but on the other hand I have not the strength to work on without ceasing as I used to be able to' she wrote to Levi on April 23, 1879, deeply involved in private lessons as well as her quota for the music school. 'Before breakfast I walk for half-an-hour, and again after my lessons between 1 and 2 when I pay calls, do my shopping etc; then at 4 I give lessons; 5 to 6.30 I am at home to callers – say yourself what time is left to me? I have all the correspondence with Härtel's and Brahms about the complete edition of Schumann, and all my other letters to write. This goes on and on, and at the same time I must practise'.

In May she was still more occupied: unable to find a suitable golden wedding present for her Dresden friends, the Hübners, she was delighted when Marie suggested that she should compose them a March in the form of a duet. Beautifully bound in blue velvet embossed with gold, and with each page of the manuscript delicately gold-bordered, her presentation copy[1] was inscribed 'Den lieben Freunden Julius und Paulina Hübner, als Festgrüss zum 21 Mai 1879'. The ceremonial main theme in E flat alternates with two trios, the first hinting at what she described as Robert's duet, 'Grossvater und Grossmutter' (in fact his setting of Grün's poem, 'Familien-Gemälde' for soprano and tenor, Op.34, No.4) to evoke the peacefulness of the grandparents surrounded by their children, the second recalling a nostalgic theme from *Manfred* which, as she put it 'is enshrined in my heart and calls up the past oftener than any other memory'.

The Frankfurt house, No.32 Myliusstrasse, its French windows and balcony opening on to a rose-filled garden, was attractive enough to lessen the wrench of saying good-bye to their old Baden home when it was at long last sold in the summer of 1879. After further massage in Kiel and a visit to friends in Düsseldorf Clara chose Wildbad-Gastein for her own summer rest-cure with Marie (in her turn recovering from a broken knee), though pressure from Härtel's over the complete Schumann edition allowed little true relaxation. Anxious not to have the job hanging over her for ever she enlisted the conductor, Ernst Franck, her half-

---

[1] Now in the Schumann-Haus at Zwickau.

rother, Woldemar Bargiel and Alfred Volkland (a musicologist and ublisher from Basel) as extra collaborators. But it was to Brahms, hilosophical enough to recommend discharging it all without undue rush r stress, to whom she incessantly turned for all basic editorial advice – ven as to whether she was right in insisting that Schumann's German xpression marks should not be translated into Italian. It was again to 3rahms that she appealed for time-consuming help during her 1880 ummer holiday (mainly divided between Schluderbach and Berchtes-·aden after visits to Munich for an exhibition and to Oberammergau for he Passion Play) in preparing a selection from the four volumes of :zerny's Exercises he had sent them on learning that Marie and Eugenie /ere taking over Clara's preparatory classes.[1] He had similarly been her ·rime source of strength in Bonn that May when Donndorf's new 1emorial to Schumann was unveiled, arranging a chorus from *Paradise nd the Peri* for wind instruments (since the clergy considered the words 1sufficiently Christian) for the ceremony itself, conducting splendid erformances of the 'Rhenish' Symphony and *Requiem für Mignon* at the elebratory concert that same evening (May 2), and even joining Joachim nd others in the E flat major Quartet at a chamber music matinée the next ay – though because of limited time for piano practice his contribution to his caused Clara (already much pained because Levi had absented imself) to feel as if she was 'sitting on thorns'. Her greatest indebtedness o Brahms at this time was nevertheless for his own music – not just the 'iolin Concerto, which swept her off her feet after hearing Joachim play it 1 Frankfurt in December 1879, but works which she could at once add to er own repertoire without fear of strain. The Eight Piano Pieces, Op.76, he Two Rhapsodies, Op.79, the G major Violin and Piano Sonata, Op.78, nd before long a Piano Trio in C, Op.87, all helped her to regain her ense of mission at a vital moment of need. With Joachim as partner she ntroduced the G major sonata at a Frankfurt Museum concert on)ecember 20, 1880, having already played it with a local violinist, Hugo Ieermann, at a smaller chamber concert that April.

By now she had at last heeded warnings and resolved to cut out all oncerts involving over-arduous travel, which thanks to interest accruing ·rom the Schumann Fund and to unexpected royalties from Peters in _eipzig and Durand in France on top of her Frankfurt salary, she was able o do without undue worry. Despite the physical penalties of en-roaching age, she was aware of certain compensations. Outstanding uccesses in Frankfurt in October, 1879 (Mozart's D minor Concerto), in .arlsruhe two months later and in Basel early in 1880 (the *Davidsbündler*

---

[1] This subsequently appeared as 'Exercises and Studies from Carl Czerny's *Great ;chool of Piano Playing, Op.500*, selected and edited by Clara Schumann (published by \ug. Cranz)'.

and Brahms's F minor Piano Quintet) were capped, in her estimation, b
her performance of Beethoven's 'Emperor' at the Frankfurt Museur
Concerts on October 8, 1880, which she believed she had 'never played s
well . . . the new insight I had gained, the sense of complete mastery of th
whole, made me happy all the evening. There is something exalting in th
consciousness that in spite of age one advances steadily. I often think tha
my feelings have grown colder, but today I felt just the contrary. Ah!
only one's physical powers kept pace with one's powers of soul an
developed in like manner!'

By the new year she felt strong enough to accept eleven engagements i
England, unvisited, because of her own and Felix's ill-health, since 187
Again the house-guest of Arthur Burnand, together with Marie an
another friend, at 14 Hyde Park Gate, she returned to a reception of totall
unprecedented warmth, not only from the general public 'who welcome
me as if I was their darling' and often had to be turned away in hundred
from sold-out halls, but also, to her much greater amazement, from Th
Times. On his retirement, J. W. Davison had been succeeded in 1878 b
the German-born Francis Hueffer. So instead of the grudging acclaim o
old she found her first Popular Concert glowingly reviewed on March
1881, not in the usual slot allotted to artistic events but on the leadin
political page, directly beneath the Court Circular from Windsor Castl
and the latest medical bulletin on Mr Gladstone: 'Mme Schuman
appeared last night at the Monday Popular Concerts for the first time afte
an interval of several years. She was greeted with an enthusiasm reserve
for a few favourites of the public, and fully warranted by her position in th
art-world. That position is, indeed, of an exceptional kind, being, as it is
connected with the career of one of the greatest composers of moder
times. It was her talent and her courage which gained acknowledgemen
for the works of her husband, when other virtuosi timidly shrank fron
introducing them to the public, and the few triumphs – few, if his rea
merits are considered – which Schumann gained in his life were to a grea
extent owing to the admiration excited everywhere by the exceptional gif
of his wife. Mme Schumann will be remembered as the interpreter of he
husband's genius when other virtuosi are lost in oblivion. It need scarcel
be added that, apart from this connexion, she ranks among the foremos
pianists of modern times. We, therefore, state with more than ordinar
satisfaction, that her power remains unimpaired by her recent indisposi
tion. Her reading is as original, her touch as delicate, her passion a
impetuous as ever, and her performance of Schumann's *Etudes symphoni
ques* can only be called masterly. The choice of this work, which the artis
16 years ago introduced to the English public, was of peculiar significanc
in the circumstances. A piece more congenial to her power she could no
have selected. In addition to this, she played, with Herr Joachim

Brahms's new sonata for violin and piano, Op.78. The applause after this performance also was unanimous. For more detailed criticism we have not at present space at our disposal'.

In the context of the visit as a whole (in the course of which she found a place for Schumann's *Faschingsschwank aus Wien*, *Waldscenen* and *Humoreske*), herself was particularly pleased with her performance of Beethoven's A major Sonata, Op.101, at a Popular Concert on March 14: at last she felt she had found the 'true warm feeling' for the first movement in which she had disappointed Mendelssohn when playing the work to him some forty years earlier. Hearing the highly gifted, sixteen-year-old Eugène d'Albert[1] for the first time (in the *Etudes symphoniques*), being made an honorary member of the Royal Academy of Music, reunions with old friends like the Townsends and the Goldschmidts, and choosing a smart little travelling trunk to take back as a present for Brahms[2] were experiences no less gratifying. But the safe arrival in London on April 12 of Elise and her husband and children (a second son had been born the previous July) from America, and their return to Frankfurt together three days later, prompted her warmest thanks to heaven. The Sommerhoffs' company in Switzerland that August, after Clara had rested at Zell-am-See and taken the waters at Wildbad-Gastein, was the highspot of the summer.

She refused an invitation from Brahms to hear him play his 'small' (as he put it) new Piano Concerto in B flat with the Meiningen Court Orchestra under Bülow in November on the grounds that because of the risk of rheumatism, travel in winter had to be restricted to her own concerts: she had already guessed that its physical demands would always keep it out of her own repertory. German engagements had in fact already taken her away that autumn more than was good for the Hoch Conservatoire. While in her heart of hearts she still felt that her public came first, her concern for the welfare of the school was genuine and deep, especially when Bernhard Scholz, a firmer disciplinarian and more generously endowed musician,[3] was appointed director after Raff's death in 1882. At the end of one particular academic year Brahms even remonstrated with her for so assiduously attending all six examination concerts, even the one in which she had no pupil playing, just so that nobody should feel slighted or hurt. Her interest in her pupils extended far beyond music into their personal lives. She was very concerned that those less affluent should in

[1] Soon often to play both of Brahms's piano concertos in a single programme under the composer's own baton.

[2] To ensure the size met his needs she requested him to post her lengths of string or ribbon cut to the appropriate length and breadth.

[3] She had learnt his Capriccio for piano and orchestra to play under his own baton at a concert in Breslau on November 25, 1875.

no way feel deprived, and quickly elicited the help of Frankfurt well-wishers in raising a fund that she could administer at will – such as to finance a summer holiday in Vordereck in 1881 for the highly talented Fräulein Houfer, then suffering from nerves. On Christmas Day she liked nothing better than inviting all pupils to her house for a party. Each customarily played a little solo, after which Eugenie, dressed up as Santa Claus, gave them presents, accompanied by her own doggerel rhymes, from the lighted tree. Supper was followed by games, with Clara herself improvising at the piano, softer or louder as the search dictated, in the popular game of 'Hunt the Slipper'. Because Brahms turned up unexpectedly in an uncommonly good mood the 1882 party was a particular success: 'I was quite carried out of myself' so Clara confessed to the diary, even though having to add that by this time his own piano playing had become nothing more than 'thump, bang and scrabble'.

At their lessons pupils knew at once where they were with her: when pleased she sat still, when displeased she fidgeted. If seriously dissatisfied, she frequently made them cry. Already by the autumn of 1880 Marie had accepted a staff appointment to take preparatory classes for her mother; Eugenie, though at first reluctant to have the Conservatoire overrun with Schumanns, soon joined her. Their primary task was to ensure a sound technical grounding so that Clara herself could concentrate on interpretation with those deemed sufficiently worthy of being passed on. It was her custom to teach a group of three together, twice a week, so that each could learn from listening to the others, with the folding doors of her large music-room left open so that away in the background Marie's and Eugenie's pupils could overhear the lessons. Visiting friends sometimes found themselves involved too. Describing a very pleasant week at Clara's 'grand new house' to Brahms in July 1882, Elisabet Herzogenberg wrote 'It was too charming to see her in her professional capacity, as, with flushed cheeks, she brought forward her best pupils to play to us – severe and lenient, teacher and mother by turns, as she listened. I could not help thinking to myself "How nice to be born again and become her pupil." '

'You will never make an artist until you have loved and suffered' was the corner-stone of her belief. When her private pupils in Baden way back in 1870 included the sixteen-year-old Emma Brandes, she had expressed the view that Emma could one day become her own successor – but only if her playing gained 'that fire and depth of feeling which springs from the joys and sorrows of life'. Even after once hearing a youthful American soprano, Josephine Bayley, sing 'Widmung' at a private reception her comment was 'Don't sing my husband's songs till you have been in love'. To stimulate the imagination she frequently resorted to visual imagery, urging her pupils to conjure up pictures of their own as they played. Yet for all her emphasis on feeling and meaning she passionately disliked any suspicion of sentimentality or affectation. 'Play what is written, as it is written. It all stands there' was a constant exhortation: she knew it was the sincerity, purity and truth of her own playing in an age of flamboyant virtuosity that gave her a place apart.

Speeding for its own sake she regarded as a crime. 'Keine Passagen' was her regular cry if figuration was gabbled for mere virtuoso display, and to avoid it she preferred basic five-finger-exercise-type fingering rather than dodges to make things easier. Her frequent question 'Why hurry over beautiful things?' applied not just to slow movements but to countless contexts where the clarity of inner parts or the subtleties of cross-rhythms could be jeopardized by speed – not least in her husband's works. Firm rhythm she judged of immeasurable importance; having chosen a judicious basic tempo for any piece or movement she felt that subsequent changes should relate to it rather than drawing attention to themselves in a world apart (as with the second subject of the first movement of Beethoven's 'Waldstein' or the finale of Schumann's G minor Sonata); rubato she never countenanced unless requested, and then in no way anticipated or extended.

In phrasing she emphasized breadth, achieved through minutely controlled dynamic gradation within a perfect legato. Slow movements had always to 'breathe deeply'. To produce melodic eloquence in inner parts or basses she advised thinking of each strand as if played by different instruments of an orchestra. Beautiful tone was a *sine qua non*, with perfect equality between fingers in chords to produce the maximum resonance (as in the opening theme of the *Etudes symphoniques*, where too much was often sacrificed to melody). Like her father, she envisaged the pedals as sources of colour rather than aids to *fortissimo* or *pianissimo* – the latter, however delicate, had to be of a clarity to reach the remotest corner of the largest hall. Again like her father she did not encourage excessively long hours of practice. But she insisted on good general musicianship, from sight-reading and transposition at the keyboard to regular attendances at all Frankfurt's main orchestral rehearsals and operatic performances (for which special student tickets could be obtained at modest price). She also inherited her father's belief that nothing was more bracing for youthful minds and fingers alike than long daily walks in the fresh air.

When convinced of outstanding talent, as notably with the sparkling and strikingly attractive young Pole, Nathalie Janotha, whom she had taught intermittently since 1871, the high-spirited Hungarian, Ilona Eibenschütz, the sensitively thoughtful Fanny Davies and Leonard Borwick from England, together with their fluent compatriot, Adelina de Lara, of whom Marie, in particular, had the highest hopes, Clara was untiring in efforts to launch them professionally. On several occasions she recommended Janotha, everywhere a Court favourite, as her deputy, even despatching her to London in her own stead in 1874. When the American student, Amy Fay, heard Janotha in Berlin in 1872 her enthusiastic comment was that 'she played exactly like Clara Schumann'; significantly in Frankfurt in 1888 Clara declined to give her further lessons, believing it essential for her to play in her own way. Eibenschütz, an erstwhile child prodigy, was another for whom she was prepared to write endless letters of introduction even though aware that she was liable to give too free a rein to her own temperament. (Admiring both in London, Bernard Shaw summed up Janotha as often too proud to bare her innermost heart to the general public, and Eibenschütz, after an all-conquering English début, as over addicted to speeding in the heat of excitement). To closer friends, including Joachim, Clara nevertheless admitted that her favourite pupil, and the one she thought would go farthest, was Leonard Borwick. Initially she feared his English reserve might stand in his way, and even advised his father to recall him for a business career. But as time went on, and notably after a performance of Brahms's D minor Piano Concerto in Vienna in February, 1891, much praised by its composer, Clara came to accept Borwick as the one in whom her own ideals of truth and proportion, underpinned by deep commitment, were most perfectly realized – not even excepting her own daughters, Marie and Eugenie, about whom she often worried since so much of their own platform potential was sacrificed in her own personal cause.

Close contact with the young soon convinced Clara of the necessity of passing down the 'Schumann tradition', as she saw it, in an instructive edition of the piano music containing detailed help with pedalling, fingering, phrasing, and last but not least, tempo. Whereas in the Schumann Gesellschaft undertaken with Brahms she had finally left metronome markings much as she found them, in the new project (emerging in 1887) she added her own wherever unsupplied by Schumann, as most notably in *Carnaval*, the F sharp minor Sonata and the *Fantasiestücke*, Op.12, as well as modifying many of his in the light of her own platform experience. The *Etudes symphoniques*, the C major *Phantasie*, the G minor Sonata, the *Arabeske*, *Blumenstück* and *Humoreske*, the three *Romances*, the *Fantasiestücke*, Op.111, besides many other miniatures, emerged practically untouched. In several other contexts her alterations were small enough scarcely to seem worth making at all, such as when 68 is replaced by 69 for the Theme and Variations in the Sonata-for-the-young written for the eight-year-old Julie. But elsewhere, and particularly in the *Davidsbündler*, *Kinderscenen* and *Kreisleriana*, her modifications, now faster, now slower, are sufficiently personal to make it a matter of regret that she did not print Schumann's markings alongside her own throughout the edition as well as indicating where he himself had chosen not to supply them. For while pieces like 'Bittendes Kind' and 'Träumerei' from

Kinderscenen arguably thrive on the extra breathing time she allows them, a liberty such as changing his quaver marking from 84 to 108 for the *Lento assai* (No. 6) in *Kreisleriana* is seriously open to question – the more so since he cared enough about this and the *Molto lento* (No. 4) to use the metronome for just these two slow numbers of the work alone. Her removal of dedications unpleasing to her, such as the G minor Sonata to Henriette Voigt (Schumann's confidante over Ernestine), the Op.12 *Fantasiestücke* to Robena Laidlaw (the British pianist who liked him enough in the mid 1830s to send him a lock of her hair), and the C major *Phantasie* to Liszt, was a more understandable, albeit reprehensible, human foible.

Every hour devoted to the task was of course motivated by love, and the passionate wish that posterity should understand her husband's genius in a way many of his contemporaries had not. It awakened a nostalgia so strong that, re-reading his youthful letters at much the same time, she felt compelled to prepare an edition of these for publication too – a task completed with Heinrich Herzogenberg's help in 1885, bringing her countless messages of thanks. Billroth, sent a copy by Brahms, felt that nothing ever revealed more of Schumann's soul than his letters to his bride-to-be. As he put it 'One can believe Clara could exist without Robert, but one couldn't think of Robert without Clara'.

Frequently asking herself, in the increasing introspection of advancing years, where she found the strength to go on living and working, the answer was invariably 'in my children and in art – they have sustained me by their love, and art too has never played me false' as she put it yet again in the autumn of 1884. But new trials were already looming. In February, 1885, her Frankfurt house was burgled, necessitating the installation of elaborate safety devices and the acquisition of a large dog. That same October she lost her brother, Alwin, after four months of 'unspeakable suffering'. In August, 1887, Elise's only daughter, just four, died of diphtheria. She was still more lastingly disturbed on realizing that her hitherto steadfast son, Ferdinand, unwisely treated by doctors with morphia for a rheumatic condition contracted during the war, had become an addict in need of constant medical care, leaving her with the responsibility of organizing homes and schools for the three eldest of his six children – she had already had some of them to stay for two boisterous months in 1884 when their mother was ill. Another nasty fall in Berlin in 1883 provoked further panic about her own health, too, such as when stabbing pains in the chest during her English tour of 1884 convinced her that she was dying of paralysis or consumption until told by the doctor that a good dinner with some champagne would soon put her right. Two years later a German doctor banished similar bogeys by attributing all her pains to nerves rather than any organic cause. But engagements still had sometimes to be cancelled because of rheumatism or neuralgia: in 1888 she was unable to attend the opening of the Frankfurt Conservatoire's new buildings for the same reason. There was also further evidence of ear trouble: a bad attack in February, 1886, even prompted the admission 'I cannot follow any music properly, it is all blurred, and often I hear all the higher parts a semitone too high'.

Whatever her apprehensions, once on the platform her rapport with the audience invariably carried her through, even in works as taxing as Chopin's F minor Concerto, chosen for the opening of the new Leipzig Gewandhaus on November 26, 1885, and Schumann's F sharp minor Sonata, both reintroduced into her repertory at this time after considerable absence. After hearing her in Berlin in the spring of 1885, alone and with Joachim, her half-brother, Woldemar, was at once moved to salute the growing clarity of her playing, progressing from clearness of detail to 'clearness of form and the perfectly finished interpretation of works as a whole. You, Clara, are achieving this more and more as years go on, drawing ever nearer to perfection, so that under your fingers music seems ever more spiritual and more pure whilst at the same time you have remained true to your own individuality in the best sense of the word. As surely as this is the right way, which every true artist treads by instinct, so surely and sharply does it contrast with the artistic methods of the present day, which strive after sensation'.

No praise could have been slanted to please her more, for when Liszt died in the summer of 1886, she lamented him in words leaving no doubt as to her understanding of why and where their ways had parted: 'He was a great piano virtuoso, but a dangerous model for the young to imitate. Almost all the rising pianists imitated him, but they lacked his mind, his genius, his delicacy of touch, so that now we have nothing but great masters of technique and a number of caricatures. Then Liszt was a bad composer . . . his compositions lack all the qualities which have been mentioned as belonging to him as a virtuoso; they are trivial, wearisome, and they will soon disappear now that he has gone. His personal charm and brilliant execution have always turned people's heads, and so they have accepted his works. As a young man he was most fascinating, but later he let so much coquetry blend with his really intellectual and charming disposition that I often found it disagreeable'. On Wagner's death three years before she had been moved to write a letter of sympathy to Levi, knowing how much the loss would mean to him. But her efforts in Frankfurt in 1882 to come to terms with *Rheingold* and *Walküre* under the much admired, recently appointed Dessoff, prompting her to attend both twice over so that the second time she could ignore the 'boredom' of the stage action, the 'flabbiness' of the gods, the 'stupidity' of Wotan and much else, to concentrate on the orchestration, had proved as unavailing as ever – except for recognition of just one or two fine orchestral effects ('but they keep recurring') and some redeeming reminiscences of 'Mendelssohn, Schumann and Marschner'. It was Brahms who for her still trod the only true path. As she put it after a rehearsal of his D minor Sonata for violin and piano in 1888: 'I once more thanked heaven for sending so strong and healthy a genius into the world in the midst of the Wagner mania, one who counteracts it for the moment and who must soon conquer it entirely. Mankind must in the long run regain its health through the true and great works which Brahms produces as he advances along the path marked out by his predecessors'.

There were strong grounds for her confidence at this moment. Since her joyous discovery of his third Symphony in early 1884 there had been its successor in E minor and the Double Concerto for violin and cello besides songs and chamber works in which she herself could share, such as the C minor Piano Trio (she took part in the Frankfurt première on October 28, 1887), the F major Sonata for cello and piano, and two more violin and piano Sonatas in A major and D minor, which with Heermann she introduced at the Frankfurt Museum concerts on April 20, 1888, and November 1, 1889, respectively. Like the Double Concerto, the violin sonatas were primarily written to repair the breach with Joachim that had arisen after Brahms in 1880 had openly sided with Amalie on the breakdown of her marriage (long feared by Clara) in consequence of Joachim's inordinate jealousy and ill-founded suspicions of infidelity. The reconciliation was in fact effected by the Double Concerto, tried out in Clara's presence, with Joachim and Robert Hausmann as soloists under Brahms's own baton at a private rehearsal in Baden's Kursaal on September 23, 1887. But as so often before, hero worship did not allow her to apply a blind eye to her telescope. Just as she had found the second subject in the E minor Symphony's first movement too wilful and 'in no way adapted to what goes before', so now certain passages in the Double Concerto struck her as disturbing: 'it often seems as if he took delight in preventing the listener from enjoying himself too much'.

In their personal relationship Brahms's intense productivity ironically caused new strains. Recognizing Elisabet as a much more fluent score-reader as well as a younger and less circumscribed critic,[1] he by now nearly always sent her his new manuscripts first: it was she who in fact played the first two movements of his fourth Symphony to Clara for the first time at the resort of Vordereck in early September, 1885. Always he

[1] In her Memoirs Ethel Smyth recalls a conversation between Brahms and Clara as to why the theme of his D major Variations for piano 'had what she (Clara) called "an unnecessary bar tacked on", this being one of the supreme touches in that wonderful, soaring tune. She argued the point lovingly, but as ever with some heat, and I thought him divinely patient'.

urged Elisabet to forward everything just as soon as she possibly could, since, as he put it in the context of the D minor violin Sonata, 'You know Frau Schumann is very touchy'. Piqued by postal delays on top of supposed affronts to her artistic eminence,[1] Clara in fact more than once allowed self-control to desert her: 1886 and early 1887, in particular, brought outbursts of almost childish petulance. It was at this time that she asked Brahms to return all her early letters to him,[2] a request with which he reluctantly complied even though she failed to keep her part of the bargain in returning his letters to her. Yet almost overnight her irritability dissolved, forgotten, into pleas for his advice and help – whether over editorial uncertainties, or what books to read, or asking Billroth's opinion about a new doctor recommended for Ferdinand, or finding a special brand of Austrian cigars for Ferdinand's Christmas present – to which Brahms in his turn rarely turned a deaf ear, irked and hard-pressed as he often was by the claims of ever-growing success. On receiving her letter in the summer of 1888 saying that she was considering selling her comfortable Frankfurt home to raise money for Ferdinand's medical costs and the upkeep and education of his children,[3] his immediate reaction was to ask if he might unburden some of his 'superfluous pelf' by contributing 10,000 marks towards the grandchildren's immediate expenses. Pride at first forbad her to accept. But when in October some 15,000 marks suddenly arrived through the post, she relented: 'For the time being I shall put the money by and regard it as capital to be broken into and used for Ferdinand and his family without my having to feel that I am robbing the other children. This gives me a real sense of relief and I press your hand affectionately. There is sadness in my gratitude. I cannot tell you all that stirs in my soul'.

In several other ways 1888 proved a milestone. A party at Stockhausen's Frankfurt house in May, at which to celebrate his forty years on the platform he gave an unforgettable performance of the complete *Dichterliebe*, engulfed her in a flood of golden memories of all their past recitals together even though on this occasion she was not at the piano herself. The following month, on her way to visit Ferdinand in hospital at Köstritz and his three eldest sons boarded out with her niece in Schneeberg, she dropped in at Goethe's house in Weimar, and was again overcome with nostalgia on finding the Streicher piano on which she had played to him in 1831 in the selfsame place in the same room. A still keener awareness of the

---

[1] She proudly reported to him that she had received eighty-four letters on her 66th birthday in September 1885.

[2] Many of these she subsequently destroyed.

[3] For his only daughter, Julie, she had just succeeded in obtaining one of the Crown Princess of Prussia's scholarships at the Louisenstift School in Berlin after travelling to Ems for a personal audience with the Princess the previous year.

passing of time had hit her earlier that year in London, when exhausted by her eight engagements, she reluctantly decided that this, her nineteenth visit, must be her farewell to a city which, though so forbidding and unappreciative at the start, had eventually taken her to its heart more warmly than any other in which she had ever played.

Apart from brief visits to Utrecht in 1883 and Basel in 1887, England, after her return in 1881, had in fact proved the only foreign land inviting enough to dispel her growing fear of long distance travel. Her 1882 visit she always remembered for a performance of Mendelssohn's G minor Concerto celebrating the fiftieth anniversary of its première, a Philharmonic Society concert all the more pleasurable in that its second half allowed her to accompany the young soprano, Antonia Kufferath, daughter of her old Brussels friends, in her own song, 'O Lust', Op.23. But it was this March that she admitted in the diary to growing dissatisfaction with the stiff action of the Broadwood pianos she felt compelled to use in England – out of gratitude for practising facilities and much else. Just as Scharwenka had recently brought over his Blüthner, and Barth his Bechstein, so she longed for her own Steinweg (made at Braunschweig by the sole remaining German representative of this now American domiciled family) which, combining bass depth with a bright treble, had by now supplanted all previous instruments in her affection.

She was back in 1884, and again in 1886, the latter visit not easily forgotten because of a request to play in private to the dying Lady Florence Herbert which she answered with 'a number of soft movements from various Beethoven sonatas, and then a piece with broad strong chords'. For the general public that year she unearthed her own F sharp minor Variations, Op.20, and left even more convinced than before that 'the English are wonderfully responsive, though their stiff manners often conceal it. But if once they let themselves go, their feelings break out with greater energy than is the case with us Germans'. Her penultimate visit in 1887 brought a personal invitation from the Princess of Wales, when after entertaining her young daughters with some 'little pieces of Robert's', she was rewarded with a hair-piece designed as a 'swan holding a lyre, set with tiny brilliants' specially chosen by the Princess for its musical symbolism. Her ever welcoming host, Arthur Burnand, also organized another soirée in his house so that she could make amends to many English friends for her still limited command of the English language by playing to them – with the cellist from Joachim's Quartet, Robert Hausmann, as her partner in Beethoven's A major Cello Sonata. After her appearance at a Popular Concert on April 4, the 1000th of that series, a great crowd shouted 'Come back again, Frau Schumann' as she stepped into her carriage.

It was an appeal she could not refuse. She chose Chopin's F minor Concerto for her Philharmonic Society concert on March 15, 1888, again delighting in an opportunity provided by the second half to accompany a young English soprano, Liza Lehmann, in Schumann's 'Nussbaum' and 'Frühlingsnacht'. In four preceding and three following Monday and Saturday Popular Concerts, shared with star pupils such as Janotha and Fanny Davies as well as old friends like Joachim and Piatti, she found room for Beethoven's 'Les Adieux', Mendelssohn's Andante and Variations in E flat and two Songs without Words, also Brahms's C minor Trio. But Schumann had pride of place, with the *Phantasiestücke* for piano, violin and cello, the first *Novellette*, the *Humoreske*, two Studies from the Op.56 Suite for Pedal Piano, the *Romance* No.3 in B, and most notably the *Etudes symphoniques* and *Carnaval*, as her farewell choices. After her last concert on March 26 she wrote 'I was very nervous again, but I made a brilliant end with *Carnaval* – I think I never before played it as I did today, and yet I determined that this should be the end of my visits to England, and I felt sadder than words can say. How difficult it is to stop of one's own free will when one feels that one is still capable of doing something! But I am certain that I am right, I feel that my health would not much longer endure the strain. . . .'

1888 nevertheless still had its big surprise in store. Though she herself had forgotten that October would bring the golden jubilee of her platform début, her Frankfurt colleagues had not: shortly after entering her seventieth year that September she discovered that nothing less than a miniature festival was being planned in her honour. Agreeing to play Schumann's Concerto at a gala Museum concert on October 26 she had the additional pleasure that night of hearing her March, originally written for the Hübners' golden wedding, in a festive orchestral version made by Julius Otto Grimm; afterwards there were laurel wreaths, bouquets, addresses from Leipzig, Cologne, Berlin and London, and more than two hundred telegrams. Student and professorial tributes during celebrations at the Conservatoire touched her just as much. Always restless, she had not long before toyed with the idea of pastures new for her few remaining years. But such overwhelming demonstrations of affection 'put her to shame', as she wrote to Rosalie Leser. From this moment onwards she accepted Frankfurt as her final home.

SEVENTEEN

Ebbing Powers 1888–96

Her home, by now, was her castle. It gave her enormous satisfaction in the first place to have the means and comparative leisure to entertain more freely than of old, with lifelong personal friends such as Emilie List,[1] Livia Frege, Emma Preusser, Pauline Viardot and Christine Kufferath often making extended visits. Younger musicians of interest to her were always welcome too. Christine Kufferath's soprano daughter, Antonia, whom she had accompanied at a Philharmonic Society concert in London in 1882, in fact became engaged to the music-loving financier, Edward Speyer, in Clara's drawing-room. There was also the English soprano, Liza Lehmann, who having accepted an invitation to stay for several weeks to study Schumann's songs, was much touched when Clara insisted on carrying off 'La charmante Margeurite', a French chanson recently unearthed by Liza in the British Museum, to practise its very simple piano accompaniment before presuming to perform it with her even to friends. Ethel Smyth, another youthful visitor at Myliusstrasse 32, was delighted in her turn to discover so endearingly human and '*unblasiert*' a personality behind her hostess's sometimes over-earnestly high-priestess-like public mien, someone pretending to resent but in fact enjoying her daughters' teasing accusation that she only read murders and serial stories in the newspapers, someone only too eager to learn and demand the dedication of Ethel's recently composed 'Prelude and Fugue for Thin People' (so called because of rapid crossings of the hands) to prove that though well covered she was not really fat. 'A certain amount of initiative was needed to thaw her', so Ethel wrote home. 'If I hadn't taken my courage in both hands with her from the first she would never have shown me all her sweetness'.

Of all the guests there was nevertheless no one more eagerly awaited than Brahms. Clara's pupils at once noticed a quickening of pulse in the family as tastier dishes, choicer wines and prettier dresses were made ready in his honour. As Adelina de Lara put it: 'life became gayer, less formal, and it was impossible to keep to strict discipline once he was in the

---

[1] In her Memoirs Eugenie recalls the occasion when the ageing Clara and Emilie, heartily laughing at each other, had no alternative but to lift up their long skirts and climb over a gate after losing their way on a walk.

house'. She never forgot Clara's horror when just before a lesson Brahms jokingly gave her and other pupils some of the hot alcoholic grog Marie had made to cure his cold, or Brahms's pleading 'Warum bist du so ernsthaft, Clärchen?' when in early 1889, to the pupils' intense delight, the two old friends played them his Hungarian Dances as a duet, and other works too.

Musical parties at Myliusstrasse 32, often planned around special house-guests, began to recur with increasing frequency. That in Clara's eyes they had acquired a prestige akin to those of Pauline Viardot in former days at Baden was plain when to a chance enquiry from Liza Lehmann about acceptances and refusals for a gathering during her own visit, Clara replied 'We do not have refusals'. For many of those invited, not forgetting her own pupils, it was of course an inestimable privilege to hear artists of the calibre of Joachim, Hausmann, Stockhausen (who had also moved to Frankfurt in 1878 to join the staff of the Conservatoire) and the phenomenal Meiningen clarinettist, Richard Mühlfeld, in such intimately relaxed surroundings, also works that might not otherwise have come their way so soon, such as Dvorak's Piano Quintet, tried over with Clara at the keyboard in May, 1888, as well as so many by Brahms – with Mühlfeld's clarinet already as potent an inspiration as Joachim's violin. Now so dogged by nervousness in public, as when returning to Berlin in January, 1889, for Chopin's F minor Concerto and to Leipzig for Schumann's that March, Clara herself loved nothing more than making music at home surrounded only by friends, with Brahms's D minor Sonata for violin and piano, no matter who her partner, always a particular source of joy.

Holidays for the last four or five years had settled into a regular pattern of a curative summer month at the spa of Franzenbad followed by a stay at Obersalzburg, near Berchtesgaden (not far from the charming country house, 'Liseley', so much liked by her, which the Herzogenbergs had built for themselves in 1884) often with a brief spell at Baden on the way back – as also sometimes in the spring. But towards the end of April, 1889, with a seventieth birthday not a long way off, Clara felt the moment had come to venture deeper into Italy (her only previous visit had been to Venice in the autumn of 1882) as so long urged to do by Brahms, a total slave to its riches ever since his first introduction to them by Billroth in 1878. Accompanied by Marie and Eugenie, she tried first to cure a cough by going to Nice, where the Herzogenbergs were recuperating after Heinrich's long, muscular illness. From there they all went on to Florence, now the home of the sculptor, Hildebrandt, to whom Clara had grown so attached when she sat for him towards the end of 1885: she knew he was waiting to show them round – with a little camp-stool under his arm so that sight-seeing should not exhaust her. Anxious not to disappoint Brahms, even though he had shirked the responsibility of playing chaperon himself, she wrote of her pleasure in the Michelangelos at the Medici Chapel, in various madonnas, and of her journey to the marvels of Pisa through lovely pine-woods in the sun. But Elisabet, blunter than usual after the strain of nursing Heinrich, had a different tale. 'The dear thing has ten years too many on her shoulders, and has not the elasticity of temperament which one must possess if one would be perfectly happy among the Italians in spite of the dirt, fraud and general discomfort' she wrote to Brahms that May. 'Once or twice we found her miserably seated on her camp-stool before some Signorelli or Verocchio, rubbing her hands nervously and trying so hard to feel some enthusiasm. But nothing would come and carry her off her feet, nothing awake a response in her, receptive as she undoubtedly is. The truth is, we can only appreciate the best in art after a thorough apprenticeship; we have to serve our seven years for so many things in this world! But when the glorious soul did take in anything quickly, her beautiful grey eyes, dim with emotion, would light up with youthful fire, as we all live to see them, and how we rejoiced in these rare moments of happiness for her!'

To Rosalie Leser, Clara frankly admitted that she was too old for such a journey, and only too glad to get home. Her customary summer escape brought her much more pleasure, not least on reaching Baden, hand-picked for the celebration of her seventieth birthday on September 13. Laurel wreaths, medals, flowers, gifts and telegrams poured in from Emperors and Empresses and the Grand Duchess of Baden herself as well as Frankfurt colleagues (Scholz arrived in person with a floral basket almost too big for one man to carry) and precious friends such as Arthur Burnand, who had travelled all the way from England with his two nieces, and the Bendemanns, who sent a casket with his own paintings of himself with palette knife and his wife with a bouquet set in the lid.[1] Though Brahms was unable to join her until the 20th, her joy in members of her family at her side was immeasurably enhanced by the Sommerhoffs, who had recently been able to leave America to make a home in Frankfurt. On going to bed that birthday night her prayer was that 'heaven would let me enjoy the children's love for a few years longer, not in ill-health but with a body as capable of appreciating it as my heart is'.

1890 began with a bad attack of influenza and its customary aftermath of depression. But for much of the year her plea was answered. Not even impaired hearing too seriously curtailed the concert and opera going that she had always so steadfastly maintained to keep abreast of the times and set an example to her students, with novelties by relative newcomers including Richard Strauss and Saint-Saëns much more generously acclaimed in her

[1] Preserved in the Schumann-Haus at Zwickau.

diary than might have been expected from so stringent a critic of the New
German School. Stimulated by a spring visit from Brahms, in his turn
re-charged by the exploratory activity of the Meiningen Court Theatre,
she also spent more evenings than hitherto at the theatre – primarily for
the Shakespearean performances of the actor, Sonnenthal, who caused her
to 'revel' in excitement as she had not done since a girl. In her reading,
again often guided by Brahms, she was also active and responsive enough
at this time to compensate for any recent apathy and bewilderment among
the art treasures of Florence. Musically, however, it was Joachim who
made it a golden year in her book of memories by coming as her
house-guest, accompanied by a young cellist member of the Mendelssohn
family, for two parties to commemorate the 80th anniversary of Schumann's birth on June 8 and 9. After a performance of the A minor String
Quartet at the second she was so overwhelmed with nostalgia as to have
difficulty in sufficiently mastering emotion to join her friends in Schumann's E flat major Piano Quartet planned as final tribute.

When on November 7 of that same year she was enticed back to the
Frankfurt Museum Concerts to play Chopin's F minor Concerto once
more, her anticipatory nervousness was traumatic enough, though the
performance itself pleased her no less than the audience, to convince her
that she must never risk the strain of an orchestral engagement again.
Despite a bad cold, she nevertheless summoned up courage to partner a
Frankfurt colleague at a Museum Chamber Soirée on March 12, 1891, in
Brahms's Haydn Variations, arousing such applause that the whole set
had to be encored. 'They are simply glorious, and once more I stood
amazed at such art and such genius' so she wrote after this, her 1299th
public appearance[1] – destined to be her last – while eagerly awaiting a visit
from Brahms himself to hear his new G major String Quintet (No.2) at
the next Museum Concert. But already piqued by his despatch of the
manuscript to the ailing Herzogenbergs before Joachim or herself, as also
by his renewed references to the possibility of publishing Schumann's D
minor Symphony in the original version he so much admired, she was
unable to contain herself when almost immediately after his arrival on
March 20 they fell into a violent altercation over her favourite pupil,
Leonard Borwick, and his slating from the Viennese critics, notably
Brahms's revered Hanslick, after his recent performance of the D
minor Concerto – even praised by Brahms himself at the time. Register-
ing relief when he left, she likened the whole week's stay to 'a bad
dream'.

Still darker shadows were looming. Already saddened by the recent
deaths of Gade and Verhulst in the wake of other old friends including

---

[1] Insofar as can be deduced from surviving programmes.

Jenny Lind, Avé-Lallement and Eduard Bendemann, she heard in April that her devoted English admirer and host, Arthur Burnand, had died from a stroke. Eugenie was then staying at his house: he had joked with her only a few hours before. June 6 brought the further blow of Ferdinand's death in a nursing home at Gera. This was not unexpected. She even accepted it as a blessed release on learning that drugs had so weakened his internal organs that prolongation of life would have been an infinitely worse hell than anything still endured by Ludwig in his Colditz asylum. But she was troubled in conscience that she had not been with her son at this hour of need.

Worries about Ferdinand's children, together with nagging rheumatic pains and distortions of hearing, hung heavily over a summer only briefly lightened by the pleasure of renewed contact with Hildebrandt in Munich, and her first meeting, at a Berchtesgaden dinner-party, with the cultivated but sympathetically unpretentious Duke of Meiningen and his ex-actress wife, now not only generously putting their orchestra at Brahms's disposal, but offering the resources of their theatre to his Swiss writer friend, Joseph Widmann, too. When a warmer than ever invitation to Meiningen from them arrived towards the end of the summer Clara was even briefly tempted to accept, the more so since such friendly reassurance had just come from Brahms himself after her panic-stricken realization that the cadenzas for Mozart's D minor Concerto she was about to publish as her own contained some old material of his, particularly the first. Rejecting her suggestion of issuing it as 'founded on a cadenza by Johannes Brahms' his words had been 'If you did that I ought by rights to put against my best melodies "really by Clara Schumann", for with only myself to inspire me nothing profound or beautiful can possibly occur to me! I owe you more melodies than all the passages and so forth you could possibly take from me'. But almost at once she learnt that he had carried out his intention, constantly broached to her in letters ever since April, 1888, of publishing Schumann's D minor Symphony (under the editorship of the conductor, Franz Wüllner) in a score presenting the original and revised versions side by side for comparison. To Clara this was nothing less than *lèse-majesté*, an insult to Robert's memory and an affront to her own dignity and authority. Outraged, she at once picked up pen to claim that her official permission had never been sought or given in writing, and to make it quite plain to him that she found his behaviour impossible to understand or condone. Meanwhile the physical pains exacerbating her bitterness increased to such an extent that Scholz had to take over all her lessons. The start of 1892 boded still worse. January 7 brought the news that Elisabet Herzogenberg, exhausted by her husband's long illness, had died of a heart complaint. And having fallen and strained her right wrist on New Year's Day, Clara herself developed severe inflammation of the lungs. By

February she knew she had no alternative but to resign from the
Conservatoire.

*

An attempt to pull herself together in Locarno, where Eugenie, now forty,
was recuperating after a serious illness, proved useless. As she put it: 'I
had to leave her as I could not recover my own strength in the midst of all
the commotions which her fluctuating condition entails. . . . I need peace
and so does Eugenie. We got on each other's nerves and that made things
impossible'. It was not until moving on with Marie in June to Interlaken,
where their rooms at the Pension Ober (discovered some twenty years
before) looked out towards the Jungfrau, often lit up in the evening with a
most beautiful glow, that calm gradually returned. A bath-chair specially
ordered from Heidelberg allowed her to make pleasant expeditions.
Visiting the little village of Ringgenberg, with its wood-carved houses and
the church where Mendelssohn loved to play, was always a special joy.
She was still at Interlaken for her 73rd birthday that September, when
Eugenie arrived for a brief reunion with her mother before leaving to start
a new life in England, free from family pressures, as a music teacher. But
more affecting, just at this moment, was her greeting from Brahms; she
had maintained a polite enough correspondence with him throughout the
year, not least in the context of his sister's illness and death, but had never
again invited him to see her:

'Permit a poor outcast to tell you today that he always thinks of you with
the same respect, and out of the fulness of his heart wishes you, whom he
holds dearer than anyone on earth, all that is good, desirable and
beautiful. Alas, to you I am only a pariah; this has, for a long time, been my
painful conviction, but I never expected it to be so harshly expressed. . . .
After forty years of faithful service (or whatever you care to call my
relationship to you) it is very hard to be merely "another unhappy
experience". But after all, this can be borne. I am accustomed to
loneliness and will need to be with the prospect of this great blank before
me. But let me repeat to you today that you and your husband constitute
the most beautiful experience of my life, and represent all that is richest
and most noble in it. . . . You devoted J.B.'

Further exchanges in the weeks that followed made it plain that old
wounds still smarted, with Brahms no longer attempting to hide his own
hurt that her complete Schumann edition had omitted several unpublished pieces he had begged her to salvage.[1] Yet in their hearts both knew

[1] These, including movements rejected from the G minor and F minor Sonatas, and
variations discarded from the *Etudes symphoniques*, eventually appeared in a supplementary
volume.

that old ties were too strong to be severed, the more so since the nostalgia underlying his birthday letter was already overflowing in a spate of new works for solo piano – not taxing sonatas or variations as of old, but intimate miniatures within her own present grasp. 'Full of poetry, passion, sentiment, emotion, and having the most wonderful effects of tone' was her diary comment on receiving eleven of them, all as yet unpublished, that November: 'In these pieces I at last feel musical life stir once more in my soul. . . . How they make one forget much of the suffering he has caused one . . .'. By the end of January, 1893, after an absence of nearly two years, he was again a guest in her house on his way through Frankfurt, playing all his new pieces to her in exactly the same way she herself had envisaged them. Hearing his Clarinet Quintet for the first time that March broke down her defences still more, just as the première of the *German Requiem* had done at a similar moment of personal strain a quarter of a century before.

The return the previous month of her old colleague, Anton Rubinstein, after long absence from these parts, had already prompted reflections in the diary on the comparative transience of the mere performer, here today, forgotten tomorrow, herself included. Marie and Ferdinand's daughter, Julie (now living with them for musical help and encouragement) had gone on her behalf to his Frankfurt recital, reporting the same puzzling extremities of enchantment and unrestrained violence of old. For her it was shock enough to hear that in Bonn, in aid of the Beethoven house, he had played four sonatas straight off and then added a fifth as encore. As she wrote to Brahms 'One puts one's whole soul into one sonata, can one put it into five? But this is perhaps pedantic. Evidently I belong to a bygone age'.

Aware as she was that her own platform days were done, she had nevertheless not exaggerated when claiming that musical life had once more begun to stir in her soul. Already in January she had started to teach again, sometimes helping with Marie's class but also accepting private pupils of her own. She resumed a little visiting, too, so startling old friends that their effusive welcomes made her feel as if she had 'risen from the dead'. An Easter holiday at Pallenza, with frequent boat excursions on Lake Maggiore, rekindled still more of her old fighting spirit, especially when after striking up a friendship with the local, music-loving doctor and introducing him to Brahms's new pieces, he declared that anyone capable of feeling and playing with so much life could and should do more to repair her physique. It was at his suggestion that she and Marie spent July at the wooded spa of Schlangenbad before returning to the Pension Ober at Interlaken, where Eugenie joined them too for most of August and September. The return journey included the new experience of a visit to Widmann in Berne. Besides calling on them several times in Interlaken and sending them some of his writings[1] Widmann had also helped them, at Brahms's suggestion, to obtain a small upright piano which they were able to instal at a nearby peasant's house. During previous summers she had been willing enough to leave her fingers idle.

Back in Frankfurt, by the end of the year she had in fact learnt all Brahms's reflective *Intermezzi* and many of the more strenuous pieces too, now assembled into sets and published as Opp.116, 117, 118 and 119. In December she also received his newly published 51 Exercises, compiled over many years, accompanied by a warning that they were very apt 'to cause all kinds of harm and damage to the hands (sensitive hands!)'. Practising was difficult because of a droning in her ears even more persistent than before: it also tired her enough physically to have to be restricted to two daily half-hour sessions. But as she wrote to him: 'Every day my most beautiful hour is the one I owe to you', marvelling the more at the passion and tenderness combined in such small spaces since she knew the music's inner message was for her alone, just as Robert's had been in days of old. Even pieces so teeming with discords that Brahms feared her displeasure, not least the very slow, sad Intermezzo he sent her on his sixtieth birthday in May, 1893, as an intimately personal token of remembrance,[2] found her prepared to luxuriate in their bittersweetness.

By the end of the year she was ready to invite friends to the house again to share in the riches of her wonderful new 'treasure chest'. January 1894 brought the special joy of a visit from Joachim, who joined her in a performance of Brahms's D minor Sonata so rapturous that she felt she was 'floating on clouds'. On Woldemar Bargiel's arrival in Frankfurt that March she played to him too, sufficiently impressing him with her refinement of rhythm in a Schumann Canon that he even recalled it in a letter nine months later – a tribute the more pleasing because Marie and Eugenie had always singled out rhythm as one of the prime sources of her distinction.

But her deepest satisfaction, as a seventy-fifth birthday loomed even closer, was the help she could offer her grandson, Ferdinand (named after his father). With Marie her only ally, she defied his guardian, and others, by countenancing his wish to throw over his three years' apprenticeship to a chemist in favour of music, and inviting him, though aware of his limitations and the handicap of so late a start, to come and live and study with her, just as his sister, Julie, had recently done for a while too. Many years before, on once finding Eugenie immersed in Hilty's book, *Happiness*, she had observed that happiness was a very simple thing: 'You need

---

[1] Including his play *Jenseits von Gut und Böse*, which Brahms all too plainly intimated she would not understand unless her daughters could enlighten her about Nietzsche and his influence on philosophy.

[2] No opus number or key is mentioned in their correspondence.

only do your duty in all circumstances'. Now, through Ferdinand, she proved it. With both grandson and granddaughter as her guests, that year's Interlaken summer was one of her best. They rented a chalet of their own, taking their Frankfurt maids and installing a splendid grand piano. Always cheerful, good-natured and eager to learn, Ferdinand had the time of his life making long country excursions and swimming in the lake as well as keeping up his lessons in music and French. Clara herself willingly renounced the game of whist she had come to enjoy in the evenings so that good books could be read aloud, *en famille*, with Goethe's *Wilhelm Meister* their ultimate goal. The march of time could almost have been forgotten but for an unfortunate incident in early September, when, forsaking her bath-chair for a little stroll with Eugenie and a friend, she was compelled to jump clear of 'an incompetent rider on a frisky horse', painfully bruising her arm and shoulder in her resulting fall down a steep bank.

*

On their immediate arrival in Switzerland, even Marie had been surprised by her mother's determination to attend a Beethoven festival in Basel, with the *Missa Solemnis*, the Choral Symphony, the Violin Concerto and a recital by Joachim's famous quartet its highlights. But it was important to Clara to feel she 'still had a part in such things'; though defective hearing seriously curtailed her musical pleasure, she thrived on renewed contact with artists and friends. Back in Frankfurt, a similar stimulus came through Brahms's proposal that he and Mühlfeld should meet in her house to rehearse his two new Sonatas for clarinet and piano. The date was fixed to overlap with Joachim's November engagements in the city, including a performance of the Violin Concerto in an all-Brahms orchestral concert at which she proudly sat in the audience at Johannes's side. At parties in honour of the occasion, one at the Sommerhoffs', the other in her own home, she was at the piano in Schumann's *Phantasiestücke* for clarinet and a trio by Mozart, again enduring considerable secret agony because of the droning in her ears, yet emerging from it all sufficiently re-charged to welcome Brahms's suggestion of a return in February, 1895, for a rehearsal of his Clarinet Quintet at Myliusstrasse 32 while he was in the vicinity for various other concerts. This visit, too, gave rise to several convivial social gatherings. In his belated letter of thanks Brahms admitted to constantly recalling the charming circle of friends, young and old, she had gathered around her, urging her to give herself, and them, 'the pleasure of meeting and talking without restraint far more often'.

For the rest, life settled into its old routine, with, as she put it, 'here and there a pupil who gives me real pleasure'. Taking the occasional ensemble class proved rewarding, too, such as one at the start of 1895 when she played Beethoven's G major Trio to her students 'with real delight'. It was at this time that she also began to arrange some of Schumann's pedal-piano pieces for two hands with a view to publication. As so often before, Brahms's help was constantly sought: on receiving his revisions of her manuscript and his corrections of her proofs she was only too ready to admit that without his guidance she could not have done her husband justice.

For her 1895 summer she again rented a very pleasant and commodious chalet at Interlaken, installing a Steinweg semi-grand piano, though news of the death of her dear friend, Lida Bendemann, to whom she and Marie had so very recently paid one of their regular visits, inevitably gave her thoughts a darker cast. (1894 had already claimed others, including Billroth and Anton Rubinstein, on the periphery of her circle). But reunion with Eugenie, who despite her bid for freedom, always returned for every holiday, was a solace. So was her seventy-sixth birthday, bringing over a hundred letters ('not counting telegrams and cards') as well as the present of a splendid new cover for her piano from the children, and most important of all, a renewed awareness of her 'happiness in possessing such children, and of being so surrounded by love in all its fullness'. The cover even prompted her there and then to order a new piano from Steinweg for her return.

Nor, thanks to her old Brussels host, Professor Kufferath, was it long left idle. Turning up with his daughter, Antonia, and her husband on their way back from Meiningen's first festival of the three great B's (Bach, Beethoven and Brahms) he affectionately informed her that they had come not just to see her but to hear her play. Her response was an invitation to call at her house for an hour each day at noon. Though the diary for that October mentions a return to many old favourites like Schubert's C minor Impromptu and the Gluck Gavotte arranged for her by Brahms some twenty-five years ago (and scales and exercises too), her visitors wanted only the music of Schumann. 'Of failing health and any decline of power there was not the slightest sign' was how Antonia's husband, Edward Speyer, recalled these performances as an old man. 'The astonishing youthful energy and fire, the power of expression, from intense tenderness to explosive passion, and the still unerring perfection of technique, made an overwhelming impression'. When Brahms himself arrived for a night's stay on his way home, there was a party at which Antonia sang some of his cherished, recently published folk-song arrangements after much preliminary banter between them as to whether the other (Brahms was at the piano) could manage the tricky ensemble of 'Im stiller Nacht'. At supper, when the conversation touched on Borwick, Clara and Brahms found themselves totally at one in disapproval of Borwick's plan to make his Berlin début in an unknown concerto by

Stanford. Before Brahms left next morning she played to him 'most beautifully', first a transcription of an organ prelude and fugue by Bach, in whose music so many listeners had always judged her peerless in noble poise, and then an Intermezzo and the Romance from his own Op.118. They embraced in farewell, unaware that they were never to meet again.

Though recent worries about 'gout-stones' in her hands had in fact proved unwarranted, by the end of 1895 her digestion was giving enough trouble for the doctor to prescribe a strict diet not at all to her liking: 'how funny it is that even in old age one should care so much for what tastes nice - yet I am no gourmand' was her diary comment. Her condition was not helped by two new sources of anxiety – her daughter, Marie, confined to bed with sciatica for over a month, and her son-in-law, Louis Sommerhoff, in January, 1896, suddenly smitten by a stroke, albeit not fatally, while out hunting. His consideration and kindness, manifest in so many gestures of shared social responsibility, had particularly touched her on holiday at Baden in May, 1891, when he had hired her a private carriage so that she could better enjoy the countryside. Marie she could at least help by taking over some of her lessons, a task that while often totally exhausting her yet still miraculously rekindled smouldering embers. On her own recovery Marie could even report to Rosalie Leser that at a so-called demonstration lesson at the end of January, 1896, 'Mamma played some of the canons and sketches her arrangements of which she had recently published, beautifully, with wonderful strength and freshness, and with her own unique rhythm'. Ferdinand's continued eagerness and progress under her guidance was an even keener reminder at this time that life had brought her blessings to counter-balance all pain. 'Thus light and shade always go together' she observed in the diary on the last day of that month. Yet she knew that her strength was ebbing. To Brahms only twenty-four hours before she had written 'the only thing that truly comforts one is hope, and that is ever more and more denied to old age'.

In February she struggled to read a book he had just sent her about the octogenarian artist, Adolf Menzel, whom he often encountered in Berlin and profoundly admired. But her letters to her old friend grew shorter. By March she scarcely had the will to pick up pen at all, except to confide secret anguish to her diary: 'My evenings are terrible. I'm always so exhausted that I can hardly hold up my head, and the pain and sickness are dreadful. . . . I feel as if I should die. . . . Who knows how soon I shall have to leave my children? This thought never leaves me now.'

On the afternoon of March 26, having heard Ferdinand and a pupil of Rudorff play in the morning, she set out with Marie for one of those keenly awaited carriage drives, that with the trees once more bursting into bud, could still bring a glow to pallid cheeks. But as they talked Marie noticed a sudden change of expression: occasional difficulties of speech and of co-ordinated movement in the next few days confirmed the suspicion that her mother had had a slight stroke. By the 30th Clara was nevertheless sufficiently her old self to take up the burning question of where they should go for the summer. Continuing stability, despite the occasional flicker, throughout April encouraged friends to feel that heaven had granted a temporary reprieve. 'Thank God better news of Frau Schumann from Frankfurt today' were Joachim's words to Brahms early that month. 'I cannot bear the thought of losing her, and yet we shall have to get used to it'. But by now, Brahms himself was prepared: '. . . I cannot term sad what your letter mentions. I have often thought that Frau Schumann might outlive all her children and me too, but I never wished that for her. The idea of losing her cannot frighten us any more, not even my lonely self, for whom there are far too few living in this world. And when she has gone from us, will not our faces light up with joy at the remembrance of her, of this glorious woman, whose great qualities we have been permitted to enjoy through a long life, only to love and admire her more and more? In this way only shall we grieve for her'.

Reminded by Ferdinand that May 7 was Brahms's birthday, a day never forgotten by her since first they met, she demanded pen and paper to scribble one further greeting: 'Heartiest good wishes from your affectionate and devoted CLARA SCHUMANN. I cannot very well do any more yet, but or soon Your ____'. On May 8 she felt well enough for a ride round the garden in her bath-chair. The next day she expressed the wish to hear Ferdinand play. After Nos. 4, 5 and 6 from Schumann's *Intermezzi* Op.4, and then the F sharp major *Romance*, Op.28, she stopped him with the words 'It is enough'.

A second, more serious stroke soon followed, making it almost impossible for Clara to speak. But Marie and Eugenie (who had rushed back from England) just caught the words 'you two must go to a beautiful place this summer'. On the afternoon of May 20, she herself, whose eyes in the context of music had always looked 'as if she could see into a world more beautiful than this'[1] slipped very peacefully into that paradise all her own. 'Our mother fell gently asleep today' was the telegram sent at once to Brahms.

A large gathering of dignitaries, artistic and civic, assembled at Mylius-strasse 32 on May 23 for a brief ceremony of farewell, with a choir under Stockhausen to sing music including the valedictory chorus 'Schlaf nun und ruhe' ending the second part of Schumann's *Paradise and the Peri*. Joachim was among the company but not Brahms, who having boarded a wrong train in his distress, arrived too late. But the next day at Bonn

---

[1] Eugenie's phrase.

/here her coffin was taken for burial in Schumann's grave, it was not
oseph, but Johannes, who amidst children, grandchildren, other mem-
·ers of the family, and countless colleagues and friends, saw her to rest.
Eye hath not seen, nor ear heard . . . the things which God hath prepared
or them that love him' was the text chosen by Dr Sell, Professor of
"heology at Bonn University, for his address. There was a choir to sing
horales.

To Berthold Litzmann, among the mourners, death had no sting. It was
Vhit-Sunday, and before the service the bells of Bonn had pealed boldly.
n that green churchyard the song of innumerable birds mingling with
he fragrance of hundreds of floral tributes seemed to him to bring 'a
nessage of spring to all weary and sad hearts' as Clara and Robert
vere at last inseparably reunited.

Little verses to Clara from R.S., Vienna, 1838
(See page 62)

`o a certain Bride
`ho will have no man in the twenties for her husband.

1. A bride over twenty, a groom over thirty years old –
   So must the bud into the leaf unfold.

2. Years of wooing more than five,
   No true lover can survive.

3. Laurel for the queen of Art
   Is fit coronal:
   Myrtle for the maiden
   That is best of all.

4. A sweetheart true belongs to me,
   Who looks into her eyes will see
   What woman's constancy can be.

5. Truth hath never ruth.

6. Egmont's true love Klärchen hight –
   Oh name of exquisite delight.

7. Klärchen Schumann's name
   Straight from heaven came.

8. We wander afar –
   Star severed from star –
   Yet I follow alway
   As night follows day.

9. Decked with her name, my name shall rise
   And then our blended harmonies
   Will thrill the angels in the skies.

). Ransack the earth for love like ours;
   She brings me mirth in April showers.

. We have suffered enough of sorrow and care:
   Out of leaves sharp and rough springs the pineapple rare.

12. Long, long she bids me languish ere she is mine indeed.
    Peace, loyal heart, thy anguish shall win a double meed.

13. Yet not too long; you do me wrong.
    The heart grows old, and men grow cold.

14. Should Florestan storm,
    With Eusebius keep warm.

15. Florestan wild,
    And Eusebius mild,
    Sun and foul weather, Take them together,
    Find both in me –
    Sorrow and glee.

16. Jealous in truth is Florestan,
    Eusebius trusts in his brother-man –
    Which of the twain shall be dearest to thee?
    Who most true to himself and his love shall be.

17. And shouldst thou seek to domineer
    Rebels twain hast thou to fear –
    Who will defeated be?
    Who will have victory?

18. Then lead we thee with pageant to the throne,
    And humbly take our place on either side. –
    If one of us thou'rt ready to disown,
    Will a like fate the other too, betide?

19. Oft have I let you look into my heart,
    And watched how happily you gazed and gazed.
    Is it not true, that often you would start
    To find yourself there, and draw back amazed?

20. Yet did I show you all my thought,
    Dark phantoms would your spirit grieve,
    A fear that comes to me unsought –
    Question me not! Love and believe.

21. Close, close to thy breast, On thy heart let me rest:
    Then whisper, 'The best
    Of all things in God's plan
    Is an honest, true man'.

22. Treat me not too lightly,
    And do not prudish be;
    Nor coy, nor yet too sprightly –
    That's the wife for me!

3. Twilight gray, flickering fire:
   'Come' they say, 'My heart's desire'.

4. At night, when you were very small
   I oft came dressed as a spectre tall
   And rattled at your door –
   You bade me be-gone, as you shrieked, afraid.
   Ah! could I now come in a ghost's disguise
   You would open your arms in glad surprise,
   And whisper, 'A kiss all else before,
   From my lover in masquerade'.

5. In a riddle we'd involve
   Things that none of us could solve.
   Read 'Roma', mistress of the world,
   Backwards. What meaning is unfurled?
   Jus now this topsy-turvy town
   Between us two has settled down –
   A bridge of soft lips we must make,
   Kisses our messages will take.

6. You saw a duck, you thought it a goose.
   Certainly things play fast and loose.

7. 'Nay sir, let old times go;
   We will forget.'
   Not so, not so.
   Rather with fond regret
   Count all the blessed days of long ago.

8. Heaven smiles on the course of true love, they say.
   Now, kiss me, sweetheart, and hearken;
   The marriage that heaven has made, one day
   No earthly sorrow shall darken.

9. 'Together we live, together die;'
   I spoke, and silence fell.
   It was as if we looked across death's stream
   And bade farewell –
   your loving eyes, so tender and so true,
   Held my eyes in their spell.
   'Together will we live, together die:'
   In that all blessings dwell.

10. When thy fair spirit quits this earth
    I will follow thee into the dark unknown,
    My guilt shall shelter behind thy worth,
    And I shall reap where thou hast sown.

APPENDIX II
Clara's Jubilee, 1878: an appreciation by Fanny Davies

This 'eye-witness' account of Clara's performance of Schumann's A minor piano concerto in the Leipzig Gewandhaus appeared in Volume 6, 1925, of Music and Letters, *by whose kind permission it is reprinted here. Fanny Davies (1861–1934) was one of Clara's outstanding pupils.*

This is not the moment to discuss the Pianoforte Concerto at any length, but I should much like to share with any reader who may be interested, some impressions of Madame Clara Schumann's performance of the Concerto in the Leipzig Gewandhaus on the occasion of her jubilee: a record performance even for that great genius. A student, I had come from Frankfort and was privileged to be present at the private rehearsal as well as the concert.

With the first chords she plunged her listeners into the mood dominating the whole of the first movement, and one realised the great foundational line of thought: passionate aspiration. She showed us that it was not as a preparation for a sickly, sentimental melody that Schumann has chosen that elemental introduction with its precipitous descent in chords. We heard the clarinet solo played in the same tempo as the introduction, and realised that Schumann has indeed given the whole responsibility of the tempo to the pianist. No small responsibility. The solo was perfectly free, full of nuance, but without *wrong* ritenutos and sentimentality. In short, Schumann's "Allegro Affettuoso" is not an affected allegro.

At the animato (not much faster, but always "taking wing"), great importance was given to accenting, though not over-accenting, the triplets which go to form the rolling accompaniment, as well as the distinct rhythmical melodic design of the accompaniment itself. Each arpeggio rolled out to the very end, it was spacious, brilliant, but never flurried—its wings were never clipped.

Then in the great middle section, where the three rhythms each play their part simultaneously—(the melody rhythm and the two underlying rhythms of the accompaniment and the marching basses)—the values of each and all were made perfectly clear to the listener, together with the foundational line of thought—aspiration. The cadenza—from quite a simple beginning, piano, and as coming from a distance, but not overdone, unfolded as naturally as the petals of a blown rose. The coda, not too fast, by reason of its emotional value.

The Intermezzo Clara Schumann played with a certain simple and eager sincerity, and not too slowly. And on this memorable occasion one heard that the orchestra is responsible for changing, in two chords, the whole mood of the intermezzo into one of breathless suspense and tension, ever more and more pianissimo until it prepares for Florestan's exuberant outburst of triumphant victory—the finale. That she never took so fast as to lose its nobility and pride as well as exuberance. But she possessed to such a degree that rare and consummate power of dominating every mood at the moment, and the necessary technique which enabled her adequately to convey every shade to the listener.

She was very particular about rhythm, and at that rehearsal, not being quite satisfied that the orchestra was not going to run away in the fugal part, she suddenly walked from the platform half-way down into the hall, and stood and listened to the effect, until convinced that it was going to be perfect on such an occasion.

The coda she took quietly and with the necessary elegance of melody-technique, thereby creating the contrast which alone can bring out the value of the last exuberant climax for which Schumann has reserved most of his pianoforte percussion.

During the whole performance, both at the rehearsal and the concert, one could not but notice the love in the playing of the orchestra; for there were still many older men amongst them, who as youths, had played under Schumann's own direction when Robert and Clara lived in Leipzig. In other words, the practised tradition was there, and the "trifles that make perfection"—to use Michael Angelo's words—came therefore as a matter of course.

FANNY DAVIES.

APPENDIX III

Clara's diary message to her children, soon after Robert Schumann's death, about her relationship with Brahms

To every man, no matter how unhappy he may be, God sends some comfort, and we are surely meant to enjoy it and to strengthen ourselves by its means. I have you, but you are but children. You hardly knew your dear Father, you were still too young to feel deep grief, and thus in those terrible years you could give me no comfort. Hope, indeed, you could bring me, but that was not enough to support me through such agony. Then came Johannes Brahms. Your Father loved and admired him, as he did no man except Joachim. He came, like a true friend, to share my sorrow; he strengthened the heart that threatened to break, he uplifted my mind, he cheered my spirits when and wherever he could, in short he was my friend in the fullest sense of the word.

He and Joachim were the only people whom your dear Father saw during his illness, and he always received them with evident pleasure so long as his mind was clear. And he did not know Johannes for years, as I did. I can truly say, my children, that I never loved any friend as I did him – it is an exquisite harmony of soul. It is not his youth that I love, there is no flattered vanity in my affection. I love his freshness of mind, his wonderfully gifted nature, his noble heart, which I have learned to know in the course of years, as others cannot. At times he may seem rough, and the younger musicians feel his superiority of mind – Who likes to confess that to himself or to others? – Therefore they do not like him, and Joachim alone openly expresses his admiration, for he is his equal as an artist. They look up to each other with respect. It is an ennobling spectacle such as is seldom to be found in this world. Joachim too, as you know, was a true friend to me, but I did not live near him, and so it was Johannes alone who supported me. Never forget this, dear children, and always have a grateful heart for this friend, for a friend he will certainly be to you too. Believe what your Mother tells you, and do not listen to petty and envious souls who grudge him my love and friendship, and therefore try to impugn him or even to cast aspersions on our relations, which they cannot, or will not, understand.

APPENDIX IV

Clara's compositions

Op.1 Quatre Polonaises
No.1 in E flat; No.2 in C; No.3 in D; No.4 in C

Op.2 Caprices en forme de Valse

Op.3 Romance variée

Op.4 Valse romantique

Op.5 Quatre Pièces caractéristiques
No.1 'Le Sabbat'; No.2 'Caprice à la Bolero'; No.3 'Romance'; No.4 'Le ballet des Revenants'

Op.6 Soirées musicales
No.1 Toccatina; No.2 Notturno; No.3 Mazurka; No.4 Ballade; No.5 Mazurka; No.6 Polonaise

Op.7 Piano Concerto in A minor
Allegro maestoso; Romanze: Andante non troppo; Finale: Allegro non troppo

Op.8 Variations de Concert sur la Cavatine du 'Pirate' de Bellini

Op.9 Souvenir de Vienne

Op.10 Scherzo No. 1 in D minor (Con passione)

Op.11 Trois Romances
No.1 in E flat minor; No.2 in G minor; No.3 in A flat

Op.12 Three Songs (originally published as Nos.2, 4 and 11 of Robert Schumann's *Liebesfrühling*, Op.37)
No.1 'Er ist gekommen'; No.2 'Liebst du um Schönheit'; No.3 'Warum willst du andre fragen'

Op.13 Six Songs
No.1 'Ihr Bildnis'; No.2 'Sie liebten sich beide'; No.3 'Liebeszauber'; No.4 'Der Mond kommt still gegangen'; No.5 'Ich hab in dienem Auge'; No.6 'Die stille Lotusblume'

Op.14 Scherzo No. 2 in C minor (Con fuoco)

Op.15 Quatre Pièces fugitives
No.1 in F; No.2 in A minor; No.3 in D; No.4 in G

Op.16 Three Preludes and Fugues
No.1 in G minor; No.2 in B flat; No.3 in D minor

Op.17 Trio in G minor for piano, violin and cello
Allegro moderato; Tempo di Menuetto; Andante; Allegretto

Op.18 Missing (Possibly intended for unpublished Piano Sonata in G minor: Allegro; Scherzo; Adagio; Rondo)

Op.19 Missing (Possibly intended for unfinished Concertino in F minor for piano and orchestra)

Op.20 Variations on a Theme of Robert Schumann

Op.21 Three Romances
No. 1 in A minor; No. 2 in F; No. 3 in G minor

Op.22 Three Romances for violin and piano
No. 1 in D flat; No. 2 in G minor; No. 3 in B flat

Op.23 Six Songs
No. 1 'Was weinst du, Blümlein'; No. 2 'An einem lichten Morgen'; No. 3 'Geheimes Flüstern hier und dort'; No. 4 'Auf einem grünen Hügel'; No. 5 'Das ist ein Tag'; No. 6 'O Lust, O Lust'

Romance in B minor (1855)

Cadenzas for Beethoven's C minor (Op.37) and G major (Op.58) Piano Concertos

Cadenzas for Mozart's D minor Piano Concerto, K.466

APPENDIX V
Foreign Concert Tours

1832   Paris
1837/8 Prague, Vienna, Pressburg, Graz
1839   Paris
1842   Copenhagen
1844   Russia
1846/7 Austria
1853   Holland
1854   Belgium
1855   Holland
1856   Austria, Hungary, England, Denmark
1857   England, Switzerland
1858   Switzerland, Austria
1859   Austria, England
1860   Holland, Austria
1861   Belgium
1862   Switzerland, Paris, Brussels
1863   Holland, France, Belgium
1864   Russia
1865   Prague, England
1866   Austria, Hungary
1867   England
1868   Brussels, England, Austria, Hungary
1869   Holland, England, Austria
1870   England
1871   Holland, England
1872   England, Austria, Hungary
1873   Brussels, England
1876   Utrecht, London
1877   Utrecht, Rotterdam, London, Basel
1879   Zurich
1880   Basel
1881   London
1882   London
1883   Utrecht
1884   London
1886   London
1887   London, Basel
1888   London

Index